Decisions Decisions

Getting Answers to Life's Challenges

Haneefa Mateen

Copyright © 2024 by Haneefa Mateen

Compilation of the four volumes of *Decisions Decisions: Getting Answers to Life's Challenges*, copyright © 2024.

Volume 1 Getting Started: Decisions Decisions: Getting Answers to Life's Challenges, copyright © 2023.

Volume 2: Returning: Decisions Decisions: Getting Answers to Life's Challenges, copyright © 2023.

Volume 3: Sidelined: Decisions Decisions: Getting Answers to Life's Challenges, copyright © 2023.

Volume 4: Fulfilling a Destiny: Decisions Decisions: Getting Answers to Life's Challenges, copyright © 2023.

All rights reserved.

ISBN 978-1-73772-19-8-7

No portion of this book may be reproduced in any form without written permission from the publisher or author, except as permitted by U.S. copyright law.

Acknowledgment is gratefully given to the authors of the book, Physicians of the Heart: A Sufi View of the Ninety-Nine Names of Allah, for granting permission to use their list and explanations of the ninety-nine names of Allah, in Chapter 18 in this book. Copyright © 2011 by Wali Ali Meyer, Bilal Hyde, Faisal Muqaddam, Shabda Khan. Sufi Ruhaniat International.

Disclaimer: The author of this book, Decisions, Decisions' stories, experiences and opinions are from author's perspective and are not intended as medical advice or the use of any techniques as a form of treatment for physical, medical, psychiatric, mental health problems either directly or indirectly. The intent of the author is only to share experiences in a general nature in her quest for emotional and spiritual wellbeing. In the event that you use any of the information in this book for yourself, which is your constitutional right, the author and publisher assumes no responsibility or liability whatsoever for readers or purchasers of this book.

Decisions, Decisions is a non-fiction story, however some names, locations, and other identifying information were changed to protect privacy of individuals.

Book Cover art: Haneefa Mateen

Contents

Volume 1 Getting Started

Volume 2 Returning

Volume 3 Sidelined

Volume 4 Fulfilling a Destiny

Contents

Introduction	5
PART ONE: Getting Some Answers	8
Chapter 1: What are Oracles?	12
Chapter 2: Metu Neter Cards	14
Chapter 3: What's in a Name?	17
Chapter 4: Afrikan Women Warriors	23
Chapter 5: Heru Khuti (Ogun) Clan	27
Chapter 6: Rituals	31
Chapter 7: I Ching	35
Chapter 8: I Ching Destiny Readings	38
Chapter 9: Career Readings	40
Chapter 10: Native American Cards	42
Chapter 11: Medicine Cards	44
Chapter 12: Sacred Path Cards	49
Chapter 13: In Person Spiritual Readings	51

Chapter 14: Cuban Candomble Priestess Consultation	53
PART TWO: GETTING AWAY	58
Chapter 15: School for International Training	59
Chapter 16: The Drop Off	63
Chapter 17: Which Country?	66
Chapter 18: Zimbabwe	68
Chapter 19: Ndebele Language and Culture	71
Chapter 20: Village Life	78
Chapter 21: Purpose for Being in Zimbabwe	84
Chapter 22: Stout?	88
Chapter 23: Moving On	91
Chapter 24: Independent Study: Zimbabwe Healthcare	96
Chapter 25: Traditional Healers	99
Chapter 26: Before Colonization	106
Chapter 27: Personal Reflections and Struggles Living in Zimbabwe	109
Chapter 28: Americans Over Concerned About Cleanliness, Germs and Illness?	114
Chapter 29: Vegetarian Dilemma	118

Chapter 30: Reality of the Situation 125

Introduction

For those who have been frantically worried they are going to make the wrong decision, especially when responsible for other people's lives, this book introduces some solutions. What it is like to have an overall view of what is going on before you make a major decision. If you lose sleep because you're worried that you still don't know your life purpose, natural talents and career yet, there's hope. Hopefully, you are inspired to learn more about your own life purpose, as you follow along my journey with some of the tools and strategies I use to make major decisions, and to learn about myself and my life purpose. Keep in mind, I'd lived half of my life before I was introduced to these indigenous or ancient concepts. In amazement, while learning different cultures' divination and then looked back on my past, what I saw was very accurate. And you will too.

Divination provides roadmaps or a GPS that lets you know where the traffic congestion is and guides you through the detours. Sometimes we get stuck in traffic anyway. GPS gives alerts and warnings ahead of time. Divination also gives you alerts and can help you get back on the main road of your life.

Some people may wonder from reading my first book, *Mother's Love from Beyond: A Healing Journey of Grief and Loss,* how I could be so gullible and influenced so easy to follow the advice given by the mediums. Doesn't some of these messages have the same advice or apologies that could be given to anyone? Or even made up? And now seek guidance from throwing coins, bones, cards and other items? Really?

As you get to know me better, you will see I am very much a person who marches to the beat of a different distant drummer. Ask anyone who heard me drum. Punished again and again for not conforming. So why would I follow guidance from throwing coins, oracle cards, or medium messages?

As you start to see less crises in your life, as you understand how the universe functions around you, and make better choices in your thoughts and behaviors, then it is not hard, even for us who are hardheaded, to believe. Especially when your life begins to flow smoothly synchronically, and what you need simply shows up abundantly.

This is not a religious book. It is a cumulation of 30 years of studying and using various different cultures' divination methods. I use some foreign language terms because that is the way I learned them and is my way of continuing to honor these indigenous cultures and beliefs. With deep respect for indigenous cultures and the people who truly have the knowledge, I thank them and yield to them.

Hopefully this book introduces you to different perspectives as my personal stories bring understanding of how ancient and now popularized practices for making decisions — when used properly — brings improved quality of life, inner peace, satisfaction, and sense of purpose on your own life's journey.

My goal with this book, *Decisions Decisions*, as with my other books in the "Spirituality Made Simple series" is to make spirituality and healing simple. Simple to understand, and simple to apply to daily life. In the first book, *Mother's Love from Beyond*, readers learned about my childhood and early adult years, as I was prepared through life experiences to accept that there are many different ways of healing and knowing. Readers gained faith and courage along with me as I learned to trust intuitive higher guidance.

In this book, I offer tools for you gaining access to your own guidance for your own life, while continuing with my stories of how I was introduced to these divination tools and how my life changed along the way. This book is mostly written in the order I learned these techniques however, the stories are updated with my current thoughts, events, and style of writing. Previous readers asked me to go into more details about my middle years, my thirties, forties, and early fifties to explain how I got from, and transformed beyond multiple crises and obstacles from then to now.

I use several approaches to meet different readers' needs, interests, and learning styles. Some people learn best from information and research. Other people enjoy and learn from life stories as examples. Here, both approaches are combined. Take what you need and leave the rest. At different times later in your life you may want to come back to this series for more understanding.

PART ONE: Getting Some Answers

I was first introduced to the concept of oracle cards and divination through an African-centered church, the Ausar Auset Society Church in 1991. They had weekly classes where I learned about ancient African history, philosophy, and cosmology's different ways of viewing the world. They taught us about improving our health because poor health affects our ability to manage our own emotions and behavior. This included spiritual health as we wonder, what's the reason and purpose for living? Why get up in the morning day after day? There's got to be more to life than this? Why does this keep happening to me? Why do I feel so lonely and empty? Why did I keep choosing the same type of relationships, the same dudes?

    I had recently married and divorced twice making me feel lost, like a failure, and wondering how not to repeat the same mistakes. I was feeling lost too because since I almost died in 1982, there were several weird experiences that I didn't yet have an explanation for. No one close to me knew of the term "near death experience, and neither had I, until I found the book, <u>Heading towards Omega</u>. However, although the author's stories told about how people's personal values, relationships, body sensitivities, even personality changes after a near death experience, there wasn't guidance for what to do with these changes. I felt very alone.

In these Ausar Auset Society Church classes, I began to get answers to these life challenges, though I didn't understand much in the beginning, I just followed along. Attendees were instructed to first get a destiny reading also known as an incarnation objective from a priest. A "reading" is a spiritual guidance consultation. The reason for a destiny reading is to learn your purpose for having been born on Earth at this time, and what lessons you are to learn. Later, we learned how to do our own spiritual readings using oracle cards or coins.

These destiny and other spiritual readings are not meant for fortune-telling. Divination is to help you grow emotionally, mentally, heal physically, build a strong spiritual character with responsibility to community, therefore having success with true abundance in all areas of your life. After doing the initial destiny readings, then you can ask about your destiny or life lessons at more frequent intervals such as daily or monthly. Later, you can inquire about specific situations or projects that you are in, or you wish to be involved in. But all readings are to be referred back to your destiny reading. In other words, ask yourself, "How does what I want to do, and the current spiritual reading help me to fulfill my destiny?"

However, over time I did observe some spiritual readings do foretell the future. Initially it was six months, and sometimes ten years later these events would unfold, that helped me understand the meaning of the reading. Being new to doing spiritual readings, I had no idea this would happen. I began to see that spiritual readings predict current and upcoming challenges, and gives advice to assist with navigating personal as well as situations with relationships, family, major purchases, moving, career, employment, and supervisors.

Shekum ur Shekum (Ra Un Nefer Amen), the founder and leader of the Ausar Auset Society Church a Pan-African spirituality church, commented in one of his classes that one day someone should write a book showing how their own spiritual readings and understanding evolved. I was surprised when he mentioned this idea, because he previously taught that what is in each individual's "book of charms" is private. It was emphasized that no one sneak and read anyone else's notebook without permission. However, since I am in my later years of life, and knew several people who came to Ausar Auset Society Church who told me they did not understand and therefore didn't benefit from the teachings or spiritual practices, I've decided to share some of mine. I greatly benefited from Ausar Auset Society Church and it was a springboard for the rest of my life.

You May Be Wondering . . .

Wait a minute! What is it that I believe then? Isn't this against what most major religions teach? Or personal free will and independence? Let me explain. My beliefs changed for me after I had a near death experience back in 1982. Many people are having near death experiences these days, as they are surviving what used to be fatal illnesses such as heart attacks, strokes and cancer, or car and other crashes, drownings, falls, gunshots, fires, floods, tornadoes, and weird accidents. They return to tell stories of meeting with an energy of pure Love, Peace, Acceptance and Infinite Knowledge and Wisdom. They see Angels, their loved ones and others who passed on, that they thought had died. Those who have had near death experiences whether they flatlined, or their car was completely totaled yet they walked away without a scratch, see their whole life flash before their eyes. A life review from birth until now, showed that most of what they thought was wrong, and rules that were broken aren't as important as how they were kind, understanding and compassionate with other people. This helps them see their purpose for living, the need to return to Earthly life to finish what they started, change their thinking and behavior, heal and help others. Then they often choose to come back, or may be pushed back into their bodies to wake up with a commitment to do better. However, they are also told that they will temporarily forget most of the wisdom and personal insight shown to them.

Next time, on my Day of Judgement, during my life review, I want it to show that I learned what love is, how to receive, accept, and share love. That I loved, more than I hurt people, during this lifetime. That I used the talents that I was blessed with. Over my lifetime I've noticed that it really doesn't matter what religion or beliefs that I've tried out, heaven still provides for me with abundance. Perhaps this abundance comes from faith, love, sharing, gratitude and following heaven's guidance.

I've borrowed the good from several religions, beliefs, and theories. Using the example of a puzzle, this is because each culture, society, religion or group has pros and cons with only a few pieces, often missing a lot of the rest of the worldwide puzzle picture. No group sees the whole picture. We need each other. No one has all the answers for the best way to live. Together we can learn, grow and evolve.

Chapter 1: What are Oracles?

The dictionary's definition of oracles is a person who is usually a priestess or priest that is a medium through whom advice or prophecy was sought from God. The word "oracle" is from the Latin verb for "to speak." An oracle can also be a wise person. Sometimes young children bring us important messages.

Closely related to oracles is divination. Divination is the practice of seeking to foresee or foretell future events or hidden knowledge by interpretation of symbolic happenings in nature, or by the aid of people gifted with unusual insight or intuitive perception. Divination is found in all civilizations' histories.

Since most of us are not yet fully open to our own intuition, often too busy or distracted, not having extensive quiet time like our ancestors did to pay notice the environment around us, therefore using tools such as cards, coins, shells, bones and other assorted items for divination are helpful for getting guidance for life challenges.

What I noticed over the past twenty years is sometimes the oracles will give similar advice no matter what question I ask. This means there is some attitude, behavior, thinking, or behavior that I must change within myself before my outer life situation will improve. Changing one's self may take weeks or months, but the rewards with the increased abundance and helpful people in your life is worth the effort.

People often comment that I radiate peace, love, and confidence. The peace comes from doing the inner work of acknowledging all of my feelings including the anger, hurt and sadness because included with these uncomfortable feelings is joy and inner knowing. And from following through on the outer work of taking action based on the guidance received. Knowing that all is in universal order, I am able to let go of worry.

With all the different types of divination systems and oracle cards, what is most important, is whatever you choose is easy to understand and is comforting for you. Having good books for interpretation is essential. So I have about four I Ching books, and a few oracle card books. There is a list of some of the ones I use at the end of this book.

Chapter 2: Metu Neter Cards

The first oracle cards I learned were the Metu Neter cards that were designed by Ra Un Nefer Amen. These are seventy beautiful cards with colorful pictures representing the ten Kamitic African deities on the Tree of Life plus four other energies that influence our personalities and life events. What I liked about Ausar Auset Society Church teachings is that "deities or gods" are not up in the sky somewhere, they are qualities, talents, and abilities we each have inside us, in varying amounts. We can make the decision, conscious and unconscious through meditation and actions to improve our thinking and behavior to meet whatever challenges we have in life. Instead of, "this is the way I am, or "I've always been like this," or "this is the way I've always done it," or "how my grandpa did it."

It was freeing to learn there are infinite possibilities. Otherwise, I grew up like most people, feeling inadequate and stuck.

When using the Metu Neter cards, besides asking "Please give higher spiritual guidance, insight into understanding this situation and what I need to do, I also add "what energies are needed for this situation? Then for the specific card, I listened and meditated to the mantra on the 30-minute cassette or CD. I would sing the mantra aloud or in my head during the day, and especially in the situation I inquired about. I wore the specific colors, ate the foods with the energy of the deity, and did my best to emulate the positive attributes of the deity pictured on the one or two cards I selected.

For detailed explanation and instructions refer to the book, *Metu Neter Metu Neter Vol. 1: The Great Oracle of Tehuti and the Egyptian System of Spiritual Cultivation.*

After saying a prayer asking for guidance, the first question I asked was about my destiny. I pulled the Het-Heru Hetep card. From the book and classes, I learned that with a Het-Heru destiny throughout my life I should strive to be joyful, to experience pleasure in healthy balanced ways, be sociable, harmonious with others and nature, and appreciate the beauty in all. Further, I'm to be aware of how I use my imagination in my thoughts and daydreaming fantasies as these could come true in life. Strong inner joy and pleasure raises the life-force which will inspire and motivate me towards passionately fulfilling my goals. Best to decrease tendencies to be timid, seeking too much pleasure, wanting to feel good all the time by daydreaming or using intoxicating drugs, alcohol, sex and other addictions to avoid unpleasant tasks and responsibilities. Careers to consider are all kinds of artists: dancers, musicians, singers, writers, entertainers, make-up artists, fashion designers, interior decorators, drawers, painters, graphic designers, and animators. Het Heru is also known as Osun in the Yoruba traditions.

Some of these Het Heru traits I already naturally had. My mother was an artist and introduced me to drawing and painting at a very young age. As she read us storybooks, I was inspired to dream of becoming a children's book illustrator. Family said my mother was famous for her singing. An elementary school teacher told me I had a wonderful singing voice, but I was too shy to get up in front of a classroom so certainly not an audience. During my teen years, I designed and sewed clothes and dolls, and drew pictures in solitude. As an adult, I love to dance, occasionally until 4 o'clock in the morning at non-alcoholic parties. People who observe me move, tell me I am a natural dancer.

Het Heru's day is Friday. So on Fridays I do creative art activities, put on music and dance, get out in nature, call and do fun activities with friends. My money donations are usually multiples of $5. I also do Het Heru meditations and purposely eat sweets on Friday's.

Chapter 3: What's in a Name?

Next we were instructed to select an African Kamitic name that expressed the values of our individual Metu Neter destiny card. I initially choose Hetep Ab Meri-t which means having a peaceful, joyful, balanced heart. I selected other names, but this is the name that received a positive Metu Neter card verification to help me live out my Het Heru Hetep destiny whenever anyone says my name. Then in 1993, the *African Names,* book came out and in a naming ceremony the author and priest Hehi Metu Ra Enkamit gave me a different name AkhiaNeter-t. Akhia means joy and Neter means God. The "t" added at the end makes it feminine. All together AkhiaNeter-t means "God is my joy." The priest told me, "This name will remind you to raise your inner joy to match your smile."

In my first book, *Mother's Love from Beyond*, I wrote about the many meanings I learned about my legal name, Haneefa. My mother told me Haneefa means "inclined to righteousness." Name books and the internet say it means "true believer."

A taxi driver gave me a different interpretation than I had heard before.

He said, "It is faith so big, huge, like the faith of Abraham"

This is true. Over the years, my faith increased as I've delighted in miracles happening alongside challenges, usually after I've bravely persevered. His interpretations of my name

Haneefa matches my African Khametic name AkhiaNeter-t meaning of God is my joy.

Saturday Born

So how did I start out with a name that depicts such responsibilities of devotion and sacrifice? Perhaps because of the day I was born. The day on which you were born describes more of your personality than your astrological sun sign. It is how people actually see you and how you operate in the world. You can go on the internet to find what day of the week you were born on. Simply type in your full birthdate then "day of the week." There are sometimes printed perpetual calendar charts available to do hand calculations to determine what day.

Born on a Saturday, and during a Saturn Period meant most of my middle to later childhood was turbulent, with constant relocations and separations from my family. These challenges made me quiet, observant, a loner, with a patient determined focus on meeting future goals. I learned to patiently sacrifice and do without, because my family was poor. I like to spend time with older people listening to their stories, and I have had more maturity than my chronological age.

Naturally organized, I return whatever I use to its assigned drawer, shelf, or same spot on a table so I can find it later. The clothes in my closet are arranged by color on colored hangers, which allows me to easily wear the appropriate color for each day of the week. Turquoise blue on Mondays, reds on Sunday and Tuesdays, golden yellow Wednesdays, light blues on Thursdays, bright green and yellow on Fridays, and black on Saturdays. Similarly, as much as possible I also eat the foods of the day based on energetically hot and cold foods. My panties are still folded six inches the size of a dollar bill, and my bed sheets have mitered hospital corners from what I learned in Air Force basic training forty years ago. I make "to do" lists and use alarm clocks and timers. Calendars, I write on them but afterwards rarely look at calendars, perhaps because I've had a good memory and internal sense of time. Doing all this doesn't bother me, as it simplifies and makes life easier and convenient. Someone else would be frustrated. Not me.

Het-Heru's personality traits are the opposite of Saturday born. Het-Heru is outgoing, friendly, social, freely sexual, having to be around people, partying, spending money on beautiful clothing, makeup, hair, home, car and fun. On the contrary, I save my money and pay bills to keep a roof over my head. People I've observed with predominant Het-Heru traits, tend to put pleasure first before responsibilities. Although, I do like nice things, I'm more practical.

I learn from mine and other's mistakes, therefore I may be more cautious than other people. And my ability to change, adapt to situations and do things differently than other people who find it easier to just follow the crowd, doesn't make for me keeping many friends or having fun.

What I buy usually have to be practical and have a functional purpose too. You won't see me in miniskirts with my boobs out because I don't like being cold, or my thighs sticking to burning hot wet sweaty chairs, or my back hurting from trying to keep my legs closed. Nor will you see me in high heels hurting my toes, back, making me afraid I might fall on the ice, or couldn't get away if chased! Makeup, whenever I could find shades that matched my brown skin tones made pimples with painful white pus filled boils on my face, and lipsticks gave me an itchy blistery puffy lips. Lipstick for African Americans never made sense to me anyway because our lips are already full and beautiful. Our legs are naturally tanned, so why wear odd-colored hot, itchy stockings? Contrary to television commercials' guarantee that fingernail polish would make our fingernails stronger, my fingernails split and break each time I use fingernail polish. When I was a teenager, I begged my parents to get my ears pierced but no one told me I could be allergic to cheap metals until my earlobes immediately swelled. Luckily I was able to keep the holes in my ears. Occasionally, my ears still protest with hypoallergenic earrings. If men only knew the pain we women go through to look "pretty." Burning scalps with hot combs or perms, early balding from hair dyes that never matches the God given color and texture we were born with. Sitting for hours getting extensions of someone else's or fake hair weaved in.

Like excuse me, is the only way I'm beautiful is to look like the actresses and other female entertainers on TV and other media? With straight hair and red lips from the 1930's and 1970's?' Betty Boop?

The way most women wear makeup doesn't make sense to me, except of course to cover scars from pimples, blotches and discoloration. Eventually, I did find hyperallergenic makeup, and with the help of a young friend, we bought some from Macy's department store. Sometimes I used a pink lipstick and fingernail polish that's closer to my natural skin color. To me, makeup should enhance each individual's natural features of own shape of face, skin tones, and hair. "Extreme makeovers" on television? How is that a makeover, if everyone comes off of the stage looking the same? The same haircut, same streaked hair color, and same make up as the stylist gave the woman before her?

The only reason I might consider makeup is due to my age, my hair everywhere is thinning. You would have to look hard to see my eyelashes. Penciled in eyebrows and eyelashes frequently turn out cartoonish. Or like I had a good cry. Why do boys and men have the long eyelashes without even trying!

Surely they must know girl's eyelashes don't grow like that. But maybe salesmen do know. And that's why they persuade women that something else is wrong with them. Here's another product to buy that keeps businesses' bank accounts looking pretty. Me? I'm done with making everyone else rich but me! Besides, if men are not naked or hurting themselves to look pretty why should I?

This is my practical Saturday born energy talking. Perhaps I'm too practical and frugal for my own good. But my destiny reading is to be more like Het-Heru, how do I do this?

What did I know about romance? When I was married, my husband took me out to dinner. He ordered the lobster, salad, baked potato entrée for the both of us. Sitting in a dimly lit corner at a table just for the two of us. From the window we could see the calm water and boats docked on the river. Quietly enjoying talking and laughing.

That is until when the waiter brought the check and I saw the bill – $32 — and as my husband pulled out a big wad of dollar bills, I yelled at him.

"Do you know how many groceries we could have bought for that much money? And after you take the shell off, for a little bit of fish and only one baked potato! And don't carry around all that money in your back pocket!"

I embarrassed him (and myself) as I continued to fuss at him on the way out the door.

Well, I never had lobster before. Nor had I been to an expensive restaurant before. I didn't know that's what couples do as a treat on special occasions, when he takes her out and pays for the meal. Not grateful he would spend that much money and time on me. (Back in the 1980's that was a lot of money).

Honestly, I do try. Just prior to the 2019 COVID pandemic crisis, I was doing more socializing. I bought pretty clothes, was giving more attention to my hair, and discovered one day that I needed to clip the long gray hairs on my chin. The hairs on my chinny chin, chin, that probably everybody else noticed but me. Now I clip these little hairs twice a week on Monday's and Thursday so l remember.

Socializing? It seems there are always situations that are perfect excuses for not fulfilling our destinies. Throw in using a wheelchair so can't get in most people's homes to visit. Apartment buildings usually are walk-ups with several flights of stairs, as do party venues.

For Het Heru, true beauty comes from within. Joy and peace glows outward. I've actually experience joy after doing Het Heru meditations, rituals, or more often after simply experiencing fun or witnessing amazing beauty, and especially after healing past traumas therefore freeing me of worries. Apparently I glow. Unconsciously aware of this wonderful energy men flirted with me, sometimes using vulgar language, ask to marry me but just met me, told me how beautiful I was, even complemented my fingernails. Actually this joyful, loving energy is what everyone wants to have. But this has to come from inside yourself and lasts longer when it is real. Can't charm or steal joy from others, expecting to keep it for yourself. As usual, I wasn't wearing makeup nor fingernail polish on my short length, clipper trimmed fingernails. So other than my gorgeous smile that people tell me I have, what was the sexual physical attraction?

Another example of the how the day of the week you were born on might be influencing your life or people you know I will explain using the popular movie "Black Panther."

Chapter 4: Afrikan Women Warriors

There are some people who expressed disagreement with the portrayal of strong women warriors using martial arts and weapons in the movie, *"Black Panther"*. This discontent was stated by men and women. However, if we understood indigenous cultures before colonialism, we would not be surprised, or be caught up the current controversy over the demand for non-binary and transgender identities to be recognized. Let me explain this further from my understanding of indigenous African perspective that I learned in 1991 from the Ausar-Auset Society.

West Africa has the tradition of naming children by the day of the week they are born on. These natural personality traits occur regardless of gender. In addition, everyone has all of the abilities of all of the seven days of the week within us, just on varying amounts with some traits more natural than others. So, we really should not be surprised when a mother sees her child in danger then suddenly has the incredible strength to leap across the street in a microsecond or lift a two-ton heavy car off of her child! Or to fight off an attacker! Or a father to tenderly understand and nurture a sensitive child! Over time we have gotten away from being fully present in our bodies, aware of our environment, and connection to self, community and the universe for guidance. Guidance that would intuitively give us the ability to do whatever needs to be done in the moment.

The day of the week you were born is also the clan that you would be assigned to in the village. This way everyone is valued and needed. No clan or personality traits are any better or worse than another clan. Not like European or capitalistic societies who promote everyone has to be a doctor, lawyer, or computer geek to be successful and accepted! The example I like to give to describe how everyone is necessary is when the village decides to have a party or celebration. The clan that would head up the committee would be those born on a Friday, who are the natural partiers with the natural ability to have fun, bring people together in harmony, are the artists, musicians, entertainers, and decorators, with beautiful clothes, makeup, sexy and sensual, to make sure there is dancing, wonderful food, and soothing beverages. However, Friday born people like having fun, but are not into doing hard work. They would need Wednesday and Saturday born people to help with logistics, financial planning, and audio-visual technology. Thursday born people who have the faith and optimism and ability to bring wealth and make sure the event is spiritually correct. Sunday born people to take the lead in delegating responsibilities. Monday born people for cooking, nurturing, dedication, and dreaming the party into being. Tuesday born people for security, the bouncers for when people have had a bit too much partying.

So yes, Tuesday born people no matter whether they are male or female would be the warriors and protectors of the village! They would be trained from childhood to be warriors and protectors. They have the natural ability to see the overall situation, analyze and strategize what needs to be done. The warrior personality is not necessarily aggressive. However, if fighting is required, so be it. Most of the time though, the warrior clan is tasked with upholding the laws of Maat. This requires being honest, speaking the truth no matter what -- hurt feelings or not. They are fearless, adventurous risk takers. They do not tolerate injustices. Tuesday born people's job is to help the village let go of what is obsolete and move on to what is required in the new current situation. They are pioneering and innovative. Most other people are reluctant to change, even if it is for the better, so there can be a lot of arguments. This is a "masculine" or yang energy" that allows us to follow through on our goals. The warrior women in the movie, *"Black Panther"* fearlessly stood up for their community, and with the law of Maat announced the community came first, and then those that were physically able, yes, with martial arts and weapons fought. The Maat principle inherited in Killmonger and the other African tribal leader guided them to eventually put the future of the African nation first, although by Western standards this would be considered "weak," "soft" and "feminine." We know it as balance. The balance of masculine and feminine energies within all of us and for our communities' wholeness.

Another of the African-centered contradictions with Black Panther being one of the Avengers, is the use of brute force and fighting as a way to settle disagreements and to establish dominance. Even who was to become the king of Wakanda was decided by which brother killed the other brother. This is not the traditional African way. Kingships and other disputes were settled by consulting with the elders, the ancestors, and God through the use of trance and divination wisdom systems using cowrie shells, bones, and other sacred items. Personal opinions, emotions, and consensus were not essential for decision making. A better perspective would be gained through divination consultation to know who was most suited for a position, what was needed for the current situation, what may happen in the future, and the consequences of wrong behavior. Therefore, higher guidance was sought for impartial decision-making for the higher good of the entire community. Much could have been learned by all from both Killmonger's and T'Challa's initial return. In addition through consistent spiritual practices, the priests and priestesses would have already known ahead of time the father would be murdered, that T'Challa and later Killmonger would be coming home to Wakanda and would have prepared for these situations.

Chapter 5: Heru Khuti (Ogun) Clan

The other influence on my personality, that is the opposite of Het Heru's sweetness and dislike of any argumentative confrontations, is my moon sign. The planet that the moon was in at the time of your birth, also describes more of your personality than your astrological sun sign. My sidereal moon sign was in Scorpio which is a Mars energy. Although some computerized charts indicate a Sagittarius moon, I was born in the wee hours of the morning in the darkness of the night, while the moon was still in Scorpio. Mars is a warrior energy. West Africans would say, Ogun. Ancient northern Khametic Africans would say, Heru Khuti warrior energy.

"You don't look like you are in the Heru Khuti clan."

I smile. Quiet, with a charming smile instead of a menacing frown, I understand why people would ask, "You? In the Heru Khuti clan?" and laugh. They didn't see or hear of me loudly arguing, starting fights, or going around making trouble. Always slender, I didn't appear to be able to beat people up.

It was from classes taught by Ur Aua-t Sha-t Shemsut, the Queen Mother of the Chicago Ausar Auset Society Church community, I learned the more subtler characteristics of Heru Khuti as a fearless, risk taker. The fact I was there in the class, having rode a Greyhound bus or Amtrak train, got on subway trains and buses to travel to the Southside of Chicago was a hint. I'd been on New York City subway trains too. Never even occurred to me to be afraid until my brother said, "You were on the subway in New York? Don't do that again!"

A brief fear came over me, as I briefly remembered the movies and news reports of people being robbed or stabbed in the subway. But wait a minute! I hadn't seen any violence on the buses and trains in Chicago nor New York. Yet, in my brother's and my hometown, I saw a man grab a purse from a young woman sitting in the front of the bus behind the driver, then run out the door. She began sobbing and wailing, "He took my insulin. He has my insulin. What am I going to do?"

Occasionally, there were fights on the buses, but I'd seen none of this violence in the big cities. For years, I worked night shift, occasionally second shift, and even on dayshift having to be at work by 7 AM, it was dark going to and from work. I simply said a prayer and kept going. What's there to be afraid of?

Self-disciplined and focused, it is easier for me to immediately stop a behavior or habit cold turkey whenever I learned that it is wrong. Or I would steadily work hard to change over a few months or year. This takes courage and perseverance. You will certainly risk losing relationships, because close family and friends are used to you being the same. I'm always learning, growing, changing, and on the move. No one knows what I will do next, including myself!

Only another Heru Khuti person can be with a Heru Khuti person! That's what Ur Aua-t Sha-t Shemsut taught us. Their blunt, at times brutal honesty keeps away those who don't want their feelings hurt. Listening, I hadn't thought of myself that way. I do believe it's fairer to gently tell people privately to help them rather than joining others in talking behind their back. I don't tolerate injustice especially when watching others being mistreated. Therefore, people are shocked when I do speak up. Did I say "gently?" The wrongdoer(s) often wished I had argued, yelled and cussed at them. Instead, I simply tell the truth of the situation of what I observed. They become hurt and angry frequently avoiding me afterwards.

In the past, I gave people three strikes of disrespecting me and then I left. Took my few belongings and left. Not caring about what I left behind because my freedom and dignity was more important than the stuff or invested time I accumulated. And sometimes I've also left people behind, like I did two husbands.

Herukhuti's role is to point out what is obsolete, no longer useful, even old traditions and to pioneer new better ways of doing. However, many people are reluctant and afraid to change. This is where I've gotten in trouble with leaders in communities and organizations. "We've done this for years. Why can't we just keep doing it this way?"

Over the years, I've toned this tendency to criticize down a lot by telling myself it is their organization, they have the right to do what they want with it. Except when it comes to injustices, then I speak up. This is also why I rather not belong to any one organization or religious group. Now that I'm older, I have stayed longer. Can you imagine? Some places I've stayed 10 years or more. Hard for me to believe this myself. Sometimes you have to be a part of the change you want to see in the world.

Heru Khuti children often get a lot of beatings and punishments. Not so much because of their impulsive, exploring and experimenting but because they know when their parents are lying, are unfair or being hypocritical by telling the child not to do something but the parents are doing it. They will fearlessly argue with their parents and teachers. My stepsister told me that when I was little, I had a reputation for not being disciplined and was like a wild child, according to my stepfather. Maybe, maybe not. Most of the beatings I remember receiving from him was because his rules didn't make sense. He would accuse me of lying when I told him, I honestly didn't do what he wanted to punish me for. Previously, my mother bragged that I was not a good liar so I'd already given up trying to lie. My defense was to not cry. Just stand there and look at him. It didn't make sense to me, to mentally accept punishment for what I did not do.

Chapter 6: Rituals

All African descent churches, yes even CHURCHES use music, the rhythm of the preacher's voice, tambourine, drum going faster and faster until lured into a peaceful trance until you feel like getting up dancing. Filled with the "Holy Ghost" from Gospel praise songs extended longer and longer and longer. In Africa, and elsewhere, African spiritual religious rituals it is the same, except everyone is up dancing and singing.

Each month, Ausar Auset Society Church's classes taught us about a different deity from the nine Paut Neteru deities on the Tree of Life. Auset, Sebek, Het Heru, Heru, Heru Khuti, Maat, Tehuti, Sekert, and Ausar. Each deity symbolizes beliefs, personality traits and behaviors that everyone has within self. The goal is to have the ability to change and do what is required for whatever the specific situation and challenges life presents us with. During the specified month we did our best to personify the deity's good qualities, wore their colors, ate their foods. In addition, we each did our own individual oracle readings on what to personally focus on throughout the month.

On the full moon we came together in an African style ritual, singing the deity's mantra and dancing to their specific drum rhythm. This was similar to the music on the meditation cassettes and CDs but was much more powerful live. The combined group energy and music took me easily into trance. Initially, the priest and priestesses were astonished at my ability to dance and easily go into trance, since I had not been exposed to African traditions before.

Ausar Auset Society Church doesn't do animal sacrifices for rituals. Instead, each individual is encouraged to sacrifice problem thinking and behaviors and replace it with better understanding and appropriate behavior for a better self, family and community. The following example is what I gained from a Sebek ritual.

***

Sebek (Elegba) Ritual

Sebek is described as a dog, a clever fox or coyote. The priest instructed us to see ourselves as having the head of a dog as we danced to the sound of the drums and Sebek mantra being sung. Many indigenous traditions have a trickster or joker to get us to laugh at our own foolishness. Sebek had me laughing as I saw myself as a dog digging and digging long tunnels outside at night, looking for my bones. An image of my checkbooks came to my mind. At home I couldn't find my checkbook for weeks. I intended to tuck it away safely but somehow hid my checks from myself. Usually I know where everything I own is, because I have a designated place for each item where I consistently return it. I couldn't even hide money from myself. Other people are happily surprised when they find five dollars or $20 in their pockets. Not me.

At the time, I was a roommate with someone whose son often had parties with his friends in our absence. I'd return to see people had been in my room and slept in my bed without even the courtesy to make it up before they left. On the other hand, at least then I knew someone had been in my bed. But this wasn't the first time, that I had misplaced checks. Hid them from myself, thinking I was putting them in a safe place. It happened twice, years before when I tucked my income tax checks away, even forgot about them until I found them a year later. I had to call the IRS and ask if I could still cash it! They luckily said, "Yes." Sebek's number is three. This was the third time this happened to me, so obviously I still hadn't learned my lesson yet. I was going overboard with trying to feel safe, but was it true? Perhaps I was only tricking myself. Realizing this while in trance, I laughed and laughed vowing to let go of worries. Later that week, I found my checkbook.

The unseen healing energies from the Ausar Auset Society Church group meditations and rituals gave me some of the incredible inner love and peace, I had longed for since during my near death experience in 1982, when I experienced Oneness with total love, peace, acceptance and understanding. I repeatedly prayed asking, how can I have this inner peace in Earth life? I felt driven to heal emotionally from past traumas and grief, after trying to push away the grief feelings by working hard in college and on the job didn't help. So I tried different types of alternative psychotherapy modalities. Then in 1991, I discovered the Ausar Auset Society Church meditations, yoga, healthy Ayurvedic diet, homeopathy and rituals healed my emotional distress, toned down my psychic empathic sensitivity, so much so, I no longer needed talk psychotherapy.

A note on animal sacrifices: killing animals have a different meaning and reverence for cultures who herd animals for food and wealth, than for U.S. Americans who think their food comes from the local grocery store, and children believe money is free from ATM machines. My mother used to ask me when I was a child and begged her for money or items, "What do you think? Money grows on trees?"

What may be a sacrifice, emotional, or financial hardship for one person may not feel like a sacrifice for someone else.

Disclaimer: What I write here in this book about Ausar Auset Society Church's teachings is from my own understanding and perspective. Much has probably changed in the 20 years I've been away from Ausar Auset Society Church.

Chapter 7: I Ching

The second divination method I learned was the I Ching. My first I Ching reading was, of course, for getting more understanding of my destiny life lessons. Initially, a teacher showed me the book, *The Illustrated I Ching Workbook*, which uses a simple method using three cleaned regular pennies method for determining the six lines of an I Ching reading. Other books' methods require mathematical calculations. You throw the pennies or I Ching coins gently onto a tabletop, then write down either a straight line or a broken line to indicate yang or yin lines. You do this three times, pause, leave a space, and then throw the I Ching coins another three times to get the upper second trigram. You use the chart in the back of the books to determine the numbers of the combined six lines, that make up the hexagrams.

In a short time, I began to love the I Ching as a way to receive guidance from God. This is because the I Ching explains the overall situation. Perhaps it is problems with the supervisor, or a business's finances, or business practices or national or global economic or political influences. Sometimes it is not the right time to do what you are inquiring about. For me, knowing this was a great relief. Through religions and schooling, we are so used to thinking that each of us personally is to blame, when what we trying to do encounters obstacles. Instead, the I Ching helps us remember there is a larger world around us. Many happenings in the environment influences our lives, which we are unaware of, and couldn't have control over. This allows me to let go of worries and be peaceful knowing that there is truly a divine plan, and all will be well.

From I Ching classes, the book, *The Harlem River Arrangement: The I Ching Transcripts,* by Ra Un Nefer Amen, and personal experiences I learned there are up cycles and down cycles in life. This means there are months or years when we have more energy to do activities then at other times. For example, similar to the seasons of the year, we are less likely to feel like doing a lot of work in the winter when it is very cold or in the summer when it is very hot. On long summer days we would harm our health working from sun up, to sun down especially in the heat. Additionally, we extend the day even longer with artificial lights, air conditioning, and heating in the winter. Our businesses, schools, and extracurricular recreation activity schedules demand continuous productivity year-round, without regard to the changing seasons or individual needs. Pushing and pushing our bodies, yet somehow, not expecting our bodies to break down and demand a rest from all the overthinking and exhaustion. An I Ching message will warn us when we need to rest.

The other observation is the I Ching would sometimes give me the same hexagram or another hexagram with similar interpretations no matter what question that I asked. After a while I understood it meant the message was about me. Therefore, I needed to change my behavior or my thinking. Soon, there would be situations to test and challenge me. For example, the instructions may be to be quiet and patient, but I felt frustrated, righteous, and wanted to advocate. The I Ching may indicate it is a situation where those in charge aren't able to change yet, won't listen, nor understand. Therefore, I would be wasting my time or even making the situation worse. Then there are times when the message is, I do need to speak up but I am afraid or tired, or I don't know how. The I Ching gives me the encouragement to learn how.

The book Ra Un Nefer Amen published in 2014, *I Ching Praxis: Forty Years of Practical Insights into the I Ching*, in my opinion doesn't have the spiritual depth of his class lectures. Well okay, the title does say "practical." This opinion of course is based on my comparison to his previous book, *The Harlem River Arrangement: The I Ching Transcripts*, which is all I knew when I started.

Chapter 8: I Ching Destiny Readings

My I Ching Destiny Reading

Hexagram 34 (lines 3 and 6) into Hexagram 38

Hexagram 34 Power of the Great. Has a potential for great strength and power. However, I'm being warned there is danger of me relying on my own willpower and forgetting to ask what is right and fair before proceeding. May tend to push forward without waiting for the right time, and to see the overall perspective of the situation. Need to persevere with patience and calmness.

Line 3: gives the image of a goat butting its head against a hedge, and getting its horns tangled and stuck in the branches. Well, my mother did say I was stubborn and hardheaded when I was a young child. And that I did actually used to bang my head!

Warns against pushing ahead anyway thinking and boasting you can do it.

Line 6: The goat is stuck and can't go backwards or forward. So eventually relaxes, considers its mistakes and yields. Therefore, good fortune as now are able to go forward.

Hopefully, will evolve to being able to let go of feeling the need to always defend yourself and be so stubborn because of fears and being insecure.

CHAPTER 8: I CHING DESTINY READINGS

Hexagram 38 Opposition can lead to misunderstandings and disagreements. But opposites are natural dualities that often causes us to reach out to others to seek union.

Later, after the class was introduced to the book, *The Astrology of the I Ching*, I learned there are more ways to obtain an accurate I Ching destiny reading than just throwing the coins. Here instead your destiny is based on your birthdate, location and time of birth. The book has complicated math and charts for determining your birth hexagrams as well as degrees of auspiciousness or good fortune. Again, each hexagram describes the best personality qualities to aspire to as well as possible weaknesses and troubles in your life. Decades later with the invention of the internet and ability to google anything, there are I Ching websites that will do the math calculations for you. Gratefully, I discovered my math was all wrong! And stunned with mixed feelings in 2021 when I read the correct destiny hexagram, that I will discuss in a later chapter. For now, learn along with me.

Chapter 9: Career Readings

The next important spiritual reading you will want to know, is what your career path should be. This is what I got for mine in January 1993.

Geb tem tchaas/ Amen hetep. Hexagram 40 Deliverance (lines 2, 3, 5, and 6) into hexagram 33 Retreat. Geb means physical health or the health of the situation you inquired about. It also represents the physical world and material needs. At the time I did this reading I was having problems with asthma.

Hexagram 40 Deliverance as obstacles, difficulties and tensions are beginning to be resolved. Return to normal life as soon as possible but don't overdo. Correct and forgive mistakes.

Line 2: By developing one's own inner strength and correctness this helps overcome obstacles in public life caused by those persons wrongly placed in official positions.

Line 3: When going from poverty to experiencing comforts, have to be careful not to go beyond one's means or usual personality and position.

Line 5: Have to leave behind people that are doing wrong. This means mentally letting go too.

Line 6: There is a person in a high social position who is wicked and preventing progress. He should be forcefully removed.

Hexagram 33 Retreat. It is best to retreat from the situation temporarily. Meanwhile prepare to return later.

October 1994. What energies are governing my career this incarnation? I forgot I already did this reading the previous year. At that time, it was my understanding it was only to be done once in a lifetime. Breathed a sigh of relief later when learned you can do career readings as needed. Nonetheless, this is the answer I received:

Metu Neter cards: Tehuti tu tchaas /Tehuti tem maat.

Hexagram 58 The Joyous represents true inner joy. Joy along with gentleness and friendliness influences other people. However you shouldn't get caught up in excessive amusement, charisma and social pleasures.

Since I was just beginning to learn about the I Ching, I didn't know yet what these hexagrams meant.

Please Note: The I Ching interpretations and insights came from reading several I Ching books, listed in the back of this book, which I used to summarize the main points here and in later chapters.

Chapter 10: Native American Cards

Medicine Woman Cards

A friend, Anna asked me if I wanted her to do a reading for me. At that time, I didn't know of any cards except the Metu Neter cards. I accepted my friend's offer of advice because of curiosity and I didn't know what I was going to do with my life. Having withdrawn from art school because it was too expensive and was about to resign from a minimum wage job working in the deli kitchen of a natural foods store, I didn't know what to do next.

The seventy-eight cards set that Anna used was the Medicine Woman Tarot Deck. It came with a small paperback, *The Medicine Woman Inner Guidebook: A Woman's Guide to Her Unique Powers Using the Medicine Woman Tarot Deck.* Ann pulled the usual three cards for past, present and future, the Pierced Shield, Eight of Arrows, and the High Priestess Seeker: Inner Reflection/Wisdom cards. I made brief notes from what she read to me, however after all these years, I only remembered the turning point guidance and that I needed some R&R (rest and relaxation/ recreation). Both the past and future cards Ann pulled for me mentioned "turning points" especially my future card the Seeker: Inner Reflection and Wisdom card.

I went home and followed the instructions to make a list of what major events happened every seventh year of my life from when I was seven, fourteen, twenty-one, twenty-eight, and thirty-five years old. The major events could occur a year before or after.

7 years old: My mother married my stepfather and we moved to a city in another state.

14 years old: Sent to foster home at age 13.

21 years old: Air Force. Married.

28 years old: Near-death experience at age 26. Graduated nursing school at 28. Divorced at 30.

35 years old: Joined a new religion. Moved to Chicago to go to art school.

Chapter 11: Medicine Cards

Another friend, Paula, and I went looking for the Medicine Woman Tarot Deck at the Healing Earth Resources bookstore. The store didn't have it. So instead, when we found among many other cards, *The Medicine Cards: The Discovery of Power Through the Ways of Animals* book, we each bought a set. The original card deck had forty-four cards and was later expanded to fifty-two cards.

Another Destiny Reading: My Nine Totem Animals

The behaviors and attitudes of these nine power or totem animals represent abilities, talents, and challenges you have had throughout your life since birth. Some abilities still need awakening and developing, yet the potential is here. Connecting to these nine power totem animals in each of the seven directions East, South, West, North, Above, Below, and Within will help with understanding the lessons of each direction. To learn about yourself and for a detailed explanation and instructions refer to the book, <u>The Medicine Cards</u>.

East: Butterfly/Transformation. The East direction represents accepting guidance for our greatest spiritual challenges and illumination. I gasped and briefly sobbed as I read the interpretations for both the Butterfly and the Snake Cards because these accurately described the past 40 years of my life. It seemed I was continuously in the process of some type of transformation. The butterfly metaphor was my inspiration to not go backwards when life got tough, because it's not possible anyway for a butterfly in the chrysalis stage to go back to be a caterpillar. Plus I've loved butterflies, embroidering, painting, and drawing butterflies to me.

South: Snake/Transmutation. The South direction is our childhood trust and innocence that needs to be protected. People with true snake energy medicine are considered rare because they are able to symbolically go through multiple snakebites, being poisoned, shedding one's skin and still survive and thrive. Healing on all levels physical, mental, emotional and spiritual. Although you can fear changing one's being and life situation yet again because change can be uncomfortable, you know this won't last long. Ongoing life-death-rebirth cycles. These transmutations bring about the ability to create through enhanced psychic, sexual, and spiritual energies. Having survived childhood abuse, domestic violence and ongoing racism it felt like I was getting bitten again and again. Therefore, it's been hard for me to trust other people and my talented abilities.

West: Grouse: Sacred Spiral. The West is our ability to be introspective going within to know own personal truths, answers and goals. Grouse symbol of a spiral brings awareness of personal power. In meditation, visualize yourself spinning in a spiral pattern towards the center. This reminds me of how children love to spin yet don't seem to get dizzy. In high school modern dance class, I learned to spin without getting dizzy by looking at a specific chosen spot on the wall with each turn. Nowadays I can spin with my eyes closed, and when opening them occasionally but not fall down. The Sufi whirling dervishes spin in a spiral circle that brings on a state of ecstasy when they connect to the oneness of the universe. Dancing is another way to ground myself because I can be too much in my head daydreaming, mostly problem-solving and analyzing. Grouse also symbolizes death and rebirth! (groan). Sekert too.

North: Turkey: Giveaway. The North is wisdom gained. Turkey is an acknowledgment you have transcended the self. To now be able to be of service to others. Turkey energy medicine is similar to the principles of Maat that I learned from Ausar Auset Society Church: sharing, helping others knowing we are all one, that what you do for others you are also doing for yourself. But not to give to receive. Knowing heaven always provides for all — gives inner peace, faith and optimism. No need to want and hold onto stuff or talents you aren't using that someone could make use of. Willingly give away what you are not using.

Above: Hummingbird: Joy. Above us is the Great Star Nation from where we came and will return. The attributes are very similar to those of Het Heru/Osun. Pure inner joy and love, spreading joy with your presence, along with harmony, and an appreciation for outer beauty. Hence, I was given a Khamitic name meaning Heaven is my joy.

Below: Antelope: Action. Below is the Earth, the Inner Earth. The importance of being connected and staying grounded with the Earth. Antelope energy medicine gives mental clarity and physical strength with the ability to make quick decisions and take action to get tasks done. Antelope provides guidance and solutions when we listen and act. Have the courage to trust and speak truth, being willing to go a new different way instead of automatically following others. I did mostly listen and follow my intuition. What I needed in order to follow through, synchronistically showed up: the money, time, the information, and people to help. But I was timid in groups and institutions about doing things differently. I would speak up but if leadership kept doing routines as usual, I followed too. Most initiatives I did in the privacy of my own home.

Within: Swan/Grace. The Within direction symbolizes your own heart's joy and your own personal space within and around you. You have a choice of what and with whom to share your personal thoughts, energy and space. Be faithful to your own personal truths. Swan energy is being able to accept a greater divine plan and going with the flow. It is the ability to go into the dream time, with different levels of consciousness to know the future. Again more transformation and healing as a result. For me, that means when I feel sleepy, to stop doing whatever I'm doing, take some deep breaths, perhaps a little nap, and also reminds me to meditate regularly. Accordingly, when I need to be fully present and accounted for, Swan energy reminds me I need to do regular grounding exercises to connect with the Earth. And to know the difference between what it feels like to be grounded versus daydreamy.

Right Side: Elk: Stamina. The right side direction protects our masculine side similar to how a good father would. It gives us our courage and warrior energy. Elk represents stamina which is increased by pacing yourself, although this may take longer to accomplish your goals, you will be less likely to become burnt out. Elk is also having companionship with those of your own gender. In my case sisterhood. On the other hand, Elk is doing activities with the opposite gender because it is important to have a healthy exchange of masculine and feminine energies.

Left Side: Coyote. The left side direction protects your feminine side. The feminine qualities of receiving abundance and nurturing and connection in relationships for yourself and others. An appreciation of mothers.

Coyote is the infamous trickster. But most of the time we trick ourselves. When we don't learn from our mistakes, or self-sabotage and fool ourselves by not facing the truth of how we really feel with the present situation. Coyote gets us to laugh at ourselves. It can also warn us somebody else is trying to deceive us. However, I wondered how coyote traits would protect my feminine side? So I pulled another card asking for clarification. Dog: Loyalty. Dog medicine energy is loyalty. Being able to serve others and humanity and explore deeper ways to serve. Being loyal to friends. Yet maintain allegiance to your own personal truth. Thank you Sebek!

Chapter 12: Sacred Path Cards

Later we discovered there were spreads in the Medicine Card book that used both the Sacred Path Cards and the Medicine Cards. We decided to buy the Sacred Path Cards too. The Sacred Path Cards became my favorite cards. I prefer the *Sacred Path Cards: The Discovery of Self Through Native Teachings book to the Medicine Cards* book because the accompanying Sacred Path stories explain the Native American spiritual teachings in an easy to understand way. Therefore, easier to apply to my everyday life.

One of the first Sacred Path cards I pulled was the 1 Pipe: Prayer/Inner Peace Card. It reminds us of personal responsibility for creating one's own inner peace or discord that flows out into the world. We radiate the feelings and thoughts we hold inside whether we say or act on them or not. We can make the choice to aid world peace by healing our own inner conflict, hatred, doubt or anger. At that time, I had a lot of sadness and loneliness.

In 2009, I found the *Sacred Path Cards Workbook.* It has questions to ask yourself. Now, I use it more often than the initial hardcover book that came with the forty-four Sacred Path cards. The workbook has additional card spreads for specific questions. However, I rarely do card spreads. One card is challenging enough to understand and live out in everyday life!

Combination Readings

I began adding both the Medicine Cards and Sacred Path Cards to using the I Ching, when I did my every six months' solstice readings on June 20 and December 21 each year. Sometimes the I Ching only has one hexagram with no specific line stressed to help me know what information applies to me. Similarly, if I pulled only Uatchet or Nekebet cards from the Metu Neter cards deck. With time I saw that the Sacred Path cards with additional other oracle cards helped me understand both the I Ching and the Metu Neter readings much better.

After a while I stopped using the Medicine Cards because I was rarely out in nature to connect with animals to follow through with the recommended exercises. It was even difficult to visualize my totem animals. This made me feel I wasn't honoring the Native American culture. Whenever I do encounter a bird or animal, then I pull out the Medicine Card book to read the interpretation.

Usually I only pull one card from a deck instead of doing the additional card spreads of laying out three, five, ten cards, or more. For me, it is much easier to understand and follow through on lifestyle changes with just one card. Otherwise it is not possible to remember all that information anyway. Plus, I'm not purposely using the cards to predict my future. I prefer to help influence my future by taking it one day at a time, in the present.

Chapter 13: In Person Spiritual Readings

It was 1991. I was riding home in a car with an elderly couple when I felt such an intense sense of panic and fear I could barely breathe. Soon after I arrived home and got into bed, the phone rang. It was my grandmother Mother Dear, "Your father passed away. His heart gave out."

He died at 11:00 PM, the exact time when I was feeling panicked.

A few days later, feeling lost and confused as I sat across a small table in front of a man dressed in a white robe, and white trousers with a white cloth hat on his dark-skinned head. Nervously I looked around, waiting, in a large room with white walls, I've never been in before. I didn't know what he was doing as he silently tossed some small white seashells on the table. When he spoke, he advised me what to do for my father.

"Hang three bananas at the top of a doorway in your home. Leave it there until the bananas fall off by themselves. Wear bright blue clothes."

I didn't understand most of what he said or why he wanted to me to do such strange things.

Yet, he told me after he tossed and moved around the cowrie shells again, "I can't advise you about your life. You already know what I know."

Huh? What did I know that he knows? From the little he told me, I assumed this meant the wisdom he had. I was only 35 years old at the time. What did I know? Later I learned he was a Yoruba Babalawo priest. He used the cowrie shells or coconut shells to do Ifa divination readings.

Chapter 14: Cuban Candomble Priestess Consultation

On a fall day in 1995. I waited in the living room, with comfortable couches and chairs surrounded by full bookshelves. I kept myself occupied with the book, *Light Emerging* while subtly listening and observing comings and goings of people in and out of the other room. My friend who invited me, sat next to me. We chatted occasionally but I was nervous not knowing what to expect. I'd paid my fifty dollars ahead of time. After, approximately an hour my name was called, and I was led into a small room where sat a young man and an older woman. He was her interpreter. She introduced herself as Valdeci, then asked my birthdate, wrote notes then proceeded to throw an assortment of small items, shells, and rocks inside a box lined with a red cloth. She gave me a piece of paper with the following:

1st Orisha: Osoosi
2nd Orisha: Osala
3rd Orisha: Oya

The only Orisha that I was familiar with is Oya. Oya is a Yoruba name with attributes similar to Sekert.

The priestess explained to me, " Oguna rules your head. Ogun is the Yoruba name for warriors who in Africa carries a machete or sword. However, after coming to the United States living among the Native Americans, then Ogun began using a bow and arrow instead. And his name became Osoosi. You are very spiritual. Osoosi's job is make sure your spiritual path stays clear and straight. But this is a double-edge sword. Anything or anyone that gets in the way must go. Therefore you have suffered many losses. From here forward you will have minor difficulties. Your finances will clear shortly. You will find the right job. But you must first lay the foundation, to plan spiritually and materially. Stick to your goals. You must find and follow your own path. Put spiritual first. Health will improve as your spiritual is healed. She gave me cleansing herbs with instructions to mix them with water, and then pour them over my head while I'm standing in the bathtub. Based on the reading from her throwing the items in the box, she said, "I will pray for you but I can't tell you what to do. You already know."

She then asked me if I had any questions. I asked about my mother, where she might be. The interpreter hesitated for a long time and only gave me a few words compared to all the the priestess was telling me. They argued a little between them. Basically he told me, "Your mother is still alive but it will be very difficult to find her. You may not be able to accept the conditions she is in. Some people may not want to be found."

Similar to the previous Ifa reading by the Yoruba Babalawo priest in 1991, again I was told that she couldn't tell me what to do, because I already know what these priest(ess) knew. But how can this be? I still felt as lost as I did four years prior! I'd dropped out of art school and was working at a health food store as a cook in the deli section for minimum wage.

A far cry from my training as a nurse. Depressed with severe chest pains with exertion, as well as while sitting, I don't know how I had the strength and the will to continue to be on my feet all day lifting heavy pots, cooking and serving customers, putting away supplies, washing dishes and mopping floors. Plus walk for one hour home and walk another hour back to work Monday through Saturday because initially I didn't have money for bus fare. Perhaps my smile got me through. But is that all I got for my fifty dollars? I needed answers and guidance for what to do next with my life.

Well, on the positive side, at least I didn't have to do similar to some of my friends who went to the same Candomble priestess and had to pay hundreds of dollars to buy an animal to sacrifice along with continued consultations with a priest. A true precious blessing, and thinking about it now, as I write this, still brings me to tears because what the priestess explained to me immediately brought comfort, calmness and healing to my heart. I cried when she told me about Ososi, because this helped me understand why I had so many losses in my life. Over time I had become hurt and bitter. It was a big relief to have this explanation and meaning. I could stop blaming myself and others, and instead open to forgiveness.

After my consultation with the priestess, I of course went searching for information about who are the other two Orisha, that she told me ruled my head were. Osala is a Spanish language variation of the Yoruba name for Obatala. It is somewhat similar to the Khamitic description of Ausar. That's why the Babalawo priest who did my Ifa reading told me, I should wear white, and whenever he saw me afterwards, he would actually prostrate himself prone on the floor straight out in front of me. Since this was my first reading and introduction to African spirituality, before I went to Ausar Auset Society Church, I didn't understand.

At a local African American bookstore, I found a small book, *Ochosi, Ifa and the Spirit of the Tracker*, about the story of Osoosi. Spelled and pronounced "Ochosi." It seems when you have strong Osoosi energy ruling your life you will frequently get hurt by and suffer the most losses from the people closest to you. His own grandmother killed his pet bird because she was hungry, after a month with very little food. This parrot was his companion helping him hunt for food in the forest. His grandmother wasn't thinking of the consequences, nor of the special close relationship Ochosi had with his parrot. She only thought of her own needs. There's more to the story.

Ochosi had other skills and talents besides hunting, I witnessed and understand as similar talents unfolded in my own life. In later chapters, you'll learn more of what I learned.

Ochosi energy may have had influence over the Muslim name my mother gave me. Later, I learned that my name Haneefa means more than "inclined to righteousness" as my mother told me or "true believer" found in name books and on the Internet. A university student from Saudi Arabia told me in 2010, that the word "hanif" means "straight, to straighten what is crooked, and to divert something back to being straight or to correct it."

My mouth dropped open, but I didn't know if I could tell a Muslim what I'd been told by a pagan priestess, so I didn't. Osoosi's job is make sure my spiritual path stays clear and straight. How is it I would be told similar meanings by different approaches, languages, countries, religions and cultures? My mother requested my name from a Muslim leader in Pakistan. Perhaps he used astrology to determine which name to give me. Aries is ruled by Mars the warrior. But where did the predicted spiritual abilities come from?

PART TWO: GETTING AWAY

Chapter 15: School for International Training

By 1996, I could no longer tolerate the concrete jungle of being surrounded by tall apartment buildings in Chicago. Initially, I thought this need to be out in nature was because when I was a young child my mother frequently took us to the large city parks. As an adult, I too spent time in parks. However, although Chicago has large parks, it also has a larger population hanging out in the parks, making having privacy rare.

In my meditations and whenever I closed my eyes, even momentarily or before sleep, I would see the beautiful bright vivid fields of red flowers I'd seen when I was on the Other Side during my near death experience. Seeing the red flowers immediately filled me with love and calmness. After a while, I began to want to go, to wherever in the world those flowers may be. In addition, I saw myself in a valley between steep tall mountains with occasional waterfalls. It was peaceful there too, so I began to desperately pray to go to both places.

During the School of the Art Institute's orientation in 1994, I learned about their student study abroad programs. Previously, traveling did not seem like an option because I thought only rich people traveled to other countries. A year later, before almost dropping out of the school because it was way too expensive, I inquired about the study abroad program when the spiritual group that I belonged to was going to go to Ghana in Africa. Couldn't I finish my bachelor's degree abroad? The Ghana study abroad program focused specifically on Ghana's art history seemed ideal. Disappointedly, she explained that it wasn't an option because it was an exchange student program, meaning students from Ghana would have to come in my place and that was not likely to happen, unless they were rich and could support themselves without working in the United States.

She showed me the School for International Training's had study abroad programs in over forty countries to choose from, including Ghana. Tanzania had the tallest mountain in Africa, Mount Kilimanjaro. Kenya was nearby. The tuition with scholarships and loans would pay for my year on campus with room and board, and include the flights to and from a country, during my senior year.

As I usually do oracle readings for major decisions, especially considering moving to another state or country even if temporary, I used both Metu Neter cards and the I Ching coins for guidance and insights into the situation:

What energies are needed to be successful at the School for International Training (SIT)? Metu Neter card: Herukhuti hetep. Being courageous, hardworking and fair to others will help remove obstacles.

And then later, "What is my purpose or goal for being here? Metu Neter card: Maat tu tchaas/ Amen tem maat. To have an optimistic sharing attitude, and to learn to let go of old conditioned behavior patterns.

I Ching: hexagram 13 (line 3) into hexagram 25.

Hexagram 13 Fellowship with Men. Focus is on maintaining relationships and friendships with the need to continuously cultivate one's own emotional and spiritual growth to have pa-

CHAPTER 15: SCHOOL FOR INTERNATIONAL TRAINING

tience and understanding with others. To be able to transcend one's own fears, selfishness and unreasonable expectations. Most of all, we must strive for higher spiritual clarity, a unified universe as guided by oracles, being open and honest, towards what it means for everyone to be treated equally.

Line 3: May have mistrust and difficult getting along with others, especially when there are differences in perspectives. Being defensive brings humiliation.

Hexagram 25 Innocence. Our true nature is inherently good, especially when we are connected with our divinely guided intuition, inner peace and joy. Success, if don't try to be other than authentic self.

I decided to enroll in the World Issues Program at the School for International Training. It had a bachelor completion program with the junior year on campus, then the senior year away, usually in another country, or in the United States for international students to do independent study. All of the classes offered were so interesting it was difficult to choose only three classes for the first semester from either Population Studies; Peace and Conflict; Community Society and Development; Human Ecology; or Economics concentration courses. I did I Ching readings on each class to decide but I won't be detailing them here now. The classes I chose were Population Studies; Human Ecology; and Peace and Conflict. All students were required to take the Intercultural Communication class along with some brief introductory economic, grant writing, and teaching English as a second language workshops. The next semester I took the second part of each course: Women, Health and Development; Mediation Skills; and Human Ecology.

As I looked at the teacher at the chalkboard and then around the room at my new classmates, I realize I've seen all of them before – including the teachers. But how could that be? Half the class was from other countries, and the other half of the twenty-six students were from other states. The international students were two from Cambodia, two from Zimbabwe, one from Kenya, one from Eritrea, one from Germany, one from Ecuador, three from Japan, and one from Taiwan.

Chapter 16: The Drop Off

We were only on campus for three days when our teachers explained to us that we would be going to visit nearby Vermont towns. A van would come at 9:00 in the morning. I thought we were going together as a class. However, they informed us that students would be dropped off in pairs or trios in separate towns. We were each given a roll of Lifesaver candy and a five-dollar bill. The van will return at 9:00 the next morning. As the van drove off, Sara, Chifen, and I stood on the corner looking around us at the very quiet town with only a few people walking on the streets. Who could we even ask for help? It's good we already had breakfast, but five dollars wouldn't buy lunch let alone dinner! We walked a little way but then decided to sit in a small park in order to not draw unnecessary attention to ourselves. A Chinese, African American, and white young women in a state whose population was ninety-nine percent white. We nervously joked about it.

As the sun began to set, we started to worry. Where would we spend the night? We still hadn't eaten, and it was dinner time. Across the street from the park was a small church. Together we decided to go knock on the door. The pastor invited us in. His family lived in an attached house. We sat at the table with them as his wife served us a casserole for dinner. Then off to church we went! Not quite what we bargained for. The pastor had already preached to us during dinner, and he continued preaching to us after church while we were preparing for bed, then during breakfast the next day. He yelled at me for doing my usual daily morning Tai Chi. He didn't want to expose his children to anything else but fundamental Christianity, and that's why they home schooled them. He was preaching nonstop to an atheist, a Muslim and a Buddhist! We ran out the door after breakfast. Our ears full, we were glad to get away. Relieved to see the SIT van on the corner.

The School for International Training Campus is located approximately 5 miles away from downtown Brattleboro, Vermont. Our classes were in large houses, as were our dorms, therefore giving us a family style community feel. Even the newest building with the cafeteria looked like a large house. Alongside the paths and roads were bubbling streams, waterfalls, and wooded areas. Surrounded by rolling hills, the hills looked like mountains to me. I loved hiking through the woods and up the hills. In the fall, the bright spectacular colors of the autumn foliage was breathtaking. We often had classes outside, while moose looked on.

"Mud season? What's a mud season?" I asked.

I guess I should've known the answer, because the pretty white boots that a friend gave to me, became brownish as my feet got sucked in with each step in several inches of snow. Hey, who could complain? I'd truly gotten away from the tall concrete apartment buildings and skyscrapers of large cities.

A Different Perspective. While I was at a bookstore in downtown Brattleboro, I found another I Ching book, *I Ching: a New Interpretation for Modern Times*. Reading this new version of Hexagram 34 Great Strength made me feel much better about my incarnation destiny reading. I learned I have lot more influence on other people than I ever thought. Having grown up with a lot of criticism by my fathers and from negative racial stereotypes by others, I was a quiet introvert. Protected from the streets, I always felt I had to catch up with everyone else. I wondered why anyone would pay attention to me. Still hexagram 34 warns me to not to take advantage of people using my influence. Nor ignore I do have influential power. My lacking self-confidence, awareness and social skills would have people confused and bring them down. Being more outgoing than usual would actually give other people strength. This was a surprise to me. Line 3: cautioned me to not become overconfidence from past successes, and to not try to force situations.

Chapter 17: Which Country?

During the School for International Training's application process, potential students were asked to list three countries they wanted to go to and with short essays explain why. Of course, I couldn't say it was because I saw visions of fields of flowers, mountains and waterfalls. I had to learn more about each country.

To decide, I inquired of the oracles about Jamaica, Australia's aboriginal culture, Kenya and Zimbabwe. Zimbabwe was the best reading. I actually cried because I hadn't heard of Zimbabwe, didn't know anything about it. Later when I went to the library to do research, I calmed down when I saw Zimbabwe actually did have fields of flowers because the Dutch grew and exported tulips from Zimbabwe. It also has the enormous, famous Victoria Falls. In addition, I was interested in indigenous medicine and Zimbabweans often go to traditional healers. Since I was a registered nurse, I wanted to study healthcare systems.

Deciding whether to go to The School for International Training's College Semester Abroad Program:

Metu Neter cards: Sebek tu Maat/Het Heru hetep. Some of Sebek's attributes are travel and education.

I Ching hexagram 37 (line 4) into Hexagram 13. Line 4: Great good fortune and well-being when expenditures and income are balanced. In public life, this is the person whose sharing benefits the general welfare of all. Again hexagram 13 counsel on how do I make and maintain friendships with people whose culture is different from mine?

Zimbabwe Organization Rural Association Progress (ORAP) SIT Study Abroad Program?

I Ching: Hexagram 21 Biting Through (lines 5 and 6) into hexagram 17 Following. Hexagram 21 is about removing obstacles to unity in the community because of someone's misbehavior. They will need correcting or punishing. Each line of the hexagram helps determine whether the penalty should be mild, harsh or severe. Line 5 is more about the judge being too lenient with punishment. Line 6 is a person who's behavior is incorrigible and they need to be removed from the community and denied privileges. Hexagram 17 Following: is when someone more experienced helps someone less experienced. Usually this is an elder helping. Learning to share and serve others. It also means following the natural cycles and laws of the universe.

I decided to go to Zimbabwe anyway, although I didn't understand who's behavior needed to be corrected, but I was encouraged by the I Ching changing into a positive situation if there are elders there to assist.

Chapter 18: Zimbabwe

After a sixteen-hour flight from New York, we stayed the night at a hotel in Johannesburg, South Africa before flying to Bulawayo in the morning. Resting in bed, whenever I closed my eyes, I saw red flowers with green leaves. I thought, as I looked at the bright vivid colors behind my eyelids that I must be getting close to where there will be endless fields of flowers like I seen for years in meditations and dreams.

Upon arrival in the city of Bulawayo, I observed the scenery from the van's windows. The land seemed semi-desert with green cactus plants that resembled aloe vera. It was the end of winter in the Southern Hemisphere, so there were miles and miles of bare short trees with crooked limbs. The houses had stucco on the outside in various colors of white, tan, blue, green pastel colors. Most of the houses had small gardens surrounded by red dirt. In spite of the bare trees, there were large bushes with beautiful bright red, light or hot pink flowers. Perhaps in the spring after the rains, I will see the endless fields or bushes of real red and other color flowers.

Synchronistically I was led to choose Zimbabwe. Soon after coming onto the ORAP Zenzele College campus, I suddenly felt like I've been in this area before. The way the air felt, the furnishings even in the bathroom and kitchen. Very peaceful, safe feeling atmosphere. Perhaps from memories of my great aunt Lil's farm, when I was a little girl, where my family stayed for a few weeks each summer. Maybe my history goes back much further. It was an overwhelming peaceful, yet confusing feeling because somehow, I could just be with these intense feelings, while in a group of mostly young white women who were in the habit of talking and moving constantly. I could not explain my awe, as I looked at the shrines in each corner of the large room, and one in the middle of the room divider composed of small pebbles on the bottom, then somewhat larger stones on top of that, and large red stones topping the whole pile. At the base of each of the corner's shrine were also gray pebbles, an old wooden stool, a wood shelf covered by a long-draped cloth hanging from the ceiling. On the shelves were intricately woven baskets that appeared empty, and other assorted unfamiliar items with a different colored cloth made each shrine unique. One shrine was draped with a long string of leather medicine bags strung close together.

   I looked at the ground outside, saw the red soil and burst into tears. I felt like I had come home. This was confusing to me because my family did not come from down south in the United States, and I don't remember seeing red soil before. I had only heard about it. In addition, slaves weren't known to come from southern Africa. Whatever the reason, I had an overwhelming feeling of being home.

The Second Drop Off

Ten days after arriving on the ORAP campus, the van dropped us students off in a rural village for our first homestay. Being on campus, in a small city neighborhood, despite being in a foreign country was familiar to us. Our dorm building had twin bedrooms, washing machines, dryers, and hot showers. The rural villages did not. No paved roads, no electricity, no indoor plumbing with running water to sinks, nor toilets. Houses were round, colorful, but small. Very few people spoke a even a little English. Scared, in shock we were immediately immersed for three days in different languages and customs.

Chapter 19: Ndebele Language and Culture

While I was waiting to go to SIT, I went to the downtown Chicago public library language department and asked for audio cassette tapes and manuals for learning Shona. Later, in Vermont on the SIT campus, there was no one who spoke Zimbabwean languages so I chose to continue learning and improving my Spanish from classes that I had many years ago in high school, because every student at SIT had to pass a foreign language fluency qualifying test in order to graduate. In the ORAP semester abroad program I was surprised I had to learn another new language. I did not know there were two major languages in Zimbabwe. Shona is spoken predominantly in the north and Sindebele in the southern region of the country. The Ndebele people originated in South Africa when it was Zululand. The invading colonizing British unfortunately privileged the Shona peoples over the Ndebele people. Therefore, books and newspapers were written in Shona or British English.

We learned more about Zimbabwean culture and customs in the Ndebele class on campus than the language. Each student had an interpreter in the villages who tutored us. There were times when we were out in the villages for weeks more than we were on the ORAP campus in the city of Bulawayo. For class events, there were a few different interpreters, besides the one that I was personally assigned while I was in the village. Some words didn't translate directly to English. People seemed to talk for 30 minutes, yet the interpreter would only give me two sentences. Is it because Ndebele is more of a story language, that I seem to hear the same words being repeated by the person who was speaking? Maybe the interpreter wanted to spare me the repetition. The reverse happened in the first village I went to, where I would say several sentences and interpreter will go on and on and on in.

It is true there was a lot of repetition in their explanations and storytelling resulting in long conversations. It took a lot of patience to faithfully listen, and when I happened to drift off, I noticed it was possible to return to listening in at a later time, and understand the main point. They would question me to hear if I understood. If I missed just one word, I had to be prepared to hear the whole explanation all over again! This happened whether they were speaking Ndebele or English. Later interpreters explained that indeed the thirty-minute conversations they translated into English in ten minutes, was because they did reduce the repetition.

The problem, I learned later was also because of differences in cultures, beliefs and points of reference for the topic that was being discussed. Especially when the topic was about health or more abstract spirituality. It was hard work to ask questions for interviews, be understood or to understand answers. When I asked the seeming simple questions, the elders would give me the entire history of the situation surrounding the inquiry from its inception to hopefully the present. I then had to pick out the answers I needed for my independent studies report, from within their story. I learned a lot of interesting information from stories that would last a day or two. However, only a few sentences pertained directly to my initial question. The elders had incredible memories for specific details and were impressive oral historians. I wrote abundant notes. And I decided then, that in the future, I would love to help people write their oral histories.

Ndebele is an expressive language, with the whole body used to tell a story or to express strong emotions. Hands, arms and facial gestures move constantly while speaking. In addition, Ndebele has clicks where you have to use different parts of your mouth and nose to make sounds similar to the Zulu language of South Africa. The villages I stayed in are located close to the South African border. There is also a form of sign language used at a distance for signaling a commuter omnibus minivan, which resembles a taxi and to find out what direction a vehicle is going for example. Whistling is used to call people from a distance. Names are sung within the whistle sound. It is also used to give commands to children and domestic animals.

The other language I hadn't expected to learn is British English. Words spelled or pronounced the same in British English, but have a different meaning than in the United States. Some examples: napkins or nappies are cloth diapers for babies, pigeon-holes are individual mailbox slots, and surgeries are doctors' outpatient clinics. Knocked off is when you leave work at the end of the day, retrenchment is when you are laid off or fired from a job. Somewhat similar to American English words are: a sugar basin is a sugar bowl, a lay-by is layaway credit at store, a jersey is a sweater, Scotch is plaid fabric. Humorously, an eraser is a rubber, the hood of a car is the bonnet, and the trunk is the boot of a car. Chronometer is a clock or watch. Men will be offended if you said they were wearing pants because pants are thought of as the little panties for women. Even more confusing is the word trousers isn't even in the British English dictionary.

Zimbabweans commented that I looked like an African (after acquiring a very dark tan from walking in the bright sun), until I opened my mouth and talked, then they realized that I was an American.

Men and women shake hands when initiating greetings. The handshake has three parts: first the fingers, then the thumb, and palm as an American handshake, and then the fingers again. Depending on how familiar the person is with you or when meeting for the first time, the length of the handshake can vary from a brief touch of the fingertips to wondering when the other person it's going to stop the sequence. With friends, the handshake can begin with a near–miss hand slap.

Compared to the American way of maintaining eye contact, the Zimbabwean eye contact varied from none at all, where the only way I would know that two or more people were talking to each other was from observing the sound of their voices. Or very intense staring, making me uncomfortable as they questioned me about my appearance.

All the while I was in Zimbabwe, I felt whole for the first time in my life, because I could be myself. It was wonderful to be surrounded by people of my own skin color. The Zimbabweans were open, honest, and still had their innocence. By innocence, I mean since most people in the villages did not go to school, the natural affection, honesty and intuition that children have was not taught out of them. Boys more than the girls go to school because parents cannot afford education for all of their children. Yet everyone there has a Ph.D in comparison to what we actually learn in United States' schools. Starting with the babies who crawl outside, exploring, intimately getting to know the rocks, soil, and the plants, instead of only reading about rocks. Zimbabwean know the weather and have incredible hearing and eyesight. With no street signs to guide them they can see many miles away. Zimbabweans use whistling with different codes to communicate to people and animals at a very far distance. They rely on each other with farming, harvesting, and building homes collectively as a community.

Students returned to ORAP Zenzele College campus for two months of classroom instruction, reading and writing assignments. Then in October 1997, students in groups of two or three were sent to separate rural areas for our village field studies. They sent me alone as the only African American. We toured nongovernmental organizations and observed grassroot development projects.

Women in the Nkanyiso sewing project group explained to me how they begin to work together collectively:

"Before independence we had some problems concerning life. There was severe drought and famine. In the past days, they were not so smart and had no money to buy clothes. Children were sometimes naked. We didn't know how to make our homes beautiful or even clean. Because of poverty we could not send our children to schools. We had no money for school fees.

So unlike now, back then we were not loyal to each other. We were not working hand-in-hand with each other. So people would just suffer in their homes without going for assistance from neighbors. As a result of children not going to school we are still suffering. If children were educated, they would support the elders. Usually a child is depended on us until 15 years old. Later the elders also depend on adult members of the village. But now adults are unemployed.

Before independence we lacked knowledge of collective working, but after independence we came together to discuss our matters and concerns of poverty and wealth at home. In this case, a woman could share ideas with her neighbors. They found they could start by planting tomatoes and sell them to generate income to support their families. After selling tomatoes we look at each other's families to see which family suffered the most, and then use the money to assist that family to buy food. From the success of this collective approach, we continued to use this method and to improve on it. We also discussed how to build our homes, so they look beautiful, how to keep our homes clean, and each woman then did similar to their own homes. We worked as a group to build each home. Also at this time, we discovered we could use clay to build our homes. These beautiful houses made of polished clay appears to be built of cement, but it shines. Then looking at their beautiful kitchens, we realize we were lacking plates. So we came together and put our money together to buy say for Mrs. K ten plates, then the next time Mrs. S ten plates, etc. until all of us had enough plates. The whites saw us working together and were attracted to learn how we worked too, and they even helped. With working collectively together, everyone realized that everyone is equal. No one is better. No looking down on anyone."

ORAP teaches and promotes the revival of the concept of amalima, which means people meeting together and working collectively, loving each other, with unity of purpose to pull together not only their labor and resources but also their thinking to solve daily problems. Traditionally they used to work collectively with plowing, planting, harvesting and were encouraged by ORAP to extend this cooperation to work together to solve all problems in the community.

CHAPTER 19: NDEBELE LANGUAGE AND CULTURE

From my observations and experiences in the rural villages, collectivism was still very much deeply rooted in the culture. So much so as an American, I felt very overwhelmed and culture shocked over the loss of my individualism that at times I felt I had to defend, yet felt left out of family and community activities, because I naturally was not a part of the group thought processes. So ingrained was my colonized, privileged conditioning of selfishness, entitlement, and narcissism I wasn't really aware of my dumb individualistic thinking and behavior back then.

Their young African men were more mature than American males because everyone in the family has responsibilities from a young age. Gratefully, missing was the competition, low self-esteem, edginess, and the palpable constant anxious tension of sizing each other up behaviors of men in the United States, although Zimbabweans also went through colonialism, apartheid and a recent Civil War. They had only had their independence for fifteen years, when I was there in 1997.

Chapter 20: Village Life

The people of Gwanda came out to greet me upon my arrival, welcoming me saying, "We are glad our daughter has come home."

Women took terms being interpreters. They served me plenty of food and very tasty greens. There was open expression of unconditional love and nurturing with both men and women, even with strangers. Where, as you're talking to someone walking down the road or the street, they will hold your hand whether you are male or female. With the same innocence when a child holds your hand. Nothing sexual. Just that you care and like that person in that moment. They frequently held hands as they talked and walked together. Without the fear of being called "gay." They shared their meager food and belongings even with those who had more than them. I'm crying now as I remember this. In the villages, Zimbabweans spoke to each other on the road, not just "Hi, how are you? I'm fine" then quickly get on their way, instead, they also asked each person, "How is your family? How is your farm? How are your animals? How is life, etc.,? Their greeting in Ndebele language translates to, "How did you sleep last night?" This is a better question then asking a person how they are. Answering honestly how you slept includes whether sleep was refreshing with peacefully dreams or pain or worries or nightmares kept you awake. This was true "CP time" or colored people's time, because you got where you were going, whenever you got there. People are more important than your destination.

When you are ill and visit a traditional healer, you will be first asked, "How do you get along with your family? How do you get along with people in your village?"

Then they inquire about where your hurt is in your body or what's troubling you. Traditional healers were respected for their divination with "bones," and trance work, as well as use of natural medicines. I did not have to hide my psychic abilities, I could be all of my true self.

Ndebele Religion

I learned from the language and culture teacher that Ndebele people believe in the Creator and ancestors. Priest mediums are used as intermediaries to communicate with their ancestral spirits to give and receive messages. The Creator is seen as too great for people to go to alone. From further recent research of an article about the National Shrine Njelele, I read Zimbabweans come together as a nation to pray in times of disaster through ancestor spirits there. Only elders, ages 66 years and older, can pray for the nation. Matobo hills, a large area with two billion years old granite rock formations, has the National Shrine Njelele. Inside a cave with hidden tunnels, elders ask aloud for guidance for healing illnesses, settling disputes, and making political decisions. They ask what the people need to do and to learn in order to stop doing specific behaviors. These elders actually do hear answers. Therefore, the Njelele shrine is considered an oracle. Usually rituals are done at the shrine at the beginning of the rain season. And when the people did what the elder recommended for changes in their lives, then their requests are answered, such as for rain—it pours down raining.

Back in the village, I observed families come together to pray in their home compounds. My host family, the Dubes, held church in a hut. Other people came. The service began with European style hymns and reading from the Bible. I saw each person kneel and say a personal prayer aloud or singing. Participation in the service, appeared egalitarian. Children had a large role in singing, leading, reading from the Bible, preaching, testifying and giving thanks. Women as well as men preached, danced, led songs, did healing. Later, the worship became traditional African. Men lead the dancing with boys carrying shepherds' staffs or tall sticks.

They start the day and end the day with prayer. All events begin and end with prayer. Meals begin with prayer. There were large churches of different denominations in the downtown city of Bulawayo. However, traditional spirituality, rituals, and honoring one's ancestors is still a larger aspect of Zimbabweans's lives.

Creatures Great and Small

One of the children came running into the kitchen hut to tell us there was a snake in the chicken house. The interpreter said usually the chickens sleep at night, but now they were squawking. Some snakes suck out the inside of eggs and then will use poison to kill the chickens. The family went together carrying big sticks. They set some wood on fire inside the fowl run of the chicken house. The snake ran out and the men hit and tried to burn the snake, but the snake went inside a hole. Somehow they got the snake out of the hole. When they threw the snake on the ground, in the large open yard between the huts, I was surprised at the size of the snake. It was a good two meters long. They were beating the snake with sticks and poking it. I thought it was dead but then the tail began to move. I pulled the small children and myself back further away, although we were way on the other side of the yard. The man used an ax to cut off the head, tail and then the body of the snake in half. The head and tail were saved, while the rest of the snake was taken into the fields and burned. The family said it was a black mamba snake — the second longest, most venomous deadliest snake in the world.

At night, I slept on the mud floor in the kitchen with the other women each on our own blankets, except I used a large army green rain poncho that opened up into a tarp, on top of that I had a foam mattress to cushion my protruding bones, and then blankets. I put my shoes at the end of my bed. One morning, I stuck my foot in my shoe and felt something cold and wet. Shaking my shoe, astonished as a large frog jumped out. From that day forward, I turn my shoes upside down before going to bed.

We were out for a walk, when I saw a giant millipede on the ground. At least giant to me, since in the United States millipedes look like a tiny black worm only an inch long. Shorter than an earthworm. For size, I asked if Mrs. Nube would put her hand next to it, so I could take a photo. She instead calmly put it on her hand. The millipede was as long as her hand, approximately six or seven inches! When I was younger, I didn't understand how centipedes could be bigger than a millipede and have longer legs. Doesn't centipede mean 100 legs and millipede mean 1000 legs? Actually house centipedes only have 30 legs. Millipedes have up to 300 legs.

Well, one afternoon Mehuli and I were sitting alone on the built-in bench along the wall of a hut. He was helping me study the Ndebele dictionary and language book. He looked up and told me not to move. When it was safe, he pointed out a large six-inch centipede up higher on the wall behind me but off to the side. We slowly got up and left the hut. Mehuli explained centipedes were poisonous in Zimbabwe! The big centipede looked like it had less legs, each with a hard, outer shell. Extremely different from the harmless, tiny, thin legs of the one and a half-inch-long centipedes in the United States. Later, I read that larger centipede's bites can be very painful but only dangerous if you're allergic to them.

Chapter 21: Purpose for Being in Zimbabwe

Insight into my focus, purpose, and role for while I am in Zimbabwe?:

Metu Neter Cards: Auset hetep. I Ching: Hexagram 55 Abundance.

Auset is the universal archetype of the Mother. I was nurtured and cared for while I was in Zimbabwe. Perhaps because I was the only African American female in our ORAP class of eleven students, I was the only student given a "matron" while in the villages. There were four men from other African countries: one from Malawi and Ghana, and two from South Africa. By the way, the assumption that all Ghanaians were poor wasn't true, since this student told us he was from royalty, a prince, and paid his own way. The matron cooked my meals and provided boiled water for drinking, bathing, and washing my clothes. When in the village I followed like a child the matron's and the interpreter's directions, and went wherever they went. I did not know where we were going each day, because I didn't speak the language. Further without streets, nor street signs in the wide-open land between homes, I would be lost.

In Zimbabwe, you are not a woman unless you have birthed and raised children. Here I was, a woman in body, but had almost died twice when miscarrying babies. Am I not a woman? It would have been difficult to explain this in a different language. Eventually, after several months when I became reasonably fluent with Ndebele language, the women insisted on having time alone with just the women to have conversations with me without my young male interpreter. Many topics were taboo to discuss with the opposite sex. It was the aunties, not mothers that discussed menstrual cycles and sex with daughters approaching puberty and adulthood.

The women in the villages were physically much taller, heavier weight yet solid and stronger carrying the heaviest loads on their heads. Men did not come along and say, "Here give me that. Let me carry that for you." Men were shorter and thinner. They had the sexiest muscular body builds without forcing themselves to get up and go to the gym. They pushed the plows through the rocky soil and herded the goats and cattle over many miles. Men milked cows too.

Women carried almost everything on their heads. They carried water, bundles of firewood, heavy sacks of grains and mealie meal, furniture and tables. They fetched water from the rivers and bore holes. Occasionally the matron woke me very, very early in the morning to go with them to fetch water and small branches for firewood. Initially, they wouldn't ask or let me help carry the water. When they did let me try, I could only carry a small bottle of water a short distance as my head and especially my neck hurt. The second time, I was bravely able to carry a child size small bucket of water on my head all the way home. But I spilled water down one side of my dress. Embarrassed that now everyone would know I didn't know how to carry water! One of the women put leaves on the top of the bucket to prevent the water from spilling out of the bucket that I was carrying. My neck hurt for a whole week! I wondered how the women are able to do it. Perhaps it's because they start the girls very young therefore building up strength and endurance. There was a little girl five years old who came along. If I had learned to carry water and other things on my head as a young girl, I would have been strong enough to have carried the load of water with ease. Later, I learned if a girl could not carry a full jug of water on her head, then the amount of her loboda or bride's price dowry could be cut in half.

My interpreter Mehluli's mother, Mrs. Mhlope was assigned to be my matron. She carried my luggage from the bus to my home in the village. She slid and caught the heavy suitcase from the rack on top of the bus onto the top of her head. I chuckled in awe, because previously an older man fell over backwards trying to reach up to catch my suitcase with his arms. I had to catch both the suitcase before it fell and broke my camera, and the man. Most of the time my huge suitcase was hard for most men to carry in their hands, arms, or on their shoulders. Yet it seemed very easy for her to carry my luggage on her head. Her only complaint was that something in the bottom of my luggage was sticking her in her head. It was my deck of oracle cards.

I loved the bitter tiny green leaves that looked like the weeds that my village home mother Mrs. Dube picked from the garden surrounding her home. She mixed it with onions, peanut butter, and a little red hot peppers. During the times that students returned to campus for classes, the cooks would occasionally cook the greens. They were surprised, frowning as they asked me, "You liked that?" Afterwards, the staff would give me bags of the dried greens that they didn't particularly want because the dried was, of course, several times more bitter than the fresh greens.

CHAPTER 21: PURPOSE FOR BEING IN ZIMBABWE

It was a relief when Mehluli told me I was not required to finish everything on my plate. In the United States, if you don't finish everything or most of what is on your plate, then the cook would be insulted and think you didn't like their cooking. If you acted as if you did like it and smiled, then it backfired on you because they would happily bring you a second helping! So in Zimbabwe, initially I was forcing myself to eat the huge servings of food given to me. Isitshwala is made out of finely ground white corn and cooked stiff similar to American grits is the Ndebele people's main staple food. There were times, of course, when the isitshwala got boring to me having to eat it several times daily, and some foods were foreign to my tastebuds which naturally I didn't like. Mehluli explained that the food I didn't eat from my plate was passed along to the next person in the hierarchy. The elders eat first, then the next person in age, until the children eat last. All very grateful to have what I didn't eat! That's why the plates given to me was piled so high with food.

Chapter 22: Stout?

"I want you to be stout." Mrs. Mhlope told me one evening. What does stout mean? I asked Mehluli.

"Fat. She wants you to be fat. Do you want to be fat?"

Well, I said, "Not fat, just a little rounder."

Sounds simple enough. But little did I know what the implications were of having a matron who thought it was her duty to "make me fat."

Mrs. Mhlope arrived back in the village two days after I did. First thing she did was to ask me to make a shopping list. Then she sent someone the next day to buy the groceries. I should've known when they returned with 10 and 20 kilograms (20 to 50 pounds) bags of mealie meal, oranges, potatoes and more. The only items that were small, were the two tiny jars of peanut butter and that was only because the shop didn't have a larger size!

For breakfast it was porridge. Then barely two hours later she served "tea." Tea would've been fine alone, I could always use the extra fluids in the hot weather except she served me five or six small sweet potatoes with it, and sometimes groundnuts (peanuts) too. Then she would expect me to drink no less than 3 cups of tea. I was still stuffed from the large bowl of porridge. I don't know where she expected me to put all that food!

Everything she dished out for me and her son were in large serving bowls. She didn't seem to know the meaning of, "May I please just have a small amount?"

She would still fill the bowl piled to the top but not overflowing.

I tried for a week to convince her to not cook a large heavy meal for me after 6 PM. I was having stomach aches from the gassy potatoes or beans or in a tomato gravy she would serve after 8 o'clock at night. I would be tossing and turning and expelling gas all night. I don't know why she didn't notice as she slept on the mat next to me! The smell was offensive even to me. I would be irritable the next day from lack of sleep.

She then would say at 7:00 PM, "How about just some rice?"

"Okay, but just a little."

I agreed thinking okay rice is light. But I forgot with her there was no such thing as, 'just a little' and she really didn't know how to cook rice, it was always hard to chew.

We had just walked 16 km (10 miles) during the day therefore I was really too tired to think, let alone chew. I should've been hungry, but I was really too tired to eat. So I asked her to take some of the rice from the plate.

I ate it, which may have been a mistake because the next night she asked me again "Will you have rice?"

I agreed. "Yes, thank you."

What she gave me was a bowl of rice with chunks of potatoes with a little cooked chopped tomatoes and onions. Potatoes and rice was a strange combination to me and did not agree with my taste buds at that time.

After this incident, I refused to eat anything after 6:00 PM. The next night she came with a plate of isitshwala with cooked greens after I told her I would eat a few ground nuts and maybe an orange.

She asked, "What am I to do with the food I cooked? I am going to serve it to you for breakfast."

The next morning, I had porridge as usual. Porridge is thinned cooked white cornmeal. Mehluli said to me, "She's going to serve last night's dinner to you for lunch."

By then I thought it was going to be all dried out. But she didn't give it to me. So I worried she would give it to me for today's dinner.

Later he told me, "She fed it to the dogs."

I felt very guilty. Certainly, my conscious bothered me for wasting food, especially since food was scarce in Zimbabwe.

Really, she was only being like a good mother feeding me because I would be totally exhausted after walking all day, sometimes two hours walk towards and two hours from distant villages. Probably also slowing down their pace. Surely I must have been really skinny from burning more calories than I was taking in.

I did become stout. For the first time I had a "shelf" to rest my arms on my buttocks, under my enlarged breasts became chafed, and my thighs stuck and rubbed together when I walked. I had forgotten Auset's motherly energetic body shape is being pleasantly plump. When my skin darkened from five months of sun rays unfiltered by pollution, Inviolatta proudly commented, "Now you look the way you are supposed to, African."

Chapter 23: Moving On

The Dema village community came out to see me off. I would be going to another village.

"Thank you for coming, and your good behavior. We wish you could stay and we wish you farewell. We will miss the times our groups have come together."

The best I could I responded, "I will miss being here too," as I tried to hold back the tears.

I was just starting to relax and enjoyed being there, as they told me I should do from the very first few days when I arrived. I never really had to ask for anything. People here, have been very good to me and to each other while I've been here. They worked hard to teach me and show me about ORAP and to help me explore my interest in healthcare. Life here is very busy and often difficult, yet they took time out to spend time with me and the rest of the community. Some walking very long distances. I did not have a chance to tell them how much I appreciated their inviting and welcoming me into their homes and community, because I had to go to the toilet and a delivery truck arrived at the Vice Chairman's home and the people left to help him. Perhaps this is good, because I would have cried throughout all of my giving thanks.

Second Village Stay

The first few days I was without an interpreter. I was surprised I could speak and understand more of the SiNdebele language than I previously thought. The people were also really excited to be able to speak directly with me. There was more interaction with the family this time. I got up earlier to help plant maize (corn) and bean seeds in evenly spaced holes, to cultivate and hoe the soil around the maize plants while removing weeds as we went along. We picked the indigenous green vegetable called olude. Some afternoons I went with them to fetch water and firewood. These activities gave me more time to talk with the family.

Mehuli tended to talk most of the time. I do learn a lot from him about the culture, farming, his life, etc. but from his perspective only of course. However, his talking to me also shut others out. This family made an effort to speak more English to me.

Glad there weren't males present, the women told me about child rearing and food taboos for children. One of the daughters said, "I am only expected to do domestic work as a career. I hate ironing."

I naïvely said, "There are other things you could do."
She asked, "Like what?"

I couldn't answer her. Not because she wasn't capable of doing other types of jobs but because she hadn't been exposed to other opportunities. I also couldn't answer her because I was thinking about all the domestic jobs I had simply because that is where older women told me I could get a job. Never mind that I took college prep classes and I wasn't dumb. Even in nursing school I excelled in the sciences in theory and

CHAPTER 23: MOVING ON

medical technology, management, etc., but still nursing itself is traditionally a "women's job." And involves all of the chores male doctors wouldn't want to do.

She continued, "I was forced out of school because I had a baby. Pregnant women are expelled from school. But even so, the amount of work I'm required to do: breastfeed the baby, wash clothes every morning, cook, fetch water and firewood, clean the house, bath the baby plus work in the fields would prevent me from attending school."

My tongue was paralyzed. What could I really say? Here I was a foreign woman, a student doing what I wanted to do, resting on my laurels while she cooked and washed my clothes and cleaned up after me!"

A teenager asked me, "Do you know of a whitening cream to make my skin lighter so I can be light like you?"

I was shocked! I told her, "There are creams to lighten but not whiten skin. But why would you want to be white? I wouldn't want to be white because the ugliness of their harming people. Plus their skin ages sooner, sunburns and they have straight hair they can't do much with. I have the skin color I have not by choice, but because of white slave owners."

She said, "I understand because I read the books, Native Son, and also The Color Purple. Do you have a house girl?"

Laughing I told her, "No, in the United States, Black women are the house girls. There is no one to do anything for me except me."

Looking back as I write this book now, I am ashamed of how ignorant I was in my 40's. Realize now, they treated me as if I was a fragile white woman, gave me privileges without asking me if I needed or deserved these services. And l didn't know to pay them. This is what these Zimbabwean young women saw and wanted for their selves and their futures.

Several men told me, "You're to marry before you leave Zimbabwe."

Very scary! Especially after being told by one man that I was learning to be a Zimbabwean woman — to fetch water and firewood, to hoe, etc., — as he gave me a shovel to help dig, to find water for a well. This would've been okay if I wasn't hearing stories about some men drinking, not bringing money home, wife beating, everything is theirs' and demanding respect "in their home" when most of the time they were absent and didn't contribute to the labor and upkeep of the home. Sounded extremely familiar to me because I've been there and done that already in the United States. In Zimbabwe, while a few men stay in the village, most go to cities or to South Africa to work, only coming home on weekends, sometimes months or years later. I'm not blaming the men, that's what happens when colonizers come in and steal away your land, culture, values and dignity with forced labor or humiliating random underpaid employment.

And this matter of everyone telling me to get married or have a child "so as not to be lonely," why get married if I was going to be lonely anyway? In the United States, I'd have to work outside my home and neighborhood. Even in Zimbabwe, the workload doesn't allow for our idea of "quality time" with the children. However, infants and toddlers are carried on their mother's backs almost everywhere she or an older sibling goes. In the United States we may work on the other side of town or city and put our children in the best school far away if we can afford it, or in daycare with strangers. I was afraid my children could grow up with problems or even hate me for a lack of bonding, love and genuine concern.

Comparatively, what I received in Zimbabwe was pure unconditional love. Surrounding me, they truly made sure I didn't miss my family and friends too much. While Zimbabweans did not have an abundance of material resources, they shared whatever they had, along with an abundance of valuable priceless, healing caring and love. Hence, I experienced the meaning of hexagram 55: Abundance.

Chapter 24: Independent Study: Zimbabwe Healthcare

Students had to write out a learning contract listing their goals and how we were going to accomplish ORAP Zenzele College class assignments, as well as, research personal interests. We were to help the villagers do research on what was needed for their chosen projects, write down our observations, impact on us, and what we each personally wanted to investigate. At the end of the semester we were to write a ten-page paper that could be of use to the village and ORAP.

I also had to do written assignments to fulfill my independent study requirements for the School for International Training. Back then, access to a computer was rare. Therefore, I had several sheets of black carbon paper in my notebook to send copies of handwritten weekly reports to my academic advisor. Mail was very slow. She would receive my letters two to four weeks later, if at all.

Since my personal goal was to learn about the Zimbabwe healthcare system, I interviewed health care workers and villagers. I learned most villagers treated themselves with local herbs and prayers or went to traditional healers. The community health worker invited me to come along as she did her rounds in the village. I asked her, "How do you know when someone is ill? Do others tell you? Or does the patient send a message or a note with a child?"

She said, "I go door to door visiting, asking about people who are ill. Sometimes the sick person comes to my home. I go to visit people who are sick and see if their illness is mild or severe. If minor, I treat them with available tablets or pills. If severe, I take the person to the clinic or hospital."

Common illnesses she's seen were: headaches, stomach aches, diarrhea, complications of self-induced abortions, and pregnancies with twins and triplets.

At the clinic are the nurses. People called the head nurse "Sister" because she supervises the other nurses and staff. She wore an all-white dress and hat, similar to a navy uniform with stripes on her lapel and the shape of her hat. There were long waiting lines inside and outside the clinic. The doctor only visits rural clinics once a month and he only came to examine serious cases. Pregnant women go to the hospital by ambulance if there are problems. The Sister is the only trained midwife in the area. I accompanied her on home sanitation visits. She said she had already visited nine homes, traveling by foot, when I met her on the road. She checks inside each home for cleanliness of the toilet and kitchens, to see if the water containers are covered and the pot rack is high enough to protect it from animals and blowing dirt. Outside, she checks the cleanliness of the toilet, and that the rubbish pit not overflowing and is divided into what can be burned and what could be composted for the garden.

Later, I joined the Sister at the Gwanda Outreach Baby Clinic outdoors in the village. Babies and young children were weighed in a hanging swing scale attached to a tree branch. Their weight in kilograms were recorded on a line graph on both the mother and the official yellow cards. I assisted with marking the mother's copy. Thirty-five children were in attendance. They were also given vaccinations for polio, measles, or diphtheria/tetanus/pertussis (DTP). Sister said last week no one came to the clinic, so she had to go to their homes and give baby vaccinations. She was glad to see the children at the outdoor clinic this week.

Ausar Auset Society Church introducing me to African culture and spirituality in the United States helped me to be more comfortable in the Zimbabwe villages. I also previously experienced being poor. All of my other study abroad classmates who were white, had difficulty adjusting and demanded to return home to finish out the year at their respective universities. I, instead, begged to stay in Zimbabwe to learn more about traditional healing.

Chapter 25: Traditional Healers

Two traditional healers introduced themselves and explained what traditional healers commonly do, and what they each did. Their stories were very similar. A traditional healer is a prophet (seer) with the ability to see the sick person, and what is wrong that is causing the sickness often before the sick person even comes to the door. When the sick person comes to their home, they will wait outside while the healer prepares to meet the person by making a protection. A protection for the healer and the healers' home if they see the sick person is carrying an evil spirit. I asked them questions about spiritual healing for behavioral as well as physical healing. Communication was difficult due to differences in culture, personal beliefs and points of reference. For example, I personally don't attribute problems to evil spirits. To improve communication, I showed them some of what I did as a healer.

During holiday break, I lived with these two women traditional healers; Mrs. Nube and Mrs. Moyo and their families. They had to get permission first from the village chief. He took several days to make a decision, but finally agreed. I insisted on not having a matron this time, which was also reluctantly granted. Mehuli still came along. I observed hem as they went about their daily chores and as we walked, they gathered herbs, they explained to me what the plants were used for. Many plants look like aloe vera to me. I wondered how the women could tell the difference since they told me some of these were poisonous!

One day, we walked to Mrs. Moyo's home, where we were greeted, but then were left alone for a while in the empty hut. All of a sudden, we heard loud growls and the floor shook. Bursting through the doorway were the two traditional healers dressed in native attire with animal skins and feathers. Although I'd seen trance and spirit possession in rituals in the United States, I wasn't prepared for being so scared. Mehuli was trembling too, as we sat back-to-back on the mud floor holding tightly onto each other. We watched not knowing what would happen next. They seemed to be in trance with their eye gaze elsewhere. Eventually the two traditional healers left. Alone again, I asked Mehuli to explain. He said he had never experienced anything like this before. The two traditional healers returned, with their usual selves. We gradually calmed. They tossed the six small wooden piece "bones" divination to inquire about my family ancestors. However, I didn't understand most of what they were telling me of what the bones reading meant.

They also invited me to a special ritual another time at night where lots of n'angas came together. They sang and danced in line formations, stomping hard in Ndebele style with each n'anga holding a small sword. Later, as a going away present, they gave me my own sword, along with a small wooden mortar and pestle. All of these were symbols acknowledging me also being a traditional healer.

In turn, I invited them and their families to a small Auset ritual. I wore teal blue and white clothes. I started the ritual by pouring libation outside. Then the small group of healers and families went inside a hut. There I chanted the Auset mantra and went around the room hugging while briefly rocking each person as a mother would do to comfort a child. They had tears in their eyes and thanked me. We prayed for healing for our families and peace for the country.

Later, Mrs Nube told me the plants grew bigger on the edge of the garden where I poured water for libation. Nonetheless, I was surprised when they later started referring patients to me. I also occasionally did oracle card and I Ching spiritual guidance for the traditional healers and patients. They asked me to name some of their babies, so of course I did destiny readings first.

During the second semester, I lived in Bulawayo. It wasn't the Spring semester because Zimbabwe is in the Southern Hemisphere, meaning their seasons are the reverse of in the United States. Therefore Christmas is in the summertime. Zenzele College teachers arranged for me to intern at Zimbabwe Traditional and Medicine Clinic. The medical doctor was British, the other health practitioners were local traditional healers n'angas, certified by the Zimbabwe National Traditional Healer's Association, who had their own offices in the clinic.

N'angas are usually certified members of the Zimbabwe National Traditional Healers Association. Some practice on their own. They use herbal remedies, guided by a "healing spirit," and diagnose spiritual problems that have not yet become medical problems. Each specializes, therefore they will refer patients to other healers where needed or when their own method did not help.

As a registered nurse, I helped the British doctor examine patients, listen to their chests, monitor blood pressures and check their ankles for swelling. I taught the nurses' aides how to read a thermometer, feel for a pulse, count heartbeats, and use a stethoscope to check blood pressures. These were mostly patients with health insurance. The other patients went to see the traditional healers. I sat and observed the faith healer in her office across the hall. An n'anga showed me how she determined cause of and cured infertility without modern tests, medicine or surgery. I didn't understand most of what she was telling me because it was mostly invisible energetic healing. A male n'anga used herbs, and special prayers with rituals. Imagine seeing a huge python snakeskin stretched across the back wall in one of this n'anga exam room.

Zenzele College also arranged for me to train at a maternity clinic. The nurse midwife showed me how they determine how many weeks pregnancy by measuring the length of the woman's extended abdomen to her umbilicus navel since ultrasounds weren't available. Later I helped deliver a baby, coaching with breathing and trying to convince the nurse to allow the mother to sit up more rather than telling her push while lying flat on her back with her feet up in stirrups. There were some complications as the mother had bleeding from tears and the delayed delivery of the placenta. I showed the nurse natural ways of hastening the delivery of the placenta, by asking the mother to nurse the baby, but she was tired and in pain, so she refused. Instead I had to massage her nipples which gratefully successfully produced the placenta and the bleeding ceased. The grandmother thanked me afterwards and asked if they could name the baby girl after me.

Later I attended an International Lay Midwife Conference with midwives from Denmark, Sweden, Australia, Canada and New Zealand, along with representatives from South Africa. The purpose of the midwife conference was to promote collaboration between Western trained medical doctors, nurses, and the lay midwives in the villages. Emphasis was on maintaining cleanliness during the birth to prevent infections with proper hand washing and sterile new razor blades to cut the umbilical cord. However, true collaboration meant acknowledging the wisdom of ancient traditional birthing methods. Allowing the mother to squat or get into whatever position was comfortable for the mother and the baby, instead of being forced to lie flat on her back on a table with her feet strapped to stirrups. Lying flat slows down the natural gravity descent of the baby and requires more hard pushing to get the baby out. Lay midwives knew what herbs to give and how to turn the baby in the womb to the head down position. European midwives complained about unnecessary medical procedures that harmed mother and baby such as excessive medicine induced labor and unnecessary cesarean sections. I told them about homeopathic remedies, such as Sepia, for postpartum depression and prolapsed uterus. Sepia naturally pulls the uterus back up into correct position and decreases the mother's fears or apathy about caring for the baby and her family after childbirth. It is possible the lay midwives already had similar herbs for this purpose. Due to language and cultural differences, it was difficult to communicate ideas.

***

Navigating downtown Bulawayo was easier because of street signs, as I went on my own to obtain health statistics from the education officer of the Ministry of education offices. English is the official language of Zimbabwe. It was wonderful having the familiarity of a downtown city to restore some of my independence as I rode buses and walked around.

I visited the modern city hospital and separate psychiatric hospitals. The buildings were small but similar to any hospital in the United States.

A couple of days each week, I went to a local n'anga and his young daughter Leticia's home in Bulawayo. They had a separate room attached to the house filled with shelves of assorted jars of herbs and other medicines. He was a tall, large man who always wore a long black dress. Everyone called him, "ubabamkhulu" which was confusing to me because the Ndebele name for God, "uNkulunkulu" sounded similar to my ears.

I spent most of this time in the medicine room learning from Leticia. She and I wore white. I was pleasantly surprised to see she also had drums! She showed me how to play special prayer rhythms on her drums. One day, her father excitedly ran inside the room saying, "It's raining! It's raining!" Since we have been waiting for rain for months, repeatedly disappointed when the skies would darken with clouds, yet no rain, I thought that's what he was excited about. Leticia explained to me that my playing the rhythm she taught me on her drums, caused it to rain!

Meanwhile, I lived with my former classmate Inviolatta at her home in Bulawayo. She lived in a large, beautiful three-bedroom brick ranch style home. Inviolatta shared her home with her sister and brother, a maid, and a girl from Botswana whom she helped to attend school in Zimbabwe. I slept in a twin-size bed with the maid. Similar to in the village everyone here helped each other.

When Inviolatta discovered I loved her steamed, buttered white pumpkin with the leaves, she prepared it often for me. Unlike in the United States, where we throw away the leaves, here everything is eaten, including most parts of animals. Okra leaves are cooked too. What I had difficulty getting used to was, the small servings of collard greens, only a couple of tablespoons on my plate, versus having a full bowl or two of cooked greens with the pot liquor to dip my cornbread in, like in the United States.

As you can see, being in Zimbabwe allowed me to experience the Metu Neter card Auset energy of the mother, fulfill the role of teacher, nurse, midwife, witness the ability to go into trance and purposely dream for guidance. I had to manage my emotions, not giving into indulgence as Zimbabweans were willing to give me anything I wanted.

Chapter 26: Before Colonization

In a bookstore in downtown Bulawayo, I found the book, *Guardians of the Soil: Meeting Zimbabwe's Elders*. Reading it helped me understand and believe the elders' stories about how Zimbabwe used to be before colonialism. In the chapter interview with the chief from Matabeleland in the southern area of Zimbabwe, he confirmed as the traditional healers previously told me, the land used to be very fertile, like a green rainforest. Instead of what used to be a large river, it had become so dry the villagers have to dig under the sand to get to the water. The white man's plow made rows deep into ground, as they cleared the land for fields and mining, causing the soil to be easily washed away. Animals and birds disappeared. In addition, whites killed off herds of wild animals, whereas the villagers only killed an animal when needed. Zimbabweans used to live in union and communion with their ancestor spirits and God. They believed the land only belongs to God and it was created for all the people to use. But when the whites came in, they took choice large areas of land and fenced it off as their own private property, and told the native people they had to buy land. Having no money, the African people were soon pushed off the land. The elder emphasized that not having land destroys people's humanity.

Thereafter, too many people began dying from unknown diseases for which there was no cure. Previously, the traditional healers had herbs to cure every disease, but now with the drought, the trees, bushes, and plants are gone. In addition harmony among the people was considered the most important for true health.

Elders see their God as superior to the Christian God especially in regards to, the concept of burning in hell for sins because Zimbabweans believe that everything and everyone can be forgiven. They had forgiveness rituals whenever there were disputes between people. Therefore the idea that God is not forgiving doesn't make sense. Other elders in the book, added that their Creator did not have heaven or hell since the dead do not die. Christian missionaries taught them that acknowledging their ancestors was evil, so now their ancestors' voices are not heard.

Zimbabweans also had utmost respect for women, especially their mothers. The womb of a woman is a shrine. A man is only successful because he consults a woman. And if he is beating his wife he is a coward, and in doing so is also disrespecting his parents. Getting angry with or raising his hand to his mother will cause him to be cursed.

Whites brought greed and taught greed and individualism to young people in their schools. Children don't listen to elders, nor know their history and culture of how to live in harmony with each other and nature. Along with the land drying up, so did the people's dignity, independence and sense of responsibility.

As I read the book, <u>Guardians of the Soil: Meeting Zimbabwe's Elders</u>, my heart was filled with both awesome love and sorrow for the people, culture and land of Zimbabwe. I bought two more copies of the book, gave one copy to my village family for the children, and gave the other copy to Mehluli. I urged and hoped the book would inspire him to write his own book about the many fascinating stories he told me of village life.

Chapter 27: Personal Reflections and Struggles Living in Zimbabwe

While in the village, I'd been wanting to write freely for days, weeks, months. My Zimbabwean family tried to read everything I wrote. Have they not heard of a journal or diary which has a person's private thoughts and is kept locked at all times except for when writing in them? I really needed a creative outlet. I couldn't even cook without other people interrupting as if I didn't know how to do anything. Never mind, that I was almost 42 years old. Otherwise, I was just sitting around staring at other people sitting and talking to each other, except when we were doing chores. They seemed honored to remove all tasks from my hands. This was literally very, very boring. I'd sit there thinking of all the other things and responsibilities I had to do, like school assignments.

Later, by the questions they asked me, I began to understand Mehuli, and the few other young people who could read some English, were watching me write in my notebook because they had not seen anyone write in cursive before. They did not join their letters together. My writing was even more mysterious because I wasn't doting my i's nor crossing my t's as I tried to write as fast as I could, transcribing the history or stories the elders were telling me. While taking notes in college, I had gotten into the habit of going backwards later, after a couple of sentences to cross my t's and dot my i's. I didn't realize this was foreign to them, until Mehuli asked as he pointed at my notebook, "Oh, is this a t? Oh, that must be two t's." I showed him, by first writing each letter separately and then making small strokes to join the letters that I was doing the same as he prints. Cursive writing can be faster than printing after you get used to it. My worries that they were spying on me were unfounded since they couldn't read my handwriting. They were only curious.

Even having some time to just sit and reflect, composing my many conflicting thoughts would have been wonderful and worthwhile. But where? Whenever I tried to get some quiet time here, someone comes knocking to ask if I'm sick, or to tell me to come and cook or bathe. The husband of the family and Mehuli seemed to think it was their job to criticize whatever I did. "You can't cook. You can't wash pots." They never even let me get started to see what I can do or what I know how to do already. Like with the drums, the men criticized and then left, but the women and I enjoyed playing the drums together.

Zimbabwean sit, stand and sleep close together. They do the same with strangers. Shoulder to shoulder. If they like you, they will grab your hand while walking There is a shortage of transportation so when riding in any vehicle, expect to be packed in like sardines. There is no difference where men or women sit. I had to get used to sitting partially on men's thighs occasionally, or even have a man leaning on me. Having to sit in the boot of a commuter omnibus minivan or the back of a pickup truck, especially in your Sunday best gets interesting.

Coming from a family and a society that does not touch much, I had to get used to the Zimbabwean close personal space. Sometimes I was embarrassed, not quite sure of the other person's intentions. Usually the innocent touches were brief similar to how young children touch while they talk. I got used to the closeness, but I found it hard to initiate touching. Sitting close did not bother me much except with men, since I was raised as a Muslim.

Having other people handling, and at times going through "my" belongings is something I never quite got used to. I always felt shocked and annoyed, although the intensity of my feelings decreased with time.

Collectivism was both an area of my keen interest and a source of frustration, as I struggled to balance the advantages of collectivism with my perception of it being seeming rigid as compared to United States' individualism freedoms of privacy, own opinions, questioning, and wandering from place to place. I was raised in a Black American extended family, in a segregated collective neighborhood. As a result of racism and discrimination, parents couldn't allow their children to have an opinion nor choices. Therefore, as an adult I cherished my "independence" although it could be lonely and isolating.

Mrs. Mhlope would tell me when to get up in the morning, when to take a bath, and then inspect me while saying, "You didn't wash your lower legs and feet." Or, "How could you have bathed without a towel?"

I was afraid of taking my shoes off in the concrete outhouse because I didn't want parasitic worms to enter through my feet. I hoped she wouldn't come into the outhouse and inspect me while I had no clothes on but she didn't, unless she peeked.

She would tell me, "Your clothes and shoes are dirty. Take them off so I can wash them."

They wouldn't let me do anything, so I wondered how could my clothes be dirty? Usually, in the United States, I would wear my clothes two days before I washed them. My socks and underwear I would otherwise change daily. Here they wash everything including backpacks and purses. Perhaps, it is because of the dry dirt roads scattering dust everywhere.

When I returned to Zenzele College campus in the city of Bulawayo, the other students told me they experienced similar from their house families. Some were told to bathe two or three times a day even though the family didn't bathe as often. I imagine the white students' skin might appear dirtier. It was explained Zimbabweans treat all visitors that way. Visitors should be able to rest since they work hard at their own homes. One of the African students from Malawi told us, this was also true in his country. They just want the visitor to be comfortable and to have the best the family can offer, even if they go without the items or services themselves.

There were times when I cried quietly in my bed because all my time was planned by someone else, even going to a church on Tuesday, Friday and Saturday nights and from noon to 4 PM on Sundays. There was no privacy, I couldn't even go to the outhouse by myself. Sometimes I refused to go to church because some services would begin late at night, it was all in the Ndebele language, and Mehuli since he was a male he sat on the other side of the church with the rest of the men. I was given an English Bible to read while they read the same verses over and over again from week to week.

Sometimes when I stayed back in the hut, because I had awful headaches with heavy menstrual bleeding. They asked me, "Aren't you afraid to be alone?"

I simply told them, "No."

But really, I was just so glad to get a chance to rest, to just think and reflect. They didn't realize how exhausting it was to have to try to interpret and understand everything anyone said or did.

This is how the hexagram 17 Following's advice for deciding to participate in the Zimbabwe Organization Rural Association Progress (ORAP) SIT Study Abroad Program, unfolded all the while I was in Zimbabwe. I had no choice but to humbly follow along in the yielding role of Auset. I didn't know the rural area, language, laws, nor culture. Never thought to run away. How could I anyway?

Chapter 28: Americans Over Concerned About Cleanliness, Germs and Illness?

When I went to the villages after a while, I began to question my beliefs about cleanliness, germs and illness. Is what we were taught about hygiene and disease true? There is such a total lack of concern about the transmission of the invisible bugs and other organisms we call germs. I rarely saw the people in the village wash their hands except for before meals, when everyone shares the same large bowl, passed from person to person to swish our hands. But I cringed knowing we used the toilet, and even the public toilets in the city didn't have soap, worked in the fields, changed diapers, polished the floor with cow dung, milked the cows, and handled other animals before putting our hands in the same bowl, and dried with the same towel that is passed around to everyone in the room. After eating, the same towel was then used to dry the dishes. This was upsetting to watch.

I asked to have my water boiled as was advised by the School for International Training's nurse and in the health document she gave us, and then wondered why I still became ill. Fortunately, I only had mild stomach cramps, headache, and brief diarrhea for a couple of days. I asked for boiled water for washing my hands after that and refused to use the towel. It wasn't until much later, I observe the "dishwashing" methods. Culturally, they insisted on visitors not washing dishes. I let it be, since I hadn't gotten seriously ill, although some of my classmates did get serious diarrhea and dehydration. When the women washed dishes and pots outside, they used the river water and the sand for scrubbing. No choice but to use the same water the chickens, dogs and goats have walked and relieved themselves in. When they could fetch water from the borehole wells, that we were told it was safe water for us to drink they also used sand to clean the inside and outside of the large metal can they used to carry the water. When I asked a young woman about this, she said the sand removes the rust." After that, I insisted on boiled water even if it was from the boreholes. And I assumed my hand-washing water was from the borehole well but weeks later Mehuli who usually helped me wash my hands said, "You've been using river water before now. Why are you upset?"

  I was shocked, of course, thinking I had explained the rationale and expressed my dissatisfaction to Mehuli, as my interpreter, many times. He himself didn't use soap even if I brought it to the table. He showed me plants they rub their hands on that is like a soap. Weeks later, he did use the diluted commercial dishwashing liquid with me when we washed our hands outside. I should've known because he asked me several times, "Wouldn't you get used to the water in Zimbabwe? It is hard for people who live there to understand, since the water doesn't seem to make them ill. Yet their babies often have "running stomachs." Perhaps they think diarrhea in babies is normal, not an illness.

Leftover food from the prior evening's meal, served on plates was left in the oven overnight and eaten the next morning. There weren't refrigerators in the rural areas. But I thought it odd to see the same practice in the city where there are refrigerators available. Eggs are not refrigerated.

People became defensive when I tried to teach about the concept of bacteria. Someone at the clinic mentioned she didn't believe in germs. The water and the food didn't seem to make them ill. Perhaps because they were probably better nourished, rested more because when the sun went down, they went to bed. They were very strong and hard-working and could outwork me many times over in just a single day.

I thought I had made a conscious choice to not waste or over consume the Earth's resources, but here I was being made to live up to their image of how rich person should live. Meanwhile, I was thinking of people who didn't have clothes or soap or water to wash clothes or bath every day. This was hard to explain to them. I tried explaining that more is not always better when the matron insisted that I add more and more laundry powder in addition to the laundry detergent already in the large plastic basins, where the water was already full of thick, sticky suds. Probably from seeing extra bubbles in television advertisements. Then the soap would be hard to rinse out, because of the drought, there wasn't enough water to rinse the clothes well, so the rinse water was also very soapy. Since they immediately dumped the wash water into the garden or around the lemon and other fruit trees, to me they were poisoning the soil. In America, fish were dying in the lakes from chemical pollution.

Reality

This again shows how naïve and privileged I was to even think this way. Water and firewood to boil my water was scarce, plus it wasn't on my sore back, feet, and neck that the water was carried. Why was I being so picky? Did my then 86-year-old grandmother not tell me stories about when there wasn't running water in the United States? She used to wash her hair in streams. People still had ice boxes in the city when I was a little girl in Philadelphia. Her family lived through the Great Depression when almost nobody had anything. My grandmother would cook for our family reunions throughout the day before and during the night. There wasn't enough room in the refrigerator for all the food, so it sat out all night and all the next day at the picnic. Nonetheless, we didn't get sick.

Chapter 29: Vegetarian Dilemma

What do you do when you are the honored guest, or one of several guests, and the hosts goes out of their way to prepare a meal especially for you? However, the food is not something you usually eat, or in some cases would rather not eat. In the village, the host places a big serving bowl of meat in front of you, after all you are one of the honored guests. You have been vegetarian for six years, not for any philosophical reasons but because whenever you would eat made your stomach revolt and give you a terrible stomach aches for two days straight, during which time you couldn't eat any other food even if you wanted to. Prior to this you had eaten meat all your life, except for pork having been raised Muslim. You had sausage, bacon, steak for breakfast. Bologna, pastrami, salami, and other cold cut deli or corn beef sandwiches, hamburgers, or fried chicken for lunch. Meatloaf, pot roast, turkey, goose, duck, lamb, veal or goat for dinner. At barbecues, you would have several pieces of each type of meat among the hotdogs, burgers, chicken, and ribs from the grill.

Perhaps your difficulty digesting meat was because of the additives, hormones and antibiotics they gave to the animals in the United States. You happen to have seen the 20/20 episode on television where a Food and Drug Administration worker was fired because he insisted on discarding chicken that showed signs of salmonella, some gross with green pus. He would put the infected chicken in the trash bin, then someone would come behind him and put the chickens back on the assembly line, cut out the obvious green pus spots, and send the infected chicken to the markets. Since then you have bought and eaten only kosher meat but later your stomach won't allow you to eat Kosher nor halal meat. Kosher chickens are very different in appearance, texture and taste them regular chickens at the supermarket. It has better flavor. Yet, perhaps a chicken is still a chicken in the United States, and the rabbi just says a prayer over the chicken, kills it humanely and sells it.

So now you are a vegetarian and a couple years later, you meet and join a religious group that promotes being vegan. This group has all kinds of logical reasons why humans shouldn't eat meat: If we were meant to eat meat we would have the same type of intestines carnivorous animals have, but instead our intestines are longer with extra pockets that meat gets trapped in and takes too long to digest and rots inside us. Hence the high incidence of colon cancer. If we were meant to eat meat, we would have fangs and other types of specialized teeth. We would salivate at the sight and smell of a fresh killed animal, eating it right then and there, getting excited about the warm blood dripping down our chins. If we were meant to eat meat, we wouldn't have to cook it to tenderize it or to kill bacteria or parasites. Carnivorous animals don't have to worry about getting sick from bacteria. Nor do they do add seasonings like salt, pepper, onion, garlic, green pepper, parsley, etc. to make it taste like a vegetable.

All of these reasons made perfect sense to you. And after years of not eating meat you don't even crave it. Except you did eat fish every once in a while. Then this year, you get tired of being tired all the time, your hair coming out in your comb, and feeling hungry all the time. A couple of your friends who belong to the vegetarian group that are supposed to be vegan eat chicken and fish. They serve fish at their home and you decide to join them since fish is the one flesh you crave. You do okay with the fish, except later you notice you become constipated and can even have a queasy stomach if you indulge in more than a small amount. Since you have been a vegetarian you have not suffered from constipation usually having two to three healthy bowel movements daily. Previously you had a bowel movement once every three days and sometimes only once a week, while growing up eating meat.

You've also read Ayurvedic medicine advises that vata constitution or slender built people are the only people who need to eat meat in order to stay grounded, otherwise they are too spacey. But you also read in the same book, vata type people have a hard time digesting food even raw vegetables, so this seems contradictory to you. So you decide to eat fish only occasionally, once every one to two weeks.

Then you sat in the first Environmental Studies class of the semester at The School for International Training, and the teacher hands you, out of all the other students, an article on fish — about how ocean fish is now being farm raised basically the same way beef is raised. Meaning fish such as salmon can be fattened or made lean to order and given antibiotics. You were shocked but you really should not have been. You thought only catfish was farm raised. Therefore you stop eating fish for a while, and then selectively occasionally.

CHAPTER 29: VEGETARIAN DILEMMA

The following summer, you feel constantly hungry. Nothing you eat is appealing or satisfying. It is hard to even think of anything exciting to eat. Now you hear in conversations with people who are from Africa, or have been there, that everyone eats meat, especially in Zimbabwe where you're going and therefore you will starve. As a result, you decide that you will eat meat, when you get there. Besides, the meat comes from free roaming cattle and chickens without additives. But now you are here, in the village, the host places a big serving of meat in front of you. After all, you are one of the honored guests. You don't want to offend your hosts, so you pick a piece of meat from the bowl and put it in your mouth. It tastes like liver and you remember that the liver's job is to clean the blood. You want to spit it out, but you don't. You take another piece from the other side of plate and it tastes more like beef, but it still tastes very much like flesh to you. Same with the pieces of chicken served in another meal. Somehow the idea that it is a leg you are biting into, is repulsive therefore only two bites is all you can manage. Why after having been a meat eater most of your life, why are you so sensitive to the sight, smell, taste and thought of meat? You push yourself to eat a little anyway. On the last day in the first village you have stomach cramps, headache, dizziness and nausea. Finally, your hosts tell the guests, after three of the four other students are also ill with these same symptoms plus diarrhea, that you do not have to eat anything you don't want to eat. They don't want you to get sick. By that time, you're too nauseated and sick to want to eat anyway. When you return to campus you rest your stomach for a day or so and then you try again to nibble on the chicken at mealtimes, rationalizing you need to get used to eating meat before you return to the village.

Several months later, near the end of the time you're in Zimbabwe, you are invited to your friend's house for the weekend. She prepares beans for you, but you are surprised when she serves you a large chicken leg on the same plate. You eat it because she's watching your every move. You tell her it has nice flavor she has seasoned it well. But looking at that leg! The next meal she serves you fish. You try to refuse by telling her that you thought she had prepared that plate for someone else. She looks very disgusted, so you say you will have a small piece. The fish is in a sauce but you can still see the head and the eyes. You eat a small piece and your friend slides the rest of the fish onto your plate.

She later serves you cuddled milk, that she says she loves, and other Zimbabweans have said it is their favorite food that's usually served for dessert. Someone had made it especially for her for the occasion of you being there. She is again is watching you closely, so you eat it slowly.

She asked you, "How do you like it?"

You say, "I will have to get used to it."

Upon which she serves you more. The curdled milk was so sour and fermented it burns your tongue. You eat it but you were feeling trapped and angry at yourself and at you friend. You like your friend very much, which puts more pressure on you than it did in the village to conform to another culture's food tastes.

You are confused because your friend knows you have food allergies and have been vegetarian for years and had urged you several times to tell the campus kitchen your needs. Perhaps she thinks maybe the food allergies are because the United States has too many additives, pesticides, hormones and antibiotics. Some Americans won't eat meat for political and philosophical reasons but even international people when they come to the United States stop eating meat. Here in Zimbabwe in the rural areas the meat is fresh. You value the friendship and don't want to argue, knowing your friend probably would not understand and would only feel hurt. Cultural shock and homesickness began to settle in, and you are depressed for most of the following week. You're not homesick because you miss your family and friends in the United States. You are homesick for your own home where you can cook your own food, and to have some semblance of a familiar routine.

What would you do? Would you decide to give up meat again, even the fish? After all they serve you plenty of fresh roasted groundnuts for breakfast and snacks. Is it necessary to eat meat protein at each meal? Would you give in to fit in?

Actually, eating meat in the village was rare because of the drought. The cows and the chickens were very skinny pecking at the few blades of grass and seeds. Zimbabweans ate reconstituted dried fish and mopane worms that are giant caterpillars. Meat was only served on special occasions. I guess in the cities, the people are rich in comparison since our student handbook had the following: "Matebeleland is cattle country and the town specialty is beef. Many Zimbabweans will not eat anything else, and steak is therefore invariably found on the menu at any restaurant, regardless of its theme. Bulawayo steak houses are famous for their generous portions of tender prime beef and most of them serve a Texan-style plank steak that defies all but the very largest of men."

Therefore, I Ching hexagram 21 literally meant "biting through" as I did have to make myself bite through the meat, mopane worms and dried fish. Oh, and even the organic beans. Taught as a teenager to "pick" beans by finding and throwing away tiny clumps of dirt, rocks, or misshapen broken beans. Well, while assisting the cooks in the kitchen, they gave me a bag of beans to pick. I began picking out the small beetles quickly discovering, as the cooks laughed at me, that there were as many dried beetles in the bag as there were dried beans. Knowing how precious food was, I took out the debris but left in the beetles. After cooking, they added flavor, were actually delicious and gave a nice crunch! Of course, I had plenty of other experiences to bite through.

Chapter 30: Reality of the Situation

Actually, Hexagram 21 is more about correcting or punishing someone for criminal behavior in the community. I personally, not that I know of, did not have a situation where I needed to punish anyone. However, while I was in Zimbabwe in November 1997, and for three days in January 1998 there were protests and food riots because of the unaffordable higher prices of necessities such as food staples of cornmeal, cooking oil, rice, bread, and gasoline for travel. Rioters broke into shops and delivery trucks to take mostly food items. Violence erupted as rioters overturned commuter omnibus minivans blaming the drivers for higher fares. The government harshly punished demonstrators, injuring them by beating, tear gas, and shooting some people. Those in jail received inhuman treatment although the Zimbabwe Constitution prohibits torture, cruel and inhuman treatment. The police were overwhelmed and unprepared calling in the military to help as there had not been previous riots of this magnitude. Allegedly, there was also some political corruption and violence against the opposition.

Unknown to me, there was also a global economic crisis occurring that started July 1997 with the Asian Financial Crisis as monetary currency became devalued in first Thailand, then Indonesia, South Korea, Malaysia, Hong Kong and Japan. This led to slowdowns in manufacturing, increased unemployment, bankruptcies, oil and food storages which also caused political instability and riots in Asia. Previously, Zimbabwe's economy had been considered stable with combined subsistence and commercial agricultural farming when it had a food surplus during the drought years. However this changed with increasing inflation, taxes, the government's huge civil service job sector amidst raising unemployment with low wages in other sectors. Therefore labor strikes occurred, including on commercial farms, with demands for lump sum payouts to disabled war veterans and more. Zimbabwe's currency exchange rate dropped 75%. As you can see, the reasons for the food riots, inhuman punishment of the rioters, yet leniency of punishments for incorrigible government corruption were complicated.

The ORAP Zenzele College closed for the next semester as American students complained about poorer quality of the class lectures and increasingly absent teachers. Wow! How ignorant we students were of the extent of the teachers', their families' and the country's struggles. Even oblivious to risks to our own safety, as we regularly traveled downtown.

Again, I apologize for my ignorance then and now. I wrote these chapters about Zimbabwe from my personal experience, diaries, class notes, and the college student handbook. After currently reading memoirs in 2022, written by people who grew up in Zimbabwe I see there is plenty history and daily life I didn't know, that I couldn't know because of language and cultural barriers. The books I read were written by people from northern Zimbabwe. Even in the north there are many more tribes and languages besides Shona and siNdebele along with those of people who immigrated from bordering countries. Zimbabwe was only fifteen years post War of Independence while I was there in 1997. Many were recovering from memories of war atrocities, torture, rape, servitude and pillage by the British and also from other native Zimbabweans.

All this I didn't know. If I had known, I would have been more compassionate and helpful. Regretfully, I didn't know how to send money to Zimbabwe. Inviolatta warned me that sending anything through the mail risked theft or her paying bribes for her to retrieve it from the post office. Cost of postage from the United States was also outrageously expensive, as I found out when I tried to send diapers and sewing supplies. I wish I had given more money while I was in Zimbabwe and also after I returned to the United States, but I was caught up in my own survival struggles.

Decisions Decisions

Getting Answers
to Life's Challenges

VOLUME 2

Returning

Haneefa Mateen

Contents

Introduction	131
PART ONE: Adjusting to the United States	134
Chapter 1: Graduation	135
Chapter 2: Reversed Cultural Shock	139
Chapter 3: Homeless	143
Chapter 4: In the Shelters	147
Chapter 5: Sent Here and There	151
Chapter 6: Men	154
Chapter 7: Gratitude	159
Chapter 8: Healing Emotionally	161
Chapter 9: Spiritual Practices	166
PART TWO: Is There a Home for Me?	172
Chapter 10: A Push Out the Door	173
Chapter 11: Family	176
Chapter 12: Not Again!	184

Chapter 13: Sacred Contracts Archetypes Cards	186
Chapter 14: More Guidance with Sacred Contracts Cards	207
Chapter 15: Where Else to Go?	218
Chapter 16: Home?	223

Introduction

People ask me, "How did you, and still do, go through tough life challenges and can smile?" They want to know what I did to survive. Divination is one of the tools I use.

No need to suffer depression and anxiety worrying what decisions to make, or did you make the right decision. Is it even your decision to make or someone else's? No need to worry what is going to happen in the future, because your guides give you insight into the situation that you are concerned about, and will show you what you have control over and what you don't. Depression and fears often comes from feeling trapped or stuck. Asking for higher guidance for what you can do to improve your situation, through the use of divination gives you solutions and putting that guidance into action, gets you unstuck. It does take faith and courage because what you will be shown is new and different. Or often what you've known all along you need to do.

"Insanity is doing the same thing over and over again and expecting different results." Albert Einstein

Fear of change or what others will think, may have stopped you. Divination gives you encouragement by showing you options. The results often better than you could have ever imagined. Miracles, lots of miracles and abundance happen.

Well, when you start to see less crises in your life, as you understand how the universe functions around you, and make better choices in your thoughts and behaviors, then it is not hard, even for us who are hardheaded, to believe. Especially when your life begins to flow smoothly synchronically, and what you need simply shows up abundantly. Divination provides roadmaps or a GPS that lets you know where the traffic congestion is and guides you through the detours. Sometimes we get stuck in traffic anyway. GPS gives alerts and warnings ahead of time. Divination also gives you alerts and can help you get back on the main road of your life.

It decreases conflicts in relationships by allowing the oracle to show us what's best. From your heart with sincerity, you can ask the following questions: How do I improve myself to have better friendships? Should I share or not? Am I enabling? Or do I tend to be selfish and not know how to share and love? Show me how to feel love and receive love. How do I get along with his or her family? Should we buy this car at this time and from what dealer? Or change employment? Or relocate? Where do I go for guidance when I'm feeling sad or frustrated? If we disagree on what to do, what is best for the whole situation? What prayers do we need for healing? And then follow the guidance, each step of the way. Relationships help us learn, grow and change.

Hopefully this book introduces you to different perspectives as my personal stories bring understanding of how ancient and now popularized practices for making decisions — when used properly — brings improved quality of life, inner peace, satisfaction, and sense of purpose. And is inspirational to you on your own life's journey.

INTRODUCTION

In the first book, <u>Mother's Love from Beyond: A Healing Journey of Grief and Loss</u>, readers learned about my childhood and early adult years, as I was prepared through life experiences to accept that there are many different ways of healing and knowing. Readers gained faith and courage along with me as I learned to trust intuitive higher guidance.

Previous readers asked me to go into more details about my middle years, my thirties, forties, and early fifties to explain how I got from, and transformed through multiple crises and the obstacles I endured described here, from then to now.

PART ONE: Adjusting to the United States

Chapter 1: Graduation

I returned to the School for International Training (SIT), after a year away in Zimbabwe. The college campus provided me with healing because it was nestled in the tree covered hills of Vermont with the soothing sounds of waterfalls and streams all along the roads. It was a nurturing small community too, but because most of the students and teachers were white, it felt shocking to be surrounded by them, although I knew most of them previously, after me living in African villages.

We had the traditional graduation ceremony with caps and gowns, however, we chose our gowns from a of variety of colors and designs from four different countries. Mine was from Kenya. The faculty giving us our diplomas wore their alumni university gowns and sashes. In the afternoon, our undergraduate World Issues Program had its own separate ceremony where we wore long white Tibetan scarves. My cousin came up from Philadelphia. I was glad to have her there with me. We have a photo of her trying to wrap her Tibetan scarf. She received her doctorate degree a few weeks later. Laughing, she accurately described the SIT campus as the, "hippie college on the hill."

I had to decide where I would live after graduation. Having brought most of my belongings with me and put them in campus storage, I would have to ship them to wherever city my new home would be. My grandmother was begging me to come live with her in Philadelphia. Stay in Vermont? Should I go back to the Midwest city where I grew up, where my closest siblings live? Continuing my education at the master's level or working in other cities was tempting but I missed my family and friends after being away from them for two years. Return to Chicago which was only a couple of train or greyhound bus's hours away from them? I did I Ching readings on all of these relocation possibilities:

***

From SIT to Philadelphia?

Hexagram 28 (line 5) into hexagram 32.

Hexagram 28 is an unbalanced situation or attitude. Line 5: Have to be able to adapt and be flexible with the current realities of the situation.

Hexagram 32 Duration indicates making a commitment to continuous striving towards goals throughout adversity and challenges. This is easier when you are able to adapt to changing situations and your upmost goal is spiritual growth of improving your own character and harmony in all relationships with others, both family and career.

***

From SIT to the Midwest city where I grew up and worked? Hexagram 50 The Caldron Transformation (lines 2 and 6) into hexagram 62 Deficiency.

Hexagram 50 represents spiritual power with the emotional and mental development of spiritual transformation of self and society. This begins with letting go of old obsolete, no longer useful beliefs, behaviors, and goals. Focus is on learning alternative spiritual perspectives and approaches to solving societal concerns. Allowing the oracles and divination to guide you. Line 2: Others may disapprove of your personal transformative changes. Line 6: After doing personal inner development, you can be of service to the community. A hexagram 62 situation is not the time to push forward or be ambitious. Will have limited resources and energy.

***

From SIT to Chicago?

Hexagram 8 Unity (line 4) into hexagram 45 Gathering Together.

Hexagram 8 is about finding and joining with others in a small group. This requires commitment and perseverance and a proper leader who can balance the needs of the individual with the needs of the group. It is important to not hesitate too long in joining because you will miss out on bonding, as well as growth, while the group develops. Hexagram 45 is a large community gathering together that is influenced by the divine and our unseen ancestors for us to come together. Oracles and divination are used to guide and govern the community.

Chicago seemed the best destination of all my choices. This was based on my limited understanding of the spiritual readings and about life at that time.

Back in Chicago, again surrounded by the tall apartment buildings and concrete, I did not feel so desperately constrained and separated from nature. It was as if my soul was satisfied after having found my people and my culture. Determined to keep that sense of wholeness I gained in Zimbabwe and maintain it, I vowed to bring this culture back with me to the United States and share this from inside me with others no matter what, not to be stolen from me again.

Remember, the I Ching Hexagram 55 Abundance was my initial reading inquiring about my purpose and role while I was in Zimbabwe back in 1996?

While in Zimbabwe and at SIT, I did experience true abundance. But I guess I forgot about the other part of the hexagram 55 advice and forewarning of decline. What goes up so high must come down. Similar to what happens after profound creative, healing, and spiritual experiences, after feeling so blissfully wonderful we must then bring the lessons we learned back into everyday life. To do this we must face the realities of our lives internally, as well as in our surrounding environments and communities.

In contrast to feeling bliss, Earthly life can feel harsh and painful. I had made an inner vow of bringing back with me to the United States, the true love and community life given to me in Zimbabwe. How was I to hold onto that love and peace and share it? Life was about to test me to the umpteenth degree more than I could have ever imagined!

Chapter 2: Reversed Cultural Shock

I was happy to be back in the United States. Readjusting, however was rough. Although the SIT counselor talked to our classes about culture shock before we went abroad and reverse culture shock when we returned to campus, I was still not prepared for the intensity of reversed culture shock. Perhaps because the Zimbabweans were true to their word that they would not let me get homesick, and while I did have to adjust to a new language and culture, it didn't shock me as much. My only clue for missing the United States was when, in the last two months I started wanting junk food like pizza and potato chips. I didn't even usually eat pizza, because of my gluten and dairy intolerance, I couldn't eat the crust nor the cheese. I did miss the crunch of plain potato chips, since the potato chips sold in snack bags in Zimbabwe had vinegar and were soft. A friend shipped a box to me with the ingredients for my favorite comfort food, homemade rice flour pancakes, the month before I returned to the United States. And yes, yes I was missing and looking forward to seeing my family and friends that I hadn't seen for almost three years.

In Chicago, my friend, Sandra invited me to live with her temporarily at her two-bedroom apartment. Everyone was glad to see me initially. However, they didn't understand or recognize how much I had grown and changed. Their lives had changed too, but I was expecting that we could still do the same activities we did before I left. They got tired of me excitedly talking about Zimbabwe. A friend who went to West Africa, and I were able to share stories, but she was only away for a month. I talked about Zimbabwe so much that people asked me, "Why didn't you stay in Africa?" For some reason, that possibility never crossed my mind. In my naïvety, I only automatically thought to finish my classes and assignments on campus, then go home to my family.

I was hoping my village experiences with being authentic and loving would help us be even closer, but instead I lost friends. Some told me that I didn't have common sense. Of course, I no longer had common sense because I was readjusting to the American society, it's routines, materialism, wastefulness and faster pace with no time to do much together with anyone. When walking down the street greeting people, people would look at me crazy for saying hello to them and asking them how they were doing. People seemed cold, self-absorbed and fake.

"She talks too slow and moves too slow." That is what a job interviewer for a nursing position at a hospital kidney dialysis unit told my nurse friend, who suggested I try there. Another interviewer said, "I see you've had 12 sick days in a year."

She judged me not knowing that I had heard a recommendation that it is the best for everyone to take "mental health days" instead of needing to take sick days off." I purposely started taking the day off before my period when I was quietly crabby and achy. Previously I rarely took vacation days, nor sick days, nor holidays. Raised a Muslim I didn't celebrate Christmas or Easter, so I volunteered to allow coworkers time off with their families. Plus, we got time and a half pay for holidays. Other people regularly bragged about calling in sick for sports games, or just because it was a beautiful sunny day, or because they partied too much the night before and had difficulty getting up the next morning. I didn't take sick days, instead accruing a nice bonus check at the end of each year, until I heard about self-care.

But the interviewers didn't know how dedicated a worker I am. All they saw in front of them was a tall, too skinny, African American woman who they probably thought was on drugs. Who had been on a strict vegan, gluten-free diet too long. That walked for miles and miles, two hours up and down the rocky terrain of Zimbabwe hills, only having had a single plate of mealie meal with a large spoonful of collard greens. Maybe if she had eaten the moponi worms and the smelly dried fish she would've had more protein, more muscle, more energy and thought clearer. Depressed with homesickness and daydreaming for the land and loving villagers she left behind. Who didn't know yet, that she had done possible irreversible damage to her body.

Unaware of how I appeared to others, I of course took this rejection personally, sinking me into depression as my friends pressured me to keep seeking employment. In some ways, I actually felt better physically than than I felt before I went to Zimbabwe and while I was in Zimbabwe. Perhaps because other than walking, I didn't do heavy labor. I did quietly get chest pain when I tried hoeing in the garden with the women or helping with digging wells with a shovel. But somehow the villagers knew and didn't ask me to participate more than a couple of times.

Back in the United States, difficulty climbing stairs was my first warning sign that something was wrong with my health. The closer I got to the top of the stairs, the more my legs felt heavy as if I could barely pick them up, and I was short of breath with mild chest pains. Because I had a history of a diagnosis of asthma that's what I thought the problem was. And so did doctors when I finally went to Cook County hospital emergency room, feeling like someone stuck an ice pick in my chest sharp pains when I tried to inhale deeply, along with the constant aching pressure in my heart. I was weak, dizzy when standing up and walking. Breathing in cold air or drinking cold liquids also intensified my heart area pain. Yet I didn't think about how irrational it was at the time, to get on buses and then two subway trains from the Southside, and through the snow to get to Cook County hospital. How I did it, was probably from sheer will, same as how I've made it through all the other crises in my life.

Without employment, I spent many days alone at home. Deeper depression was sure to follow, and it did, giving people even more reasons to be concerned, yet stay away. Only years later, did I learn that these are normal symptoms of reverse culture shock, especially for people like me who were immersed in village culture and lived far away longer.

Chapter 3: Homeless

Unable to achieve employment, my stay with Sandra lasted beyond the six months allowed on her lease. Plus like me, she was more of a loner, and she desperately wanted her privacy back. A mutual friend Paula, put my belongings in storage and helped me search the newspaper advertisements for an apartment of my own. She found a room up north, then she paid my rent and drove me there. The rooming house was close to a few major streets with plenty of stores and restaurants. Paula also gave me money for food and to call her from time to time on outside pay phones. It was winter, and I trudged through Chicago's usual first week of January blizzard leftover snow.

 My friend Paula had only paid for two month's rent. So in February 1999, I went to the Department of Human Services to ask if they would give me a month's rent so that I would not be evicted. The older woman behind the desk asked me some questions and had me fill out some forms. And then she talked on and on and on about everything else. She didn't think that my heart symptoms would qualify me for a medical card. She knew because her daughter also had a heart problem. At the end, the most I understood is that I did not qualify for the program because I didn't have a regular monthly income.

 Next, I went across the street to an unemployment program inside a church. I had called earlier. It was located in the basement. They were just closing and gave me a business card to call for an appointment. I thought, how can I call for an appointment without money? I had walked a long way to get there.

An old man came up to me and asked me if I would like to join him for lunch. I followed him to one of the circular tables and sat down. There was a younger man and two other women at the table. They asked me why I was there. I expressed my frustration and fear of not knowing where I was going to live next month. The young man started telling me about the different social services in the area and offered to show me some of them.

After lunch, I followed him around for the remainder of the afternoon. He led me a few blocks away to the Salvation Army building. The offices didn't open until 1:00 PM. Around the back of the building, lunches were also served at the Salvation Army, so we ate a second lunch there. We stood in a long line that wound around the building and up a tall steep flight of stairs. There were more stairs inside. The portions on our plates were small. With my limited wheat-free and mostly vegetarian diet, I had even less to choose from. I ate the canned fruits and vegetables. After eating, we went inside a side door, where again I waited a long time sitting on a hard plastic chair in the waiting area to see a case manager, only to be told that I needed to go to the Salvation Army on Belmont Avenue that was closer to where I was rooming.

Back out on the street, we talked as we walked. He showed me the overnight shelters in the area. There were two shelters for women. One was in the church basement that was affiliated with REST, and required a ticket to get in. The other shelter located a few blocks away, was open on a first come, first serve basis. He and I ate a delicious free dinner that night. It was getting dark, I needed to walk home. He told me to return early in the morning to speak with someone at R.E.S.T., which is an acronym for Residence for Effective Shelter Transition. It was located on the fourth floor of the building that I went to for employment services and ate lunch and met the young man who was kind enough to show me around the area. I had to be there the next morning before 9:00, since I did not have an appointment.

I signed in with the receptionist but did not have to wait long before my name was called. A counselor, who introduced herself as Jennifer, led me towards the back to a room full of cubicles. After asking me questions while she filled out a stack of forms, she told me I could get a room soon. As long as I stayed in either of the two women shelters, all I had to do is go to scheduled meetings there at REST and in the community. She handed me a sheet of paper to sign my name, where she had circled the meetings that I was interested in, such as the women's group on Monday and a women's art group on Wednesday mornings. There were also meetings that were required for everyone to attend. She also gave me a list of alcoholic and narcotics anonymous meetings in the neighborhood. She told me that the more meetings I attended, the sooner I will be placed in housing. So although I never had a substance-abuse addiction, I could go to those meetings too. Years ago, I went to Adult Children of Alcoholics' meetings, therefore I was familiar with the twelve step anonymous programs.

Jennifer called and made appointments for me while I was there. She had asked me about any history of domestic violence, so she set me up with a domestic violence support group, and for a mental health assessment later that week. She also told me where the local public aid office was.

The next day I went to the Salvation Army on Belmont Avenue, and to my surprise they agreed to arrange for one month's rent, and also gave me a $25 voucher for the Salvation Army thrift store. My friend Paula had only given me money for January and February's rent, this would pay rent for March. After that, she informed me that she could no longer help. I went "home" and packed my large denim backpack. My plan was to spend nights in a shelter and walk the twenty blocks "home" after scheduled daytime meetings to nap or shower, then walk back to the shelters. This proved to be quite an undertaking because I had to walk to get to everywhere. It was very cold outside. Other homeless people taught me that there were free meals served at different places at different times, on different days of the week. I could count on breakfasts and lunches at the Salvation Army. There was an additional lunch on Tuesdays and Thursdays in the basement where REST was. Other days I could get lunch at the community center. Big bowls of soup and bread were served for dinner at the large Saint James Church's basement located a few blocks west of REST. Besides mealtimes, I had to keep track of the new appointments Jennifer made for me and find out where they were located, since I was unfamiliar with the north side of Chicago.

Chapter 4: In the Shelters

My biggest challenge was actually getting into and surviving being in the shelter. The REST women's shelter did not open until 9:00 PM, and card holders were allowed in first. Rarely were there any beds left. I am glad that someone told me about the community center women's shelter, which opened earlier in the evening, so I did not have to stand outside in the cold too long. Being chilled has always made me feel sick and miserable. The first night I arrived at the community center, when I signed in I had to answer the same emotionally painful personal questions again. Then I was sent upstairs. The upstairs was dimly lit, but I saw rows and rows of bunkbeds with women and children. I was told to go back downstairs. The woman who registered me, thought I was a teenager although I was 42 years old at the time! She directed me to sit at one of the round tables with the rest of the women. I followed them to the kitchen for a late dinner. The food was surprisingly tasty and abundant. Then we were each given a number for one of the fifty, closely spaced, exercise mats on the floor. One of the volunteers brought me a small white sheet and a gray army blanket.

   My mat was along the main walkway going to the bathroom. The floor was hard and cold. Women kept getting up during the night to go to the bathroom. Then there were stragglers, most of them were intoxicated but were allowed in late anyway.

Since the mats were only a few inches apart, some women who were easily irritated by the slightest bump by the person next to them would start arguments. Others would steal, so I had to sleep with one eye open. My mat was also located near the noisy ice machine, so I got very little sleep at night. Just when I was starting to fall asleep, someone would go to the bathroom or turn a shower on. All too soon, it was 6:00 and the staff was waking us up to get ready to leave at 6:30 AM! There were only two sinks in the bathroom for all the women, so I didn't even try to wash up. Breakfast was served. I grabbed a quick bite to eat and back out on the street I went.

Being out on the streets was very frightening to me. Since my parents keep me indoors and as an adult I was usually a homebody, I was not street smart. Most of the other homeless people looked hard and mean to me. There were frequent fights breaking out in front of me on the sidewalks, especially when we were together in waiting rooms and soup kitchens. After prayer service at the Salvation Army, they would serve us breakfast. The Salvation Army had a warming center that opened at 10:00 AM. This meant walking the streets until then. When it opened, we had to go through a metal detector and be searched by a security guard with a handheld metal detector. The security guard stayed at the entrance of a large room filled with chairs around small tables with games to play. There was also a television. Most of the programs on the television were educational. This turned out to be a quiet, safe place.

Quiet and safe, but I felt uncomfortable surround by mostly men everywhere I went. I was friendly, polite and courteous, unlike a lot of the other women. My smile also made me attractive, but I got tired of being bombarded with personal questions because I wasn't interested having a boyfriend. I had enough problems of my own! So when I was told about a warming center just for women, I was eager to go there, but I had to wait until it opened at 1:00 PM.

The women's warming circle was located on the second floor of a large building on the corner of Lawrence and Sheridan Road. As I waited for the elevator, in the main lobby, I noticed to my left the entrance to the Cultural Center. Ironically, I had traveled there from the Southside of Chicago for a job interview the year before. They told me there were no paying jobs available. Now I rode the elevators up to the second floor with tears in my eyes. Women were already lined up along the white painted hallway. We were buzzed through the security door with the glass window, into a large sunlight room that also had white walls. When I signed in, I noticed there were over 60 signatures from the day before. The staff who greeted me were pleasant, and again I had to answer questions about my personal life. They took me on a tour. There were washers and dryers, a storage room with toiletries, bathroom with showers, kitchen and separate small support group meeting rooms. The main large room had shelves with books, games, puzzles and craft items. It also had a television and was filled with small tables and chairs. Snacks were served that day. Other days, dinner was served in the evening. The warming center closed at 8 PM, from there we would leave back out into the cold night to go to the shelters.

All of these interviews at these different social service agencies were very emotionally difficult. I felt ashamed and humiliated having to ask for help. One interview location was very claustrophobic and frightening, sitting face-to-face close enough for our knees to almost touch, being asked questions about past abuse by a tall African American male worker that kept staring at me. Gratefully, a white lady was there too, taking notes. There was no introduction as to what the interview was for, and no real explanation of the results at the end. And no place to cry after the intake sessions. Just left open and raw.

That night was horrible as memories flashed before my eyes while I tried to hold back the painful feelings and details of past abuse. On top of the emotional pain, I also couldn't sleep because of the burning pains from my waist to the soles of my feet and now my hands. My lower back, abdomen, neck and head were also aching. Eventually dozing off, I woke up late, not wanting to get up and face the day. Lying there, I realized I had an overwhelming feeling of being trapped. Trapped not only during my teenage years because I didn't know any better, but also now because I didn't know what my options were, and I was again in a very desperate vulnerable position at the mercy of others. Used to my needs verbally rejected over and over again when I did ask for help. How could I have had any energy left to face the rejection of not being hired for jobs again and again?

I felt in a daze, shocked state from all the new information that I had to learn and remember for survival. The sidewalks, waiting rooms and other places I had to go to for appointments seemed filled with mean looking and hardened street people. I do not remember ever again seeing that young man who helped me the first day. There were other men who helped me on other days to find where I needed to go. Women were distant, mistrustful and competitive. This made me feel fearful and vulnerable. Some women rudely asked me why I was always smiling. I guess smiling and being courteous was my defense mechanism, and it did help to get me things that I needed.

Chapter 5: Sent Here and There

The following weeks, I had to go to appointments from which other appointments were scheduled, so that I had appointments almost every day. I did not qualify for the mental health services at ACCESS, so I was sent to the community counseling center located about six blocks west of REST. I was assigned a psychiatrist and a social worker. After an assessment there, it was determined that I should also go to the Quetzal Center. The Quetzal Center was for sexual abuse counseling. It was located almost a mile away, to the north. I had to walk there too. Luckily as long as I had the official REST sheet of paper signed, all my appointments counted towards points for housing. In addition, I still had to go to the mandatory meetings at REST.

    The mandatory meetings at REST were boring, mostly because the repetitive topics did not apply to me. For example, almost every week at the Tuesday Housing Group, and the Immediate Support Group on Thursday mornings, we were given the same budget forms to fill out. Having worked the most of my life and a bread winner in both of my marriages, I had always been good at budgeting my money. I split my paychecks three ways – a third went to pay bills, another third went to the bank for savings, and the rest I can spend if I chose to. At the meetings there were limited participation by the other clients. There was always at least one person who was loud, negatively aggressive, talkative and tried to take up the whole meeting time. The facilitators seemed like they were afraid of these clients and rarely intervened. Women's Self-Support Group on Monday afternoons was interesting, when we could get discussions going.

The group that I really liked was Women's Art Group on Wednesdays. As a lover of arts and crafts since I was a young child, I probably would have made the best of the time anyway, but there were several reasons that I especially liked the Women's Art Group. One, there were plenty of art supplies and we were asked which other supplies we would like. The cost didn't matter. Two, although the facilitator Brian was a young man, he commanded respect and provided structure and compassion. He was during ministry from Uptown Baptist Church, but he didn't preach to us. He was a walking, living example of Christian teachings. Three, he took us on field trips to art galleries and treated us to lunch afterwards at restaurants. For example, we went to the Norman Rockwell exhibit at the Chicago Historical Society. At $15 a ticket, it would've been difficult for us to afford it. Yet, he paid our way, and still took us to lunch afterwards.

Health Talk group, on Thursday afternoons was interesting mostly because I am a registered nurse, and personally interested in a healthy lifestyle. I actually learned some new information there. Then every weekday afternoon from 2:00 to 3:00 PM REST had Alcohol Anonymous, or Cocaine Anonymous, or Narcotics Anonymous meetings. I went to these meetings there, and at the local hospitals in the evenings and weekends. The readings from the twelve step Big Books, along with personal testimonies were inspirational even though I did not have a substance abuse problem.

My goal was to get as many signatures as possible so that I could get a room or apartment sooner. I still worried and had nightmares about losing my belongings, often crying and lying awake from 1:00 AM. It was very scary and depressing watching homeless women try to carry around their remaining possessions. Many had mentally illness or were on drugs, which I was afraid I would become too if I were totally homeless. I'd lose my mind because I would no longer have a reason for living. Even though previously, after my near death experience and especially after living in rural African villages where there was extreme poverty, I had thought I had not valued possessions and I could do with less. Now, I really did not want to do away with the few belongings I do have left. Probably because what remains of what I have, and if I could have my own apartment would represent my independence, identity, and potential creativity, plus stability and having my life and my belongings organized.

Chapter 6: Men

My other challenge was the men. I've always tried to speak to everyone with respect, having friendly conversations about the weather or homelessness, and recovery in an honest manner. But the men all wanted more, asking me personal questions immediately. They would get offended when they see or hear that I "talk to someone else." A potential for fights between other men and girlfriends, which of course I would know nothing about. Even with me being upfront and honest. They had only one thing on their minds – sex. They tell me, "You're beautiful and fresh." They would say they want to marry me or shack up with me. All of which kept my abuse issues on the surface, and me struggling to stay on top of depression and my sanity.

Now I really tried to be open to, or perhaps deluding myself into believing that all men are not "bad" and that sex is not what they want from me, hoping they just wanted conversation and companionship. But then some would cling, following me everywhere I went, having me change my plans or theirs. No, I couldn't just leave them at the dinner table! And they just didn't get it, when I tried to explain.

I was too through when an older man asked me while we were walking down the sidewalk, "Is the hair on the rest of your body as pretty and thick as the hair on your head? And is it long enough to braid!"

I gave him a mean look, but he went on talking about trying to figure out how he could get a place where I could move in with him. It didn't matter how many times I had told him I was not interested in a relationship with any man, and talking to someone for two days was not enough time to get to know someone enough to invite them in. His feelings were hurt when I went on and went to the library, after telling him that I planned to spend the morning at the library and then had important business to take care of. I was glad that I left him at the other building, although I apologized and stated that it was not my intention to ditch him. But inside myself, I knew I had to find a way to get away from him, after he also complained that, I "left the lunchroom with another man."

There was another young man, I had only met the day before at an Narcotics Anonymous meeting who thought it was perfectly okay to hold my hand and hug me. Well, I will return hugs at a meeting but when he offered to carry my bag and then hugged me in front of all the ladies near the entrance of the drop-in center, it might have gotten me in trouble with them. Previously I'd talked to men for longer times during the day, and none had inappropriately put their hands on me. Other men were also watching probably thinking that I have a different man every day. Jealousy could be dangerous!

Subsequently I stopped going to the lunchroom to eat and to outside AA or NA meetings. I needed the calories and I needed meetings signed on my attendance sheet, but I didn't need the sexual harassment. Yes, I'm recovering from abuse. But no woman should have to put up with harassment even if it is "sincere." The men have no idea what it feels like. They were in recovery hopefully, but the addictive behavior was still there. They were needy and needed their self-esteem boosted, but I wasn't the one! After that whenever men offered to pay my way, house my large backpack or me —I declined.

Not all homeless people or men are that way of course. One man showed me a store that I could go to exchange food stamps for cash. I did it twice. However, when I saw that it was only a small amount of cash that the store owner gave me, I stopped, especially because this then meant that I couldn't buy groceries either. I needed the cash to pay my credit card off, which I did in a few months. Having always prided myself on paying my bills on time, I felt ashamed. After that I had no cash. No cash for toilet paper nor sanitary napkins. It was humiliating.

Love Me Love Me Not

There are several ways to ask the oracles about getting into relationships with other people. This includes friendships and romantic relationships. From Ausar Auset Society Church classes, I learned how to make healthier choices.

In separate readings, you could use the oracle cards or I Ching coins to ask, "What would my strengths and weaknesses be in a relationship with? "What would the prospective friend's strengths and weaknesses be in a relationship with me?" "How can we help each other grow emotionally and spiritually?"

I asked: Please assist with divine guidance and insight into the relationship between James and I, and the effect on my incarnation objective destiny purpose:

Metu Neter Cards: Heru tem tchaas (-)/ Auset tem tchaas (-). This means there could be a good relationship between husband and wife, except that both these cards are negative. We really didn't know what a healthy was. It was true that there was conflicts, angry words, instability, my lack of will and commitment. I would've said no to having anything to do with James, or any man, except that the I Ching reading urged me to give him a chance. Plus I needed to have a man by my side for protection from the other men. I switched from a tall 6'2" stocky built macho man Mike to a short, thin, clingy, less threatening James. Both were a few years older than I. Initially, the taller Mike tried to fight and chase away James, but James stood his ground.

The I Ching guidance was similar but more positive. Hexagram 8 Union is a time to come together and hold together. The individual personal needs must not be neglected for benefit of the union. It's best not to hesitate to join, otherwise you will suffer accordingly. Or if you're already in the situation, but don't do what you're supposed to do. Do what needs to be done, to make it work.

So I inquired again of the cards. If James and I are to unite, what energies are needed to improve the relationship:

Metu Neter cards: Het Heru tu maat (+)/ Tehuti tu tchaas (+). Being able to express joy and experience pleasure, along with having faith and optimism, while following wise counsel and regular use of the oracles.

I followed up with doing I Ching readings every two months. Hexagram 53, Gradual Progress (line 1) means I'm new, inexperienced and therefore will make mistakes and get criticism, but this is good as we learn from mistakes. Our relationship changed to being peaceful when we were together, as I gradually learned to listen to James, instead of trying to insert my opinion, or insisting on being right. In return, James was the first man to actually give and not take from me. He considered my needs and brought me useful gifts. It was his unreasonable jealousy that caused arguments. Although it was a platonic, celibate relationship James was afraid that I would cheat the same as his first wife did. We both had to learn to trust each other.

Please Note: The I Ching interpretations and insights came from reading several I Ching books, listed in the back of this book, which I used to summarize the main points here and in later chapters.

Chapter 7: Gratitude

Two months later, through their transitional housing program, REST gave me a room in the Northmere apartment building. It was nicknamed affectionately, "The Nightmare" because at night you could hear people crying, screaming, some tenants knocking on each room's door begging for cigarettes. Although it was only one small room, and I shared an adjoined bathroom with another woman and roaches it was my space, safe and warm. No more having to walk the streets in the cold, waiting for the shelters to open, hoping there was room for one more. Initially, I did have to continue walking to the now further away soup kitchens. However, as staff and new friends saw that my walking was becoming increasingly more difficult, they gave me a little refrigerator and started bringing meals to me.

Jennifer used a REST agency van to go over to the Southside of Chicago and bring me my belongings out of storage, that my friend Paula had been paying for. As I was unpacking one of the boxes, I found my *Sacred Path Cards* book. I prayed, asking for guidance and pulled the Field of Plenty card. To the best of my understanding, the Native American teachings of the Field of Plenty is about letting go of a fear of scarcity and poverty, knowing there is plenty for all. On the card is a colorful picture of a cornucopia basket full of the fresh harvest of fruits, vegetables and other produce. A reminder to be grateful now to the Creator, as if you already have it, whatever you desire, which I am ashamed to say I had forgotten in my misery, the African spirituality that the Ausar Auset Society Church had already taught me similar. Whatever you imagine and daydream about does comes true. Especially, as you put ideas that come to mind into creative problem-solving. The ability to imagine and be creative is my Het Heru destiny. How could I have forgotten?

I truly had a lot to be grateful for. My needs have been met without me purposely visualizing anything, but I had been in too much despair and hopelessness to notice. I began expressing, aloud when I was alone in my room, my gratitude and what I wanted for my future, that I could now believe was possible. Within a month after reading the *Sacred Path Cards* book, the homeless services agency moved me to a large, one-bedroom apartment with my own kitchen, where I could cook my own food.

The I Ching had previously warned me there would be a "decrease in status but not to worry about it because later I will get what I went after." I was very grateful for the I Ching and other books given to me for a divine guidance to inspire me to keep the faith and to let me know when I am on the right path, to keep going and to persevere.

The book, *Light Emerging*, also explains about cycles as "expansion and contraction." I had two beautiful years of expansion, then later in 1998 began my contraction years. The unemployment situation made me be still, and I began to be more relaxed and be grateful for this quiet, restful period in my life, only because I intuitively know the futility and uselessness of trying to make something happen before it's time.

Chapter 8: Healing Emotionally

The other part of my career guidance reading that previously in 1991 was the Metu Neter card: Amen hetep. How was I to obtain and maintain inner peace, taking neither gain nor loss to heart when my life seemed to be full of ongoing losses and health crises? Loss of my career included.

There was plenty to be grateful for, but there were some mornings when my body was too tired and in pain to want to drag it out of bed that I felt very ungrateful for waking up in the morning. I went to the 12 step meetings to remind me to take it one day at a time, and to accept the things I cannot change, being powerless over most things and people. However, I cringed hearing people answer the greeting, "How are you?" with they were "fine because they woke up that morning." Many days I wondered why I was alive, and what my life purpose was, no longer having a clue of what my dreams and goals were.

I realized I must have been still grieving, when tears came while I walked down the street as I thought about the therapist's question, "Are you feeling better?"

I responded, "A little. I'm not feeling my best. I haven't had especially good days."

I was better than a month ago because I'm not having constant emotional pain that made me want to die. But feeling blah with no excitement or pleasure, motivation or goals is not living either. It's just going through the motions, just wanting to get the day over with.

My grieving, I imagine it's similar to withdrawal when nothing ever matches the initial euphoric high. Nothing at that moment matched or measured up to the past two years of my life when I was an active contributing member of a community full of life and love in Vermont and in Zimbabwe. At least I didn't feel empty, which was a horrible feeling I had before, worse at some times than others. It's more like feeling blah, as if something's missing.

Grieving also came in the form of an inability to accept complements because it was painful to remember when I used to change my hairstyle daily, sewed and designed my own color coordinated clothes, painted very detailed proportioned pictures, had a good memory, took good care of my health the best I knew how, was a very spiritual person, just to name a few. Other people don't seem to see this side of me, although some somehow commented, "You look like a church lady. Will you pray for me?"

Returning from Zimbabwe, it was grief on top of grief. I'd also left behind my siblings when I moved to Chicago. With health problems and no income, I didn't know how to get back to them. I was just surviving. It was difficult to grieve the loss of my mother because I didn't know if she was alive or dead. Memories surfaced of missing my father. In therapy sessions, the counselors didn't focus on grieving they focused on past trauma.

When I became homeless, as a requirement for receiving social services for housing, the caseworkers at REST referred me to individual therapy at the Quetzal Center for sexual abuse survivors, as well as domestic violence therapy at another location, although these incidents occurred twelve years ago. I hadn't had therapy in nine years.

My therapist at the Quetzal Center was from Central America, so she understood some of my struggles. A few months after I became her patient, she went on maternity leave and transferred me to another therapist in her absence. The other therapist was an art therapist. When my regular therapist returned, they decided to ask me if I wanted to join the agency's women's art therapy group. It was great because the art therapists taught us a different watercolor technique each week. This was exciting for me because I had planned to take watercolor painting classes if I had stayed at the School of the Art Institute of Chicago. At $1400 a semester! Here the art therapists were teaching us for free.

For the new year of 2000, the art therapist gave us the assignment of making artwork relating to our personal goals and achievements from 1999, and then make a painting relating to goals for 2000. We were asked to make a group project from each of our previous paintings.

The therapist said, "See if you could see parts of each other's artwork that you could use in your individual artwork. Would you be willing to cut a piece out and give it to someone else?"

I said, "No, because I had just thought of some ideas I wanted to add to my painting from last week." I tried to suggest to her it would be better to borrow parts using a scanner to make a group project without cutting or destroying our original artwork.

The previous week, I took the risk of painting a picture of myself as a child in a dark terrifying place. But I didn't have time, plus I didn't feel safe to put in the dark silhouettes of the people who abused me surrounding me. When I looked at the picture today, I realized that I expected my family, even my siblings to protect me or at least stand up and say, "This is wrong." But all of us were in this secret grip of abuse together. The social workers stopped coming to check on us at the foster home, so no one reported the daily crazy happenings in that house. Thirty years later, I still felt the terror of being trapped with no way out.

I was outvoted, so I just went along with the art project. Seeing that others were able to give up almost all of their original work, helped me to lower my resistance. Some were very colorful designs that I thought would lose its meaning and image if it were cut apart and separated.

In the excitement of seeing the multiple possibilities of incorporating other's paintings, I actually forgot about wanting to complete my picture from last week. There was somehow power in being able to ask for artwork from others and being flattered that others made requests from me. But what was most powerful for me was observing the effect of cutting my dark ominous painting down to a manageable size and adding light and support from other's more cheerfully colored artwork. This is something I actually asked for help with last week; to visualize little Haneefa getting the help she needed and finding a safe way out, instead of withdrawal for survival.

I wondered if another woman in the group experienced similar, as she cut her brick wall of shame and silence from the past down to a smaller size. Last week, she told us the wall was too high to climb over and if she tried it would just get higher.

One of the therapist facilitators asked and suggested, "Wasn't there a faster way to get past that wall than axing it down? Wouldn't it be easier today to let others help and even share some of the load by acknowledging your wall of struggle in their own artwork?"

***

There were days that I felt like crying when I was out in public and on buses. Especially when I saw someone who reminded me of my friend Inviolatta who lived in Zimbabwe, and later I saw a woman who looked like Abeba from Eritrea. They were my classmates at The School for International Training. I really missed them as friends but noticed that I cry less often. Earlier I would have had uncontrollable tears streaming down my face whenever I thought of my friends along with grieving for the life, accomplishments, and potential I had before I became ill, unemployed, homeless and deserted. Memories of the above mentioned women friends, represented the best times I had in my whole adult life.

Perhaps I was feeling less hopeless as I realized I could still accomplish some of the things I had planned to do before all of this happened. Or even start new projects with some of the education and training I've had. I just would have to pace myself. I still got frustrated with the awful constant pain in my hands and back.

Chapter 9: Spiritual Practices

In the early days of my homelessness, my friend Paula invited me to an African American Buddhist group. They met regularly in a room in a funeral home. I thought about joining the group and I really thought the decision would be an easy yes. After all, wasn't this what I've been looking for and wanted? Had I not been waiting for a group of supportive like-minded spiritual people?

But the decision was not easy. When I started coming out of the depression and being honest with myself, I really felt like running in the opposite direction, far away from it and any other spiritual groups. Some teachings I did not agree with, based on my own personal spiritual experiences, especially after having a near death experience in 1982, and with the wonderful miracles and changes in my life afterwards. It is difficult for most people who have had near death experiences to accept most religions' and organizations' teachings and frightening rules about how to relate to "God" because we've already been to heaven, and met with an incredible Light of peace, love, and acceptance. Returning to an earthly body, we develop and continue a personal relationship with God. The aftereffects of a near death experience has survivors seeing the world a completely different way. Our values change so that we are not concerned so much about material things, status, or the physical body.

This just is. It's not a virtue nor makes me special. In fact, it's like a curse in a world where greed and selfishness are the expected norm. There was no reason for me to meet in a funeral home or nearby cemeteries to release my fear of death, because I had no fear of dying. Nor how to release any attachments to possessions since I was learning daily how to live homeless, without even a dollar in my pocket.

First, of my other reasons for hesitation with joining, in addition to not wanting to have to deny my spiritual experiences, is I learned the hard way that being so self-disciplined in following religious rules was detrimental to my health, relationships and my career. My commitment was extreme in comparison to most other people who pick and choose which of the rules they wanted to follow. They couldn't seem to ever find the time to meditate, they ate what they wanted to eat. For me, this was not a conscious option. The physical changes after having a near death experience make unhealthy eating a painful experience. Many near death experiencer's acquire allergies to almost everything, including food, and their digestive systems can no longer tolerate eating meat. I can't listen to radio or watch TV for long because I, as with most near death experiences can't stand high, especially loud, electronic frequencies. This can make living with people, including family and friends, complicated.

When clinic lab test results showed that my red blood cells were enlarged, I went to the library to see what it meant. I was horrified to read that megaloblastic macrocytic anemia is often from vitamin B12 deficiency, which is common in people who don't eat enough meat. Meat is the main source of natural vitamin B12. You would have to do like the old Total cereal television advertisement, and eat 10 to 20 bowls of beans, nuts, greens, etc. After learning that being a strict vegan probably caused me permanent nerve damage, that could happen in as little as six months, just imagine me being vegan for ten years! I was especially reluctant to join another spiritual group that emphasized vegetarianism was the way to nirvana.

Second, the more disciplined, the more spiritual and self-help healing and character building I've done, the less friends I had. It would be nice to think of myself as a positive role model, but the truth of it is — people resent strong, assertive, honest people. I was at the stage of my spiritual growth of having to live truth daily in the moment, in spite of what others think. But people could no longer relate or understand me, and I was having a hard time relating to them or the world since being homeless and unemployed I had no active role or place in the community or society. A very lonely place to be.

In religious organizations as well as with my family and friends, I've been such a "good girl" that the religious leaders don't seem to think I needed spiritual counseling. Other members would demand all the attention and get it, along with advice, material needs and financial help. I often helped the leaders help other people while my needs were neglected. So I felt let down and reluctant to depend on spiritual leaders. Although I was in an 'abyss' as the I Ching described my situation, where I did not know which way to turn or what to do. There is a saying, the more you know — the more you realize how much you really don't know. I truly didn't know what to do, but spiritual leaders couldn't help me.

As a result of doing spiritual practices, meditations and following divine guidance, my life has taken so many detours away from the rational concept of planned goals that I stopped making long-term goals. I did make some goals of course, daily and weekly, but in life there are no guarantees. From this perspective I wasn't usually shattered when plans didn't work out — until now.

Much of my fear of joining a new African American Buddhist group, was of my fear of being alone again, even within an organization. The worst feeling is to be alone in a crowd. If I'm going to be alone, I might as well be alone of my own choosing. Same with in my marriages, my spouses were out drinking, drugging, and partying. My husband put me on a pedestal as if I were a saint, while he was out doing his thing. I was at home alone unless I wanted to join him. Partying is boring as hell to me. Everyone looks like they're enjoying themselves except me, while I'm miserable because I can't relate to them and they can't relate to me. To me, nights are for sleeping and there is only trouble in the streets at night. When we were at home together there was little to talk about. I couldn't understand his need for the street life. He couldn't understand me. With my abusive second husband, I did not even try to understand him.

Third, I was done with male authoritarian religion leaders, especially when they criticize other religion's beliefs and practices while preaching that their way is the only way. For example, that the way I learned to meditate was wrong. He told us that it was a form of dreaming, of sleep. Never mind how much the deep breathing, music and visualizations had healed me, because he didn't give me the opportunity to tell him. By then, I had heard similar from people who had tried holotropic breathwork and not seen their past lives, and therefore said I must have dreamed what I saw. How do men get to be spiritual leaders since men have a tougher time going into deep meditation and trance, tending to intellectualize in books and lectures about what they wished were their own mystical spiritual experiences?

I had to admit to myself my strong inner desire is to live a full life, which would include family, friends, and a community. This was painful to admit to myself after knowing what it was like to always be surrounded by caring people in Zimbabwe. The village families never left me alone not even in my bed at night. Now that I was back in the United States, it seemed cruel to give someone something they have always wanted and more, and then take it away. Not some of it but it seemed like all of it! Is my life lesson to test how much that I would I allow myself to revert back to my habitual defense mechanism of the lonely child personality?

From this life lesson, in a short amount of time as I was given the opportunity to go through what very poor and possibly homeless people go through of gaining humility from experiencing discrimination, abuse, and injustices.

One person told me, "You can learn a lot from homeless people. They have no shame." I was beginning to understand why. There's a certain freedom to being an outcast from society, similar to freedom as a visitor in Africa or any foreign culture or country. Everything is so radically different from all that you've been taught to believe. It kind of forces you to give up your old beliefs and prioritize what's most important in life.

Initially, being homeless was very confusing and terrifying but it offered a liberating growing experience. Hopefully this is just a healing interval, and I will have even better relationships where there is a balance of me equally sharing and receiving unconditional love. From in the mist of my emotional, pain I can better understand other people's pain and why they do and say the things they do and be compassionate. Perhaps later

I would be able to help them acknowledge and heal the source of their pain too.

PART TWO: Is There a Home for Me?

Chapter 10: A Push Out the Door

My aunt had been asking me to move out to the suburbs with her for the past few months. Her son moved out and she didn't want to live alone. I've been hesitating because I wanted my independence. I was still hoping to have doctors fix me so that I could be employed. Plus I knew from visiting her in the suburbs, that the buses run slow, at half hour to an hour intervals, and rarely or not at all on the weekends.

Moving in with my Aunt? I Ching Hexagram 26 (lines 4 and 6) into Hexagram 34. Metu Neter cards: Nekebet tu tchaas/Geb hetep.

I Ching Hexagram 26 is again about "crossing the water" meaning traveling beyond your home territory and usual circle of friends, family and acquaintances. Line 4: don't wait until situation is too far along and causes harm. Line 6: the time for obstructions has passed therefore success. Hexagram 34 is about perseverance as the way opens up with less resistance. Warned not to force the situation, nor be overconfident. Further, what was very true in my case, was the encouragement to give up my defensiveness and insecurity since I would be going to an environmental that would not be threatening.

Transitional housing for the homeless still meant wandering from place to place. From one room with a shared bathroom, to a nice quiet one bedroom apartment, to being squeezed into a small studio apartment. The landlords could throw us all out again at any time. How much worse could it get?

One night, I woke to the sound of paper rustling and crunch, crunch. My ears perked up while I looked around the dark room. I didn't see anyone. Sounded like it was coming from the small bookshelf where I stored food near the kitchen, since there was only a couple of cabinets above the sink. Otherwise, the kitchen was simply a stove and refrigerator on one wall. It quieted, and I slept.

In the morning I found holes in bags of rice, my gluten-free flours and small boxes on the shelf. This reminded me of when I was a teenager, we woke to find on the kitchen table, a long round tunnel eaten out, through the middle, from one end of the long loaf of bread to the other, by mice.

However, after I put my non-perishable food in more secure containers on the bookshelf, the noises continued at night. I heard cans and boxes being knocked off the shelf, but I didn't hear squeaks. It would have had to be several mice together to be able to push those big items onto the floor. Now I was really scared because it couldn't possibly be mice! Did someone's pet hamster get loose?

Timidly, I reached for the flashlight by my bedside. Staying in bed, I peer into the darkness. It's huge. It's gray and menacing as it darted away. My can of cashews is on the floor. Seems to like sweets, not the plain instant oatmeal but my apple cinnamon, and chewed through my Raisin Crisp cereal box.

Terrified to go to sleep at night. The shelf was to the left of the foot of my bed. Could it be a rat? When I was younger, I had heard stories of babies in cribs getting bit by rats. Now in my one room, small studio apartment there was nowhere for me to run. Whatever it was, was bold because I couldn't scare it away by yelling and making my own loud noises, "Go away! I want to sleep!" Several minutes later, I would hear it chewing again. Maybe he was in the garbage or behind the cabinet or there could be others underneath my bed. What if it got on my bed with me!

The janitor and management at the apartment building didn't want to believe it could be a rat, insisting it was a mouse. All I knew was that that tiny studio apartment wasn't big enough fo the two of us. So my friend James brought a huge rat trap, smeared the middle with peanut butter, and set the trap. He put poison out and told me to cover the drains in the kitchen sink, make sure the sink was dry at night and close the lid on the toilet.

A couple of days later, the rat decided to eat the peanut butter and got caught. He was shockingly longer than the rat trap! I took pictures with my camera. Now we had proof.

My apartment was on the first floor across from the back door. More than the rat was a menace. Drug addicts and drug dealers living in the building kept up loud music, partying and arguments in the stairwell and hallways at night.

The rat was the last straw. Although James nailed on a metal draft stopper to close the big gap in the bottom of the door, it was past time for me to make a move. Heaven has a way of giving us all a push. A frightening push out the door. Forcing us to take that step forward and close the old doors behind us.

Chapter 11: Family

I moved in with Aunt Gussie. There were power struggles between us in the beginning. My uncle explained to me that the situation was similar to him living in a rooming house sharing a bathroom and kitchen with others. The landlord was the boss. This was difficult for me to accept because I was paying rent. Most of my life I worked and paid rent, even paid the rent when I had husbands. So I was expecting more independence. In time I calmed down, took it in stride, and gained more respect from my aunt.

From my experience and observation, when people move in with each other, as the honeymoon phase quickly fades away, the first year is going to be naturally rough with power struggles of "Why are you telling me what to do?" With time you begin to trust, learn how to lean on each other, and to appreciate each other. Knowing that this will happen, may help save many relationships whether roommates, or family members, or romantic relationships. It helped me cooperate more with my aunt.

My siblings and their children and grandchildren came to Aunt Gussie's house when Mother Dear came to visit, uniting the family. What's best about living with Aunt Gussie, is she connected me to the elder members of my family. I was getting to know her, cousins, my other great uncles and aunts for the first time. They came into town and stayed at Aunt Gussie's house for about a week or a weekend to go to visit their sister Dorothy and brother Roy in a nursing home. My paternal grandmother, Mother Dear was in her 90s at the time, smart and spry. Her brothers were ten and twelve years younger. It was difficult for me to keep from laughing as they argued, about which one of them couldn't tell them what to do. My grandmother being the oldest was of course bossing them which they didn't like, and because she was older they would try to take care of her which she didn't want because she was still quite independent.

I loved hearing them tell stories about their childhood, parents, what it was like to be back in their hometown compared to when they were younger, about historical events like the Depression and blizzards, and before there were modern conveniences. Going way back in history, considering Mother Dear was 92 years old at the time of this telling, and she was born in 1911. The following history is from audio recordings, transcriptions, and notes from Uncle Dennis, Uncle Pete and Machilla sitting around talking at Aunt Gussie's kitchen table.

Mother Dear: "My maternal grandparents were from St. Louis. Mother Dear's mother's mother was married to the son of the slave owner. She had eighteen children. The first two were by the slave owner and the other sixteen were by his son. Like his father, he was very mean. He used to take his wife out to the woods regularly to beat her. One day, she followed him submissively to the woods for her beating. Sarah, his sister said, "I'm going too." When they got to the woods, she pulled out a pistol pointed it at him, and told him, "Now you try to beat her." He never beat his wife ever again. She left him though, because he still was so mean. She took seven of her children and left him. She came to Illinois and he went to Oklahoma.

Our mother's father had a lot of land in Oklahoma. He was very ambitious. When he died, his land was divided up among his ten children.

The first house Mother Dear remembers was near the railroad tracks in the suburb where Aunt Gussie lives now. After awhile, they moved to a nearby suburb that had mostly Italians, who could be mean, but were good to our family. A large family with twelve children. Two siblings died young.

Dennis: "When we talk about family members, I give some credence to the fact that there were twelve of us children. But in actuality, I talk about only ten because I didn't know the other two. I didn't know Agnes and I didn't know Douglas."

Mother Dear: "Douglas died when he was 11 months old, of pneumonia. I was two years old, and I remember going to the funeral. Agnes was thirteen years old when she got burned. She got burned terrible, to the point where her mouth was even crisp. Our mother told us she didn't even know how Agnes could even talk, but she did tell us how she got burned. She was trying to light a coal stove. She put the kerosene on the coals in the stove, and lit the match, but the coals didn't light. She came back to it, but because combustion had built up inside the stove, it flared up setting her long pretty hair on fire and burning her face. She could barely talk in the hospital because she just had a small opening for a mouth. She lived seven hours.

They had this black undertaker, Jones, in Chicago. Mama and them, didn't know then that he had the reputation of being a swindler. When we were in the church getting ready for the funeral, there was a mouse squeaking in the casket! You could hear it squeaking and running around throughout the casket. When the funeral was over and we went to the cemetery, the undertaker was supposed to have the grave ready right? Well Agnes couldn't be buried because there was no grave dug. So, they put her in the mausoleum and told us to come back tomorrow. Mama and some friends went back the next day and the undertaker didn't even show up. The body was supposed to be in the mausoleum. Later Mama started getting all this information from people that he was a swindler anyway. So, to this day we don't know whatever happened to Agnes's body. It couldn't have been in that casket! We all said it, because the casket couldn't be open anyway. We should have figured that when we heard the mouse squeaking and when we went to the cemetery that was just a formality. He was just trying to fool somebody. Mama had given him the down payment, but they decided to not finish paying him anymore because they couldn't get Agnes buried. Some neighbors were saying Mama sold the body because Agnes had this unusual ailment, a deformity of the inside of her body. Agnes was home from school that day, because she had a medical condition that caused her to pass out, anywhere. The cause according to the doctor was that she had a uterus and vagina that lacked a "sieve." Previously there were plans made to have an operation. It could be that the doctors got together with the undertaker to get that body part.

I remember going to the funeral. I was six years old, sitting up there. I remember looking at my father with tears dropping down his eyes. Like drops of water, the tears were just that big! He loved his Agnes. Ummm hummmm. That was his joy. She was very nice looking as I remember. She had thick hair. Long thick hair down her back. It was his first daughter. It upset Mama for about a year. I don't know how she kept it together.

Let's talk about another subject. Papa couldn't carry a note as far as singing is concerned, and yet he had a brother who could really sing. Oscar was something else."

Pete: "You said Papa couldn't sing a note. Somewhere, somebody told me that Papa had a beautiful voice and sang in a couple of church choirs."

Mother Dear: "Papa did sing in the church choir. But a lot of people singing church choirs but that doesn't mean they have a beautiful voice. You are right about him singing in the choir."

Pete: "Only thing I know about Oscar, and it stuck in my mind because Mama made a comment one time, "The only time we see these people is when they are broke and they come looking for money.""

Mother Dear: "I don't know why they were like that! Even Willie Mae. You were too young to know her. She got married, she and her husband would come out and Papa had to give them carfare back home. I don't know why they thought Papa and Mama had so much money. She never came up without Papa giving her carfare back home. That was his sister, and he loved that sister too.

Well, let me get back to explaining to you what I was hoping you'd understand last night. When I was growing up, the piano had seven keys in the middle and has seven keys in other different sections. The seven keys were do, ray, me, fa, so, la, ti, do. Over the years it changed and now it's C, D, E, F, G, A, B, and C. When I had a piano teacher, she never went into that. I didn't know "do," from whatever. I didn't know the names of the keys. I don't know what was wrong with me. Miss Courtney told Mama that I couldn't come anymore. How come I couldn't come? She didn't teach me how. But when I look back over that situation, I could have had a piano teacher if she had taught me. But she shouldn't have said I couldn't come back. She probably did it because she thought I could hear, and I could hear. I was playing the notes right. But I didn't know what the notes were. Later, I did do piano recitals and drawing. Recently, I returned to playing the piano, and I am learning to play the hymns for the Jehovah Witness Hall.

Pete: Let me tell you something. When I was a college, I had some room for some electives, so I took a piano class. After about three months the teacher said to me, "Why did you take this class?" I never practiced. I didn't do nothing. She gave me assignments and I'd get up the morning before class and try to do it. So when she said to me, 'Why did you take this class?' I said to her, 'Ma'am, have no fear. I'll make sure I won't take it again.'

Life is interesting though when you look back over it. I look back at my life and I think, 'Boy, if Mama had known what I was doing, she would have killed me herself. I deserved all the 500 whippings that I got as a child. Teachers used to ask me if I was holding up the family reputation of my older brothers Dennis and Robert.

Mama would send us out to chose our own switch. I tried choosing a switch that I knew would break. She would make me go get another one. Sometimes she would beat us naked, without our clothes on with an ironing cord. I would hide under the bed. Papa didn't like disciplining us children and would only whip us if he was pressured by Mama. Most of the time Papa would just tell us to hold out our hand and he would hit it with a pencil. But there were times to be honest when he would beat our behinds.

Our sister Dorothy was so full of life. That girl sure could dance, she could roller skate too, and rode bicycles, and I don't know what else. Nothing seems to bother her. She has a good memory of family history and events. Dorothy also has a beautiful smile, and sense of humor that keeps us laughing. (Too bad she had the stroke).

I was also a good dancer. We used to "cut the rug" at the dance hall before it became Rock of Ages Church. Mama used to come and watch us young people dance.

I worked 17 years as a caseworker at a public assistance office. I tried having my own fish market, but it only lasted a year. As the youngest sibling, and the youngest boy, I had to learn to fight. I started out in life fighting more than I would have liked. I served in World War II. Was a secretary at the Veteran's Administration. Now I have three grown children. After retirement, I drove a school bus for awhile."

***

On one of the visits, Mother Dear and Aunt Gussie baked a sweet potato pie together. It was fun to watch them combine ideas for spices and other ingredients. Aunt Gussie was known as quite a baker of southern fried apple pies and assorted cakes whose names I had not heard of before.

James came a long way on buses and trains to visit me at Aunt Gussie's home. My family welcomed him in. One time he came through a blizzard to visit me. I was truly heartfelt touched that he would care that much for me. Of course I fussed at him, worried about his safety. When James didn't come for several months, my great aunts and uncles got in the car and took me to my old neighborhood on the north side of Chicago to look for James.

By the end of the year, Aunt Gussie began to trust and confide in me. She asked me questions about life and the afterlife as she talked about how much she missed her husband. He came to her in her dreams and was letting her know of his spirit presence by interfering with her radio and occasionally playing their favorite songs. She frequently asked me if these occurrences were real. Aunt Gussie worried about past situations where she had lingering guilt and regrets. Our discussions helped ease her concerns.

Chapter 12: Not Again!

Aunt Gussie taught me a lot about communication. How to talk to people. She would repeat what she said to me until I answered with real interest, with creativity instead of just nodding. Most importantly, she taught me how to listen. To really listen to what people are saying, not just with what I'm hearing with my ears but what they are say with their hearts. To go beyond words to their intention in spite of accidentally saying it wrong. Whether when only saying a few words, or going on and on and on. I learned to appreciate each person for being. Aunt Gussie also taught my ears to hear better by her talking to me from the other end of her house. I'm not sure how this was possible since I had been hard of hearing since I was twenty five years old. She herself had remarkable hearing. She could hear my soft voice from the kitchen to the living room.

I observed how she was with her friends. She listened to her family and friends any time of night or day. And I saw how her friends are friends of each other with patience and compassion. Through her stubbornness, Aunt Gussie taught me to speak up for myself and others. Together we taught each other it was okay to say our true feelings and fears. The true meaning of what it means to be strong.

I did not know then that these conversations with my aunt foretold what was coming next. She got shingles for which medicine didn't relieve the pain. Several months later, she began complaining of an awful pain in her upper leg. However, this did not stop her from doing household chores or going out with friends. Aunt Gussie increasingly spent more time sitting on the living room couch. Her doctor ordered an MRI scan but her leg was too painful for her to lie still long enough. The clinic told her to get more pain medicine from her doctor and schedule another appointment. Unfortunately, before my aunt could go for the MRI, she had a minor stroke. After admission to the hospital they did tests and were planning to do surgery on her hip. During the surgery they discovered that there was nothing to attach a hip replacement to, because cancer had destroyed the bone in her leg. The doctors told Aunt Gussie that she had six weeks to live.

Her daughters had difficulty coping. They argued. One daughter angrily banned friends and the rest of the family from visiting their mother in the hospital and later at her home. They tried to put me out and I had to scramble to find affordable housing. At such short notice, it was not possible because most affordable housing have years-long waiting lists. I could no longer climb stairs even with help, my legs would feel like wet spaghetti and would go out from under me without warning. When I walked too far, I had severe back pain afterwards especially at night. Eventually, I had to use a wheelchair and needed to find accessible housing.

Mother Dear came with a friend and drove me around to apply for apartments and to social service agencies. Uncle Dennis also came to help. All the affordable accessible apartments had long waiting lists.

Chapter 13: Sacred Contracts Archetypes Cards

In 2002, while I was living with Aunt Gussie, I discovered the book, *Sacred Contracts: Awakening Your Divine Potential.* Curious about archetypes I wanted to see how they related to the West African Yoruba deities' descriptions of human personality characteristics and abilities. The author, Caroline Myss, explains that your initial Archetypal Wheel is similar to a astrology birth chart so you only make an Archetypal Wheel once. Later when you inquire about a situation, you will use these same twelve archetype cards. Following the instructions in the book for choosing my personal archetypes, I first thought of a few roles that I have been most of my life, such as being a natural teacher, artist, nurse, and speaking up for justice. Then I read and chose other archetypes from the descriptions in the Gallery of Archetypes in the appendix in the back of the book. Each archetype represents learning experiences, and with recognition of our own main archetypal patterns, can help guide us through life. There is also an *Archetype Card* deck available with 74 archetypes by Caroline Myss, but her book, Sacred Contracts gives more in-depth descriptions than the cards.

 Each archetype, such as the Artist, has several different aspects to help narrow down whether the archetype accurately describes you or not. To assemble my Chart of Origin (Archetypal Wheel) I deep breathed, did the meditative visualization for opening to intuitive guidance, next with my eyes closed I followed the instructions to pair each of my chosen archetypes with shuffled stack of twelve numbers to represent the twelve traditional astrology houses.

Later, I started answering the long list of questions in the book for the first two archetypes that I chose but stopped because being analytical contradicts being able to be intuitive. Being too much in one's head thinking, questioning and judging prevents connecting to one's true Self and intuitive spirit guidance.

My Chart of Origin (Archetypal Wheel):

First House: Ego Personality: Amateur
   Second House: Life Values: Judge
   Third House: Self-Expression Siblings: Saboteur
   Fourth House: Home: Prostitute
   Fifth House: Creativity Good Fortune: Wounded Healer
   Sixth House: Occupation Health: Wounded/Nature Child
   Seventh House: Marriage Relationship: Slave
   Eighth House: Other Peoples Resources: Hermit
   Ninth House: Spirituality: Addict
   Tenth House: Highest Potential: Victim
   Eleventh House: Relationship to The World: Rescuer
   Twelfth House: The Unconscious: Artist

Reasons Why I Choose These Archetypes
First House: Ego Personality: Amateur. It's true that I have many varied talents and abilities, do well with each but am somewhat a "master of none." I developed many of my talents but as the definition of "amateur" indicates, I've

rarely marketed my talents nor sold what I created. Most of my creations are artistic. Some people consider art a hobby instead of a profession, probably because of low wages and inconsistent opportunities. Self-taught, I don't have college degrees in art, but I have perfected crafts, fine arts such as drawing and painting, writing, baking, sewing, knitting, also designing and sewing clothing and home furnishings. With a good memory, intuition, teaching, research and analytical abilities I might make much more income off of counseling or being an administrative assistant.

During my childhood my mother nurtured my artistic abilities. Then at age eight, all of this attention stopped when she married my stepfather. Later my foster parents criticized yet sold my artwork at art fairs, without sharing the profits with me. They criticized most everything about us children. Made me hate and not trust compliments because our talents were also exploited in other ways. Like telling me I did such a wonderful job at shining pots and pans then assigned me the daily task of washing pots in addition to my other household chores. Initially I actually did like shining pots and pans! This knocked down my confidence and later made me fearful of more exploitation if I were to sell my artwork myself.

Conversely, the ability to create was the only power and control I had in the abusive foster home. As an adult, I could give my all, while caring for patients and students in spite of bureaucracy and discrimination, as long as I had creative time at home. So I would get up early in the morning and do art or sewing before I went to work at 7:30 AM. My individual power to create that I did not have to fight over with anyone. It was mine alone. No need to conform in order to make it marketable. This gave me freedom to create, gain confidence and take risks. My connection to the divine. Remaining an amateur artist was the one area of my life where I didn't have to be competitive. The trade-off, of course is that I could have had more financial stability if I had risked selling my talents and been more willing to climb the professional career ladder. I also could've been more connected to family, community, and society instead of the many hours spent in creative solitude.

I had to quit going to the famous School of the Art School of Chicago after only one year because I was becoming literally an "starving artist." Although I had partial scholarships and loans, unlike other college majors where students buy their textbooks at the beginning of this semester and they're done, in art school teachers would require us, at least twice a week to buy and try out different kinds of paper, paints, pencils and brushes. Large sheets of tinted or textured drawing and watercolor papers were expensive. I had to decide whether to buy art supplies or groceries.

Second House: Life Values: Judge. I originally considered the Judge archetype because of its shadow characteristic of harsh criticism without compassion. I chose the Judge as an afterthought, because I thought I was supposed to choose 12 archetypes. I didn't know that I was to only choose eight archetypes, until I saw the instructions were that everyone already has the four primary survival archetypes of the Prostitute, Saboteur, Victim, and Child. I groaned when I scrambled my chosen archetypes and pulled the Judge card! But as I reread the description of the Judge, I began to see more of the positives in my character. I have been a natural mediator most of my life as a second-born middle child, the peacemaker in my marriages and at events. I try to get both sides to be seen, heard and understood. While at the School for International Training in 1997, I enjoyed the Peace and Conflict Meditation classes and activities. We role-played mediating the Arab and

Israel conflict as well as the then Yugoslavia (now Bosnia) conflict. It was difficult work because there's usually someone leading that wants to stay angry, revengeful, stepping on other people in order to maintain power. People follow them out of fear, and the more the possibility of the truth coming out, the more threatening the leader becomes. But the citizens, especially the youth who don't understand why they should be enemies have been coming together to get to know each other, for peace.

The Judge is appropriate to the second house because the second house represents life values and use of physical power. I could've gone either way with my upbringing, surrounded by lack of justice and compassion to be like my parental role models as a way to survive, or choose to have my own values and morals. I chose the latter. It has felt like hell and was very lonely, but I stuck with my values even when life got rough. In my marriage, I got tired of being placed on a pedestal, while the husband went out and did his dirt and then came home criticizing me to no end. Expecting me to be superhuman and to just put up with his behavior and lack of responsibility.

My struggles with power were mostly about values. During my younger years, I was overpowered by others who believed just taking what they wanted was just a way of life. Many times, I did without physical needs if it meant lying, stealing, or being cruel in order to get it. Or having to fight with other people. I came to believe either you want to give it to me – or you don't! I wasted a lot of years and time waiting for "loved ones" or jobs to do the right thing. After all, weren't they supposed to?

Then I discovered good people in the world and connection to the universe. Complete strangers would walk up to me and give me what I needed. Teaching me that I am divinely blessed with all that I need. Somehow my silent thoughts and wants were heard. I learned not to fear men and not to depend on them for my needs, instead of what I was previously taught from childhood to believe.

In regards to the shadow side of the Judge, I used to be critical of others because I used to be very critical of myself. As I became more forgiving and compassionate with myself, I was gradually able to do the same with others. Also I had somewhat of a unconscious "superiority complex" which is funny because my mother used to tell me I had an "inferiority complex" when I was a young child. Of course, I had no idea what she meant. Within a few years I did acquire an inferiority complex because my stepfather and foster father criticized almost everything about me. Almost everything we children did was wrong. Accordingly, as an adult some of my being judgmental was a defense mechanism to protect me from allowing others to treat me that way. It wasn't until at age thirty-five, when an elder asked me, "Why do you try to be better than other people," that I realized I have been so focused on 'trying to catch up with my peers' thinking that they knew more than I did and had more experience, that I didn't realize that I actually excelled in many areas.

Third House: Self-Expression Siblings: Saboteur. The saboteur landed in my third house and this makes sense in terms of my being able to express myself. When I was younger, I was so shy I didn't say much of anything, as a result, I was the only one of my siblings the judge ordered to have psychotherapy, labeling me as "socially retarded." I would be so self-conscious I'd choose my few words very carefully. In later years health problems caused me to speak too slow and too soft and often the wrong words came out. People did not have the patience to hear me out. However, not able to tolerate injustices, people were shocked when I did speak up, in defense of others. Then my mouth got me in trouble!

Prior to the years of 1999-2002 when I first became physically disabled, I didn't believe that I could ask for what I needed and receive it. Or that people even cared enough to listen to what I said, so this habit was probably also an unconscious reason for my soft voice. People had to lean in closer to hear me. However, becoming physically disabled forced me to become angry enough to fight for my rights and to become appropriately assertive.

It was also in midlife that I became aware of the consequences of having negative thoughts. For me, it wasn't so much being angry or resentful towards other people, as it was that I was pessimistic about wanting anything out of life. Therefore I stopped getting much of my life. By then I was afraid that other people would steal whatever I had. I'd expect the worst, since life was one crisis after another, after another. I also would leave situations prematurely because of perceived hurts. In these ways, I sabotaged myself.

Change is uncomfortable, especially with the fear of the unknown. But I don't think I really had the luxury of resisting change. I've left abusive relationships and jobs much more than other people would have. Surrounded by people who stayed in abusive situations for 15, 20 years or more, I felt ashamed and isolated. Often embarrassed because I neither lived in one place or worked at the same job for more than four years. I also followed my intuition and took the risks of going to other states to college, and even to other countries. My siblings have always lived in the same city where we grew up. Now I know moving on is healthy.

Fourth House: Home: Prostitute. Having a home has always been dear to me. So it makes sense home would be

CHAPTER 13: SACRED CONTRACTS ARCHETYPES CARDS

the area of my life where I might prostitute myself. Home is where I can feel safe enough to be myself, and to express my passions and creativity. It is where I spend most of my time and therefore will now come out fighting anyone who wants to make my home "their home." I've tried making my home with other people including my first and second husbands and it hasn't worked out well.

In many ways I did not have a home as a child. As a young child, my family moved back-and-forth to my Grandmother's house which I considered home. After age seven, I moved to different houses none of which felt like "home" because of the chaos that resided there. In addition, I was taken from my mother and put in the foster home at age 13. Somewhat my marriages were just as chaotic. I did make my apartments in adulthood "home" in terms of buying the furnishings, decorations, paying the rent, and the time I spent there in solitude doing artwork. The prostitute showed up in my life whenever I am a people pleaser, saying 'Yes' when I should say, 'No.'

It is interesting that my foster parents wouldn't let us girls go to college, and "didn't want us to work" because then we would be "prostituting ourselves." Yet, they were the ones who could have turned me into a possible prostitute in the first place by making me do sexual favors for him. In addition to having me clean up after them and their children. My people pleasing behavior carried over to my bad marriages and miserable jobs. After a while I wanted <u>home</u> more than I wanted the husband or the marriage! My second husband's wife before me, told me she actually had to act like a street prostitute to make him leave her alone.

Determined to have my own roof over my head, the jobs I had were very labor-intensive with low wages, but it allowed me to pay my rent, bills, feed and clothe myself. I'd never had a sit-down job. Up on my feet for long overtime shifts, with heavy lifting. Working gave me some "status" in the community especially since I had an education. I honestly believed that the more I gave, and accepted the poor working conditions without complaining, the more I would be respected and the more I would earn. All of which was not true. Many years of this lifestyle did eventually lead to depression and melancholy while wondering why these work ethic strategies weren't working out.

My devotion to religious organizations was probably a different way that I prostituted myself. I had a full-time job yet I was volunteering long hours, and giving my money away because I was getting some spiritual support. I sacrificed my career, financial stability and my health. After I started losing my health, I began putting my foot down and setting up limits, but by then it was too late.

Fifth House: Creativity Good Fortune: Wounded Healer. Originally chose the Healer and the Wounded Healer because I have experiences with both. I am a registered nurse, but I also inspire others to heal by encouraging them to make necessary lifestyle changes. I role-model these changes and benefits. I'm also an energy healer using reiki and prayers. The reason why I chose the Wounded Healer initially is because doctors diagnosed me with a neuromuscular disease for which there is no treatment. Therefore I would have to cure myself. Since 1988, when I read Bernie Siegel's book, <u>Love Medicine and Miracles</u>, ten years before I became ill, I've believed that personal transformation would heal me emotionally, physically and spiritually. Siegel's research and theories were based on patients with cancer. At that time, and to the present I don't have cancer. But I realized back then, that the way I was living my life would make me a prime candidate for developing cancer. So, to the best of my ability I remind myself daily to live life to the fullest, to give my body a live message.

An energy healer told me, "Physically, I didn't see a serious illness, instead your problem is mostly spiritual energy depletion. This is because you are like a sponge taking in other's negative energy. Further, it would be better for you to move away from large cities for that reason."

Soon after, I unexpectedly moved to live with my aunt in a small suburban city with single family homes.

Sixth House: Occupation Health: Wounded or Nature Child. The Wounded Child archetype of course fits for me as a survivor of childhood abuse and trauma. This is how I learned to people please, be an overachiever and perfectionist while being taken advantage of on jobs. Childhood abuse numbed me so that I functioned like a zombie. No one could really hurt me anymore because I grew a tough shell. However, I wasn't living either. In regards to occupational health, employers often called me on my days off because they could count on me to say yes. I worked long shifts without ever taking a break for a drink of water, snacks, or meals, or even to urinate. So dedicated to the patients. This continued until one day after working eleven days straight, as a nurses' aide, I was too tired to get out of bed that morning. Finally calling in sick, the supervisor gave me two weeks to rest. At the end of those two weeks, I questioned what I was allowing to be done to myself, and I quit that job.

Graduating from nursing school, my first job was as a registered nurse at a nursing home. One of my doctors suggested I apply there. The nursing home administrator hired me off the street with only a week's orientation and training. Besides having to do medication and treatments for an entire wing, later they gave me the responsibilities of supervising not just the nursing staff but for whatever happened in the whole building, along with doing treatments for patients in the rest of the building that only a registered nurse could do. Increasingly, I worked over twelve hours a day because the second shift nurse, if there was ever such a person, made a habit of calling in sick or was late. The administration informed me that I could not leave at the end of my usual eight hours because there had to be a registered nurse in the building at all times. It got to the point where I was too tired to even spend "all" the money I was making. When I had weekends off, I would go to the store but found myself wandering in circles forgetting what I came to buy. Usually I had a good memory. Previously writing a grocery list or making a mental note of what I wanted to buy, was enough to recall later.

Thereafter, I worked night shift as a registered nurse. Working nights was also not good for my health because I couldn't sleep during the day. When the sun was up I was wide awake, even though I closed the drapes and unplugged the phone and went to bed.

I also chose the Nature Child in addition to the Wounded Child because of wild animals' relationship with me, although I've not had animals as pets at home. Growing up, other family members had pets. After my near death experience as an adult, animals appeared and communicated with me as if I understood them. They are comforting and literally lifesavers for me during stressful times. I like animals but I prefer them not caged up. Loving nature came from my childhood memories of being allowed to play in the rain and going to parks. Cities can occasionally feel like concrete prisons to me. My best health, emotionally and physically, was when I lived five months in rural areas of Zimbabwe.

Seventh House: Marriage Relationship: Slave. Every time I had to say the word "slave" while reading aloud the book, Sacred Contract's description of the Slave, I got a sick feeling in my gut. This is partly because I am of African American descent but also in my marriages I was treated as a slave. I could say similar for jobs. Except for with my second marriage, people didn't boss me around. Instead they manipulated me by abusing my kindness and naiveness. They saw that I was hard-working. Some of it probably originated from my Wounded Child background that prepped me to be a voluntary slave. My father figures only gave orders and punishment. We weren't treated as human beings. They used to tell us, "You don't think. We think for you." Initially, I put the Slave as one of my shadow archetypes. As I explained earlier, I mistakenly chose 12 archetypes because I didn't know the instructions were to include the four primary archetypes common to everyone. When it came time to make my Archetype Wheel, I had sixteen archetypes. That meant four archetype cards I had to discard. Since I had to shuffle them anyway and lined them up with the twelve numbered cards, I just let intuition guide me to which of the remaining archetypes did belong to me. I was surprised of course, but in some ways, I should not have been surprised considering the American legacy of slavery and discrimination. After all, women are still treated as slaves at home and especially in stereotypical women's jobs. Paid low wages and expected to put up with terrible working conditions. Then go home and work another shift of housework, caregiving, compassion, romance, and pretend to be sexually aroused in marriages. These are difficult roles to get out of. There is a lot of negative societal pressure to keep us in our places. As a teenager, I decided I would work when I grew up and married, we would split the bills so he paid half and

I paid half, then have my own bank account because I didn't want to be trapped into abusive marriages like my mothers were because they didn't work! Women's lib didn't tell us that bucking traditional gender family roles for women meant that if I worked, I would become the sole provider for each marriage!

Even when Black African Americans are college educated, they are still given the labor intensive jobs. For example, the Black African American nurses that graduated with me told me that they went to interviews, although there were long columns of nursing jobs advertised in the newspaper for each hospital. Yet, they were told that there were only openings for a couple of the listings. These were geriatrics and orthopedics positions which require a lot of lifting and cleaning of incontinent patients. Jobs that no one likes to do. I experienced similar, but I assumed that I was an isolated case since I dressed as a Muslim woman back then.

Eighth House: Other People's Resources: Hermit (Mystic). I originally chose the Hermit because of my lifetime pattern of forced isolation and voluntary solitude for creative and spiritual pursuits. Isolation started with my premature birth, childhood years of abusive possessive step and foster families, a second husband, and later to a physical disability. The Hermit/Mystic was not one of my first choices after reading the description of the Mystic. Forewarned that the life of a Mystic is not glamorous and instead experiences great physical and spiritual suffering, hard work, and mundane activities. Would I be ready to pay the price in blood, sweat, and tears? I have had plenty of experiences with blood, sweat and tears. Sometimes I feel like I'd gladly give both the Hermit and the Wounded Healer archetypes back! Yet, I do take comfort in spirituality and solitude. There is, however, a fine line between a healthy dose of solitude and isolation for me. The shadow side of the Hermitage is a lifetime pattern of isolation.

My first impression when I looked at my archetype wheel chart and saw the Hermit in my Eighth House: Other People's Resources was that it wasn't true for me as a Hermit. I rarely used other people's resources. I just became other people's resources! I hated money and the excuses people made to do wrong whether they have too little or too much money. Probably from my ancient ancestral biological memory, Native American and African heritage, I prefer self-sufficiency in rural surroundings, although I was born in and grew up in cities and so did my parents. I sewed my husband's and my own clothes, cooked from scratch and made my own home furnishings. My siblings competed with each other trying to keep up with the Joneses. I was more practical with my dress, home and lifestyle. Borrowing was rare for me. If I could not provide my own means, I simply did without. Did without for most of my adult life. Too independent for my own good. I'm just now learning how to receive from others. Trying it out.

Family inheritance? Well, my parents didn't leave us much to inherit. What little there was from my father, my siblings argued and fought over. I wasn't even going to go to my father's funeral, but my grandmother asked me to come as a "mediator." I thought she meant assisting the family in grieving — not to be a referee! I was shocked. A few personal items given to me, and a couple items that I chose like my father's eyeglasses and a red sweater were enough for me.

As far as financial and legal matters though, I wasn't a very ambitious person. I was ambitious in terms of obtaining other goals and an education, but I wasn't a financial planner. I didn't set out planning to make so many dollars in so many years. I didn't even concentrate on the fact that an education such as nursing would pay me more money than working as a nurses' aide, I only knew that I wanted to be a nurse. And later, when I went back to college, I didn't know that I would be risking no income at all. I wasn't thinking about the consequences of school loans and being away traveling. Perhaps I didn't know, mostly because money and what I needed has always been divinely provided to me, and also because I have worked so hard previously at everything for most of my life. When I went back for my master's degree, I wasn't thinking about salaries, as much as, I knew with my failing health that I needed a sit-down job for once in my life.

Don't get me wrong, other than long-term planning such as a retirement plan, I was very financially responsible. Major credit cards were denied because I paid off my monthly balances before the interest accrued. Why should I pay interest if I didn't have to? I paid my rent and utility bills on time. I had a savings account. I split my paychecks to pay bills, with the remainder some went to savings, and some to spend. My financial future was destroyed because I let unscrupulous people take my money and possessions. As a result, I was always starting over and not getting ahead. I let other's need for money, sex, and power – overpower me. I did hire a lawyer for my first divorce, which was a good strategy, because later his lawyer advised my husband to sue me for spousal support!

Another reason for less socialization was the aftereffects of my near death experience. Most near death experiencers become less materialistic and less worried about status and ambition. It also made it hard to relate to people who mostly talk about their purchases or were planning to buy. Or drama as they engaged in power struggles.

Ninth House: Spirituality: Addict. This is kind of a tough combination to understand. Yet, in another way it makes sense. Although I have some characteristics of the traditional addict personality such as having been a workaholic, I was more of an addict with my spiritual practices after my near death experience. The near death experience started me on a quest for finding how to get back to that incredible peaceful feeling I had on the other side, and for my purpose in life. Perhaps being a spiritual addict is how I survived childhood. Of course, as a child I had not learned about spirituality, I just knew how to accept comfort from the Other Side. Also my mother gave me individual attention, that I cherished, as she supported and believed in the psychic messages that I relayed to her.

I've had both clinical depression and spiritual depression, since I had many losses in my life. It's difficult to say which type triggered which depression. Clinical depression probably came first in my adolescence. Then the near death experience gave me hope and a purpose for living. The book, <u>Heading Towards Omega</u> states near-death experiencers come back to life with an urgency to heal childhood. My second marriage forced me to relive the instant replay of trauma memories from childhood. Angry at God, I temporarily lost my faith. However, when I regained my faith, I got caught up in making emotional and spiritual healing a priority. This priority led to overzealous spiritual practices which made me neglect the rest of life, which then caused poverty and poor health. The resultant material losses led to clinical depression. I used to meditate, fast, and eat too healthy with observing Ausar Auset Society Church spiritual group practices. Without spiritual guidance from a guru or mentor, I don't know whether my physical disabilities came from poor self-care or were a result of the years I did metaphysical practices. Now I am more balanced and peaceful, determined not to go to any extremes with anything.

Tenth House: Highest Potential: Victim. Whoa! How did the Victim end up in my Tenth House: Highest Potential? I suppose it fits. It could even be comforting to know that there is some explanation for the victim role being so strong in this lifetime and several other past lives. In this lifetime it started with being a Wounded Child and taken on a passive role from there. Initially I did not know any other way to be. Gradually survival instincts taught me. And sometimes other people role-modeled how not to be a Victim for me. Except that, I couldn't understand why other people, especially other women criticized me for not staying in bad situations. Whether on jobs or at places of worship or in relationships I don't know why we try to hold each other down. After my second husband and going to therapy, I refused to go backwards to how I was before for anybody! This recovery started in 1988 and I've been making major changes ever since. Change is not easy, especially with fear of the unknown and possible loss of people and belongings. But going backwards, giving up who I am for other people, is even more frightening. It is a constant struggle, however, it got easier with time.

Coming back from Zimbabwe was when the major tests started. In Zimbabwe, I felt free and whole with amazing unconditional love for the first time in my adult life. I vowed I would bring this love back with me.

Instead, I lost my health and status in the community. My friends at the Ausar Auset Society Church were expecting me to be the same as I was two years prior being able to provide physical labor. They couldn't see or understand my pain and fatigue both physically and emotionally. They were confused, and so was I, about how much I changed. Unable to obtain employment I became homeless.

I sought help from doctors, but after a while I refused to be in the Victim role, to continue to spend my precious time waiting long hours for transportation, worried and angry because of what doctors had or had not done. Humiliated frequently because of the lack of care that uninsured and Medicaid and Medicare patients receive. I had a doctor fuss at me in 1999, when I complained of painful swollen knees and cramps in my left lower back. She said, I've seen knees more swollen than yours. You're one of those women who doctor shop."

A couple of months later I was in the hospital for 10 days, on intravenous antibiotics, unable to keep food down, a fever with a urinary tract infection and brown colored urine. On the day that they discharged me from the hospital, one of the doctors told me that if the other doctors had done the surgery that they were considering then, I probably wouldn't have made it off the operating table!

Several more years of doctors ignoring me, not knowing what to do with me, eventually taught me that I better to be my own healer.

It was only years later, that I was able to become aware of the many ways in all areas of my life where I could be sucked into complaining as a victim. A therapist asked me, "Why did you stay waiting for your friend to come? You could have left at any time. There is no sense in waiting for anyone any longer than 15 minutes."

Unfortunately, we are in the habit of waiting and waiting for others to do something or another, often knowing full well it's probably not ever going to happen. Therefore waiting becomes a convenient excuse. With time and experience, I learned I could refuse to be the victim, and instead reach out towards recognizing my own potential.

Eleventh House: Relationship to The World: Rescuer. I originally chose the Rescuer as one of my shadow archetypes. I was the rescuer with my husbands. They were not the knight in shiny armor that came to whisk me away to be married happily after. However, when I read the meaning of the Eleventh house I felt better identifying with the positive aspects of the rescuer. The Rescuer is able to assist when needed in a crisis or a difficult situation but when the crisis is over is able to withdrawal further help. Initially provide the support, strength and wisdom to help the person gain their own inner strength to carry-on. For years, I definitely have been giving people the tools, and teaching them to fish or provide or solve problems for themselves, and hopefully they will reach out and do the same for someone else. This way the world becomes a better place as everyone cares and shares what they have and know. Some people even have gotten upset because I won't do what they can do themselves, for them. I encourage them do it so that they experience letting go of their fears and gaining self-confidence. Later they thank me. Rescuers are often women. Knights of course are men. Either way, have to be careful to not keep a person dependent on you, especially with an underlying motive of fulfilling your own needs, or for pursuing a romantic relationship. I do tend to want to establish ongoing friendships and can be sad when it's over.

Twelfth House: The Unconscious: Artist. The unconscious is our intuition, dreams and knowing. Art was my connection to my unconscious. My mother introduced me to all different kinds of arts and crafts when I was a young child. So I've always been an artist. Drawing, crafts, needlework, knitting, crocheting, embroidery, sewing, designing clothes and furnishings, creative writing and watercolor painting. I'm also a cook and a baker. My overall well-being is very much improved when I am being creative.

Creativity and artwork are a form of meditation for me. I enjoyed the inspiration for projects that used to wake me up at 3 o'clock in the morning. I would return to sleep, waking up later at 5 o'clock to go into my sewing room and work until what I dreamed manifested in my hands. Artwork was also a way to find meaning and sanity during the stress of life traumas. An escape.

I rarely get artistic ideas in the middle of the night these days. My artistic abilities were still there, but I think intellectual and societal pressure "to get it right" in order to make it "marketable" blocked my creative flow. While living at my aunt's house, I bought books and followed the instructions for entering contests and submitting my watercolor paintings to art galleries, paying entry and shipping fees to unknown places across the country to the West Coast and even up to Canada. When my paintings didn't sell, I had to pay for shipping them back to me.

The best paintings I've done were those that were divinely guided. As if an unseen presence was moving my paint brush across the watercolor paper. The same happened in the past when writing letters to friends and family. It was as if my pen was moving by itself. I've longed for the flow to return. Part of the problem is, I think I have become more grounded in this Earth plane than I used to be. Most of my inspiration now comes from images in my meditations more often than nighttime dreams. One of my goals was to paint the endless fields of brilliant red flowers, that I see whenever I close my eyes giving me so much comfort, peace, and joy. These flower images are a reminder of what I saw during my near death experience. I especially see and feel this peace and love as I drift off to sleep after praying for guidance. I wanted to share this comfort, peace and joy with others when they look at my paintings.

However, learning how to paint the illusion of distance in a landscape was very challenging. I bought and read books to aid my learning how to do this faster. Perhaps relying on instructions from books, instead of intuition also contributes to artist block. Previously, I did paint a picture of the Inspiration Café, where somehow the geometric perspective of the large dining room was just right. On a positive note, books now help me work in quicker, more efficient ways for example using various large paintbrushes for special effects, that were less painful for my hands and my back and therefore allowed me to continue to paint. I taught myself how to sketch and paint reclined in my bed or in my wheelchair, similar to how I was to later learn, the famous painter Frida Kahlo did.

It occurred to me, while reading the meaning of the Twelfth House, as the unconscious is also fears, that some of my occasional artist blocks might also be due to fear of what doors may open as my artwork begins to flow. Could I feel safe enough to surrender? And be free for the rest of my life?

I did continue to paint and gain confidence. People who view my watercolor paintings say they can "feel them, can feel the spiritual energy."

Chapter 14: More Guidance with Sacred Contracts Cards

You can use your personal Sacred Contract archetypal wheel and cards to seek guidance and insight into your thinking and behavior in a situation that you are concerned about.

Working Chart: Moving On

Open to guidance on moving forward with my life, I inquired about moving from Aunt Gussie's home after she died, to an assisted living group home in another suburb. My personal reflections on my thoughts and life are based on both the descriptions and purpose of each House as well as the Archetype in that House. When I journal my spiritual guidance readings, I write or type the meaning of each House and Archetype nearly word-by-word so that it is accessible to me all in one place, when I review it later. I, of course, can't do that here in my published book due to limited space and copyrights. Therefore, please refer to the book, *Sacred Contracts,* for a fuller understanding and to make your own Archetype Wheel Chart of Origin, and later Working Charts, if you are interested.

I shuffled the twelve archetype cards and randomly matched these to the following houses:

First House: Ego Personality: Saboteur. The Saboteur has presented disruptions recently, definitely shaking up my life like an earthquake! Inside me, I've probably wanted these situations to be disrupted due to uncertainty, boredom, and restlessness, while knowing intuitively that it is time for me to move on. For sure, I have anxieties about the First House representation of all the basic survival needs in life — food, a home, and belonging to a community. Haven't been able to find a local affordable apartment in a reasonable amount of time, which means settling for an assisted living residence back in the city, away from family and friends. I worry about having enough money and food to eat. This high anxiety tempts me to take the easy way out and accept my cousin's offer to continue living alone in my aunt's home. Reading about the Saboteur as an ally to warn us to save us from making the same mistakes over and over again, helped me to reconsider. I think if I stayed here, I may be making the mistake of putting myself in the position of hexagram 56: The Wanderer, if told I have to leave at a short notice again. And I would probably honestly hate being in another roommate situation. Would I be sabotaging my own spiritual growth being a Hermit who prefers having my own apartment? People are concerned about me not getting out and doing things, yet they are worried about my safety when I do venture out on my own. Or fuss at me for asking them to do tasks "my way." Yes, I've been afraid of more drastic changes, but I have to be able to dream of better.

Second House: Life Values: Artist. I definitely struggle with the questions, "Now that I'm here, what's mine? And what do I want out of life?" I'm currently challenged with where does my power lie, when I have to rely on others for my physical care. With my own home, I would have more say. Being unemployed, using a wheelchair has really decreased my status in society. Overtime, I put aside my previous personal values, rather than be disappointed and argue with people, and I lost my desire to creatively problem solve due to feeling that this is not really my home or my life.

Art is what I usually do in one form or another. When not doing art, I feel empty, somewhat worthless, without an identity. Art is tangible and people challenged me to have more of the Second House external values of money, status, and power in society. Last year, I struggled with my self-worth while facing obstacles trying to promote my watercolor paintings as family pressured me to make use of my college degrees and creativity. I did my best as I invested in a computer, printer, scanner, software, and books to be able to work from home from my bed even as I taught myself how to use a voice recognition program that typed as I talked. Never lazy, I kept busy.

I've been visualizing and hoping the assisted living residences will allow me to continue to be as independent as possible, help provide for my basic needs, yet give me the freedom to do art. The brochure states the assisted living residence has shelves and cabinets that lower to wheelchair height with the touch of a button, and roll in shower, writing classes, workshops on starting own business, or outside employment, access to parks and transportation.

Third House: Self-Expression Siblings: Hermit. My having gotten used to being immersed in solitary activities and time alone, like a Hermit has kept me away from my siblings. However, I do blossomed in community living situations, enjoying the teamwork, as well as when I've ventured away from home and people close to me. Except for living here with Aunt Gussie, I didn't like having roommates because I need my own space to retreat, reflect and recharge. This frees me up to really be myself, enough to give of my talents to the community. It is important to me to maintain contact and closeness with my siblings and friends. My three helpers, who were Aunt Gussie's friends for years have become my friends and I don't know how I would have coped emotionally without their support and guidance. The challenge will be to keep a balance between my need to express myself as an individual, with some controls over my environment, yet not feel that I have to control others in order to have this, or to allow others to control me.

Fourth House: Home: Judge. Well, since my concern is about wanting to have a home, but will likely have to decide on living in an assisted living residence with others, I'm curious what role my Judge archetype has to do with Home. It's true many of my memories and emotions from my past experiences with home environments are a mixture of some joys and sadness. Childhood homes went from fun to frequent relocating, to chaos and abuse. Happily living in Zimbabwe followed by years of moving from place to place, I am now forced to leave yet another happy living situation with my family. Of course, I am afraid of more losses and instability. Writing in my journal, answering the questions of this working chart helps to relieve some of my depression and gives me more energy and optimism.

With the Judge archetype I am more critical and judgmental of myself than others. This probably came from the harsh criticism I received as a child. I've gotten better over the past few months, too exhausted and frustrated to be too hard on myself or others. Although this is some relief from this realization, there is some lingering guilt and sense of failure. In a sense, this could be a form of surrender in a positive way, as I let go of old habits.

Fifth House: Creativity Good Fortune: Addict. I look forward to moving out on my own, and hopefully at the assisted living place as an opportunity to return to spontaneity and abundance. A place to use my creativity, intelligence and imagination. The challenge would be to not base my self-worth on having or not having a professional career. Sometimes I lean towards acceptance that the accomplishments I've done so far in my life are enough, I've worked very hard. However, I honestly yearn to be able to do some of the things I used to do for satisfaction, self-esteem and validation.

I guess where the Addict fits in my personality, is that my creativity was done to excess in the past. One spiritual advisor told me that my overproduction of knitted and sewing items was like my father's excessive procreation. I didn't understand what she meant at the time. It's true that artwork was my escape and release to forget about my problems I had with my marriage, exploitive jobs, and inability to have children. I could ignore these situations and continue to put up with situations, that I should have left or confronted.

Sixth House: Occupation Health: Slave. Past employment contributed immensely to my current health problems because I did not know how to balance work and health. The Slave archetype, which I explained in greater detail in my Chart of Origin has a strong influence on my attitude towards employment as an occupation. As an African American Black women, I've been treated as "a slave" on the job, as well as at home and in the church. The American worker is expected to, more than ever, to do the job of several people, by working long hours plus take work home with them for less pay and benefits. In addition to sacrificing time away from family and friends and community, this makes me a Hermit when I'm at home. A part of me dreads the idea of having to constantly push my body, mind, and spirit over the edge, ever again. Actually, it's a terrifying thought! Yet I miss the income, status, and possibilities of more choices. Hopefully, the assisted living residence fulfills its promises of helping us to obtain gainful employment.

Seventh House: Marriage Relationship: Prostitute. My biggest challenge to moving on is the fear of the loss of close friends, family and partnerships with doctors. Not since I left Philadelphia as a child, and much later while in Zimbabwe, have I had such close friends and contact with family. So precious to me that this fear is enough to paralyze me. The lesson of the Prostitute archetype is to ask ourselves, "How much are we willing to sell, of our core being, to have financial security or to survive?"

Tearful as I write this, because when Aunt Gussie's health started declining, she didn't tell us she was suffering. This put pressure on me as I observed her, to be strong and not give in. I knew from my own experiences and inner truth, that I could no longer live the life of the superwoman trying to please everyone, bearing the blame for everything. I had to do my own soul searching and along the way be myself, to allow Aunt Gussie to have the courage to be herself. We learned a lot from each other that way — in a very short amount of time.

After Aunt Gussie's death, there was a lot of confusion and conflicts among family members. This is usual behavior as people process their grief differently. It was hard to think straight, to do what was right. For a couple of days, I was paralyzed by the shock of the chaos, causing me to have flashbacks to the chaos and abuse I experienced in childhood. When I realized this was happening to me, I was able to rally with others, putting our fears and personal interests aside for the good of the whole, then came peace and better solutions.

Otherwise, my survival was threatened by a desperate need for a place to live. Initially, I had to decide what I was willing to sacrifice of my belongings and finances. Later, my personal integrity was at risk. Tired from all the trauma, I wanted to do what seemed the easy way out. But it was time to "take up my bed and walk" away. Sometimes, I imaged literally having to walk — giving up my wheelchair to have my freedom.

Earlier when I saw that the Prostitute in the seventh house of my Working chart, I procrastinated reflecting and journaling because I thought the Prostitute meant bad news. However, now I'm encouraged because it all makes better sense to me now.

Eighth House: Other Peoples Resources: Amateur. One of the reasons I was almost forced to move suddenly, was some of my cousins arguing over Aunt Gussie's belongings and inheriting the proceeds from selling the house. I wasn't interested in other people's possessions or inheritance even when my father died a decade earlier. Instead, before living in Chicago, I was used to having my own money and control over my finances. However, I am an amateur when it comes to legal and business affairs, and will have to ask questions and do research especially before signing a contract with the assisted living residence. It boasts about having a business center that will train and employ people with disabilities to do medical billing. Since I'm a registered nurse, this would be easier for me.

Ninth House: Spirituality: Wounded Healer. Over this past year, I've done better with integrating spirituality with material interests. Having suffered with several recent losses, I have reasons to be clinically depressed. It could also be more of a spiritual crises, as I hunger to know what to do with my life now, and to connect to my purpose and intuition again. Rereading about the Wounded Healer reminds me that the neurologist diagnosed me with a rare neuromuscular disease for which there is no conventional cure. Frustrating, as I spent years seeking help from doctors, attempting to to have some minimum illusion of control. Symbolic of the frightening realization that I don't have control over my life now either.

As a wounded healer, I've been steadily working on healing emotionally too with a psychotherapist, and making the life changes accordingly by following the spiritual guidance interpretations from the I Ching and other oracles to the best of my understanding. Hopefully, I am coming to the end of the initiation and dark night of the soul required to become a less wounded healer.

Tenth House: Highest Potential: Rescuer. Would I be willing to make the necessary sacrifice, to leave a large part of my life behind to take the opportunity to pursue inner transformation? Yes, I could share my belongings with someone less fortunate than I, who may be coming out of a nursing home, or who I could assist with caregiving. Caretaking is what I've done most of my adult life. Some people took advantage of my kindness.

This is because I did not know at that time that I was a shadow Rescuer (commonly known as codependent). I gave to receive recognition and "love" that was rarely reciprocated. I felt resentful and hurt after awhile. Later, I realized after the divorce, that during the marriage I wasn't allowing my husband to do much giving. I often didn't ask for help, preferring to do without if I couldn't do it myself. Therefore, I couldn't put all the blame on him or anyone else. With time, I started to obtain a balance between being a shadow Rescuer and healthy Rescuer who is able to help individuals to survive through a crisis, then gradually withdraw to allow them to stand on their own feet. As also a Wounded Healer, I need to follow the advice of waiting to be asked to help. Conversely, I have been in the position of being "rescued." After a while my roommate resented me being there because I overstayed my welcome, and in my depression didn't know what to do to help myself because I'd previously always been employed. Moving to an assisted living residence will certainly test my faith.

Eleventh House: Relationship to The World: Victim. I have mixed feelings about my sense of power and the future of humanity. I used to be pretty optimistic in spite of most challenges, only allowing myself to cry or feel down for a day or two. However, with recent losses and uncertainty it is difficult to be patient and enthusiastic. Instead, I fear the assisted living situation could put me in the position of the Victim. If I were my usual optimistic self, I would remember and know that I've been blessed in previous, tougher situations that most other people would say wouldn't be possible. When man says, "No." God provides. Being at the assisted living residence could give me a new start. I can learn to set better boundaries with people.

Twelfth House: The Unconscious: Wounded Nature Child. Over the years, I'm gradually learning to be aware of and to trust my intuition. At the age of seven, I began turning off my natural intuition due to abuse. There after followed an abusive marriage as I didn't know how to use my intuition to protect me. I did get away eventually, but it took me awhile, however not as long to get away as other women I knew. This history of childhood abuse and losses gave me a fear of abandonment yet again. Although family members have been supportive and tried to right the situation, it has felt like a dark night of my soul, as I'm exhausted by now. Sometimes I feel that others have not gone through what I've gone through, would not understand. I wondered if I was putting on unconscious blinders that may have me ignoring warnings from my intuition, in regards to the reality of living here at my aunt's house or moving to the assisted living residence. Too exhausted to think clearly, no much else to do but surrender spiritually my fears from my childhood, and trust that all will be well, the ultimate task of the twelfth house.

The beautiful colorful birds like the cardinals, along with squirrels, and I will miss Aunt Gussie putting leftover food outside on the air conditioner by the kitchen window, for them and other little creatures who amazing ate together in peace. The squirrels got so used to her routine that they would come one by one and tap on the backdoor if she was late. I used to tease her, that she was turning the squirrels into junk food junkies because they loved french fries. Sometimes, I bought bird seeds and peanuts in the shell for them. The assisted living group home is located near an arboretum. An arboretum is a large garden devoted to growing and studying varieties of trees and shrubs. And of course, birds, squirrels and other creatures would thrive there too, satisfying my need and love of nature.

Change already rearranged my familiar world, as a result of the choices I made at the crossroads over the past year, or more, to pursue my life. I do look to the future as I desperately want my own place so that I can use my talents, such as leaving a legacy of inspirational autobiographies and artwork, heal and be of service to others.

The Sacred Contract cards were new to me during this time. In later years, I could simply look at the archetypes' placement on the wheel chart and immediately understand the meaning as applied to a specific situation, seeing myself and my behavior, without journaling. So obvious, I'd chuckle. Otherwise, the Sacred Contract cards are not as useful for making decisions, as much as helping me examine my thinking opening me to better clarity and hope.

Her son did eventually allow me to stay at Aunt Gussie's house after she passed on, until I found another place to stay.

Chapter 15: Where Else to Go?

A new Supportive Living apartment building was under construction and available sooner than the other assisted living residence that had a long waiting list. I sought guidance insight into situation of moving to Supportive Living apartments: I Ching hexagram 20 Contemplation (lines 1, 4, and 6) into hexagram 17 Following. Metu Neter cards: Maat tem tchaas/ Amen hetep.

I Ching hexagram 20 Contemplation is, of course, about contemplating a situation before taking action, going beyond a narrow perspective similar to "looking through a keyhole." Doing deep meditation for better insights. Also warns that when observing others know that they are also observing you. Line 1: Go ahead and do it although you may not understand the whole situation, you will benefit. Line 4: treat others with respect. Remember to consult the oracles regularly and follow this guidance with respect. Line 6: Have to view this situation from a much higher spiritual perspective of seeing the interconnected whole of society and the universe. Beyond blame and hurt. Have to consider the effects we each have on each other. Hexagram 17 Following: is when someone more experienced helps someone less experienced. Usually this is an elder. Learning to share and serve others. It also means following the natural cycles and laws of the universe. Understand and follow your destiny reading incarnation objective. Surround oneself with good people and stay away from bad influences.

Metu Neter cards: Maat tem tchaas/ Amen hetep. Remember that abundance comes from heaven. By establishing inner peace in the situation, it will change for the better.

There were many challenges, even before I moved into Supportive Living apartments. I will briefly summarize it here, because as I was reviewing my daily journals from 2004-2005, I realized that even one month of the unbelievable events that happened there will not fit in this book. When I applied in November 2004, it was under construction. Their representatives explained that supportive living facilities are similar to assisted living places for seniors, except it was for younger people ages 22 to 64 years-old. They got me excited by telling me about having my own one-bedroom apartment along with amenities of a movie theater, computer and fitness rooms. I was to choose my apartment from three different floor plans.

In February, they called to tell that me I had to share it with a roommate. March brought more disappointment as they told me the building wouldn't be ready for another three weeks. April rolled on by too. Finally, I moved in May to a tiny two-bedroom apartment. To discover that my bedroom, as another resident described it, was the "size of a 7′ x 11′ jail cell." Mind you, this is supposed to be a place for young adults with physical disabilities. My hospital bed barely fit. Transferring from my wheelchair to the bed and out was a struggle. I had to give away a lot of my belongings and put the rest in storage downstairs. What were they thinking when they chose and designed this place? There were pillars inside the apartments that further chopped the living space even smaller!

Food was served restaurant style initially when we first arrived. Fabulous menu with at least three entree selections at each meal. By June, they were serving us mostly pastas where you had to search for the sauce and the meat. As you can imagine, this did not work for me because I couldn't eat gluten foods. I ate the salads and fruit plates when available. Many days, I went hungry.

Although a nurse came out to our homes prior to us moving to Supportive Living and assessed our individual needs, making sure that our total score did not add up to requiring too much care or too little care, soon after we got there, their nurse told us that we had to be independent, to able to take care of ourselves. I was already taking care of myself, living alone, but my doctor wanted me to get some rest and not have to worry about unreliable home care aides. Ha, ha, ha. I guess we both were dreaming.

Money equals independence. With Supportive Living taking our whole Social Security checks, even if some resident's checks were over $1400 a month, and then only giving us $90 to live off of, we were supposed to be excited because if we were in a nursing home, we would only get $35! Maybe glad, except soon after we saw Supportive Living was not providing services — resentment and panic set in. Paying for telephone service and a shared cable bill for internet and television took up most of the $90. Couldn't go anywhere without bus fare, and they had minimal activities and outings for us. Although we had a little "kitchen" in each apartment, basically a one burner cooktop and a small refrigerator, management later asked us to give Supportive Living our food stamps! We couldn't even buy snacks?

It was difficult not to complain, blame and not feel hurt, especially since living there was better than being homeless. I tried to make the best of the situation. There were of course some good benefits to living there. Instead of living alone and feeling lonely, we make friends and visited each other in the dining room or in each other's rooms. I put together an art group for other residents and taught them art techniques adapted to each person's disability. For example, there were a couple of people who were blind, that I helped to do watercolor paintings.

James found me at the Supportive Living apartments. I was surprised to see him. He gave me more of his large beautiful paintings that I had encouraged him to do, when we were both living in homeless transitional housing. James had moved further north to his own apartment. The reason why my family hadn't seen him for a while is, because he was having health problems.

When I couldn't bare the conditions at Supportive Living anymore, is after a night in July, when I had trouble breathing. In the morning I went in my wheelchair to the emergency room several blocks away. I prayed all the way there. We were all afraid to go to the hospital because a lot of our apartment mates did not come back. They were transferred to nursing homes instead.

Sitting up, my breathing was easier, therefore the ER doctors didn't believe my distress during the night. Subsequently they did not admit me or even keep me long enough for observation. They didn't know what to do with me. Previously when I lived with my aunt, I had good doctors out in the suburbs who knew me. Prayed all the way back to Supportive Living. The nearer I wheeled down the sidewalks to the Supportive Living place, the harder I prayed to have my own apartment since I had to take care of myself anyway. No nurses checked on me.

Being at Supportive Living had me sicker because I couldn't take care of myself, the way I knew was best for my health.

My prayers were answered the very next day! One and a half years prior, I applied for senior housing. The manager had called a month ago and told me that I was number eleven on the list, and asked was I still interested? I wasn't enthusiastic as I said, "Yes" because I had applied for other housing too, five years earlier and I hadn't heard from any of them.

Now when this manager asked, "There is an apartment available. Do you want it?

Of course, I said, "Yes!"

A bit fearful though, because again I was saying "Yes" to an apartment that I hadn't seen.

Chapter 16: Home?

Oracle readings for moving to the senior apartment building:

Hexagram 7 The Army (lines 1 and 5) into hexagram 60 Limitations.

Hexagram 7 The Army: Line 1: Must begin with everything in proper order. If not organized, then failure. Line 5: Must have an experienced leader. Punishment is justified but not excessively.

Hexagram 60 Limitations. Usually means the need for self-limitations and self-discipline.

Metu Neter cards: Ausar tem Maat/ Auset tu maat

After another night of being awake, my alarm clock rang at 5:50 AM, because if we did not call the paratransit companies close to 6:00 A.M then all the rides would already be taken. I was grateful and amazed that the paratransit ride reservationist answered the phone on my third attempt, so I could make arrangements for my ride to the apartment interview. After I hung up the phone and made myself comfortable in my bed, I realized I've been saying, "If I were at home, I would make pizza with rice crust and mozzarella soy cheese. If I were at home, I would eat what I wanted to eat, whenever I wanted to eat. If I were at home, I would have items I need within easy reach. If I were at home, I would rest when I need to rest, without having to try to explain to the staff why in order to get my needs met."

If I am saying, "If I were at home. If I were at home, if I were at home, then that means I'm not at home. So where is home? Is there a home for me?"

Some of the anxiety and panic I felt is fear that when I move out, that it won't be home, same as being here in Supportive Living is not home for me. There's so much wrong here, that it is difficult to imagine anywhere else being better. Who will help me unpack? If I don't get unpacked immediately, how long before the real apartment feels like home? Will I have a responsible, compassionate, intuitive helper? Will she understand and help me even when I look "well?"

A Jehovah's Witness friend of my grandmother called me. She gave me inspiration by telling me, "When you pray, you need to be specific. What did you pray for before you moved to assisted-living?

"Well, I did ask for plenty of sunshine coming through the windows. That I got. The people are good here except for the management."

"I'll pray for you too, that you have a peaceful home and peace in your heart, in the meantime. You shouldn't have to live in a place that you hate. Home should be where you can close the door and be safe and peaceful. I'm shocked that you have a roommate, and she's a stranger to you. It will be good that you have someplace to look forward to moving to."

She had called to ask me for my grandmother's phone number, but I'm glad she talked to me and was very understanding of my situation. She recently moved to a lovely senior citizen apartment in a far southwest suburb to be near her children.

But what are the specifics to ask Great Mama for my new apartment? Confused now because Supportive Living "promised" many other things I asked for prior to moving there. So now I decided to pray for: a wheelchair accessible apartment with large enough doorways, bathroom, toilet and shower. Plenty of closets and storage space with a linen closet, bedroom closets, storage closet, and foyer closet. Space for bookshelves, cabinets, file cabinet and that the kitchen cabinets are large enough. Space for medical equipment and medicine. That there is proper space around my BiPAP machine for airflow, distilled water with medications close by. A real kitchen with a large refrigerator and freezer, double sink, and plenty of counter space. An art room with plenty of space for creativity, to set up my watercolor painting easel and sewing machine. Plenty of insulated large breathable windows that let in sunshine and gives me a view of green trees and gardens.

Tomorrow arrived. The apartment manager opened the main door for me and told me to wait in the TV room, while the assistant manager finished her lunch. There was an older woman, seventy-eight years old which she proudly told me, in the TV room. She quizzed me with many personal questions. Usually I'm offended by people asking me personal questions, but I curiously answered her.

"Are you married?"

"No. I was."

"Why didn't you stay married? He could've taken care of you. Do you have anyone to come in and clean for you? How old are you? You don't look any older than twenty-seven. Why don't you dye your hair black? Your hair is more salt than pepper on the top."

The benefits of tolerating her questioning is that she told me some things about the apartment building.

"I live on 11th floor. I have a beautiful apartment. But it is cold in the winter with snow on the roof, and hot in the summer with the sun beaming on the roof. There's an area out in the back with benches. There are a lot of Russians here.

They don't speak English and they stay to themselves. Who told you about here?"

"A young woman told me. Actually she begged me to put in an application, although they use a lottery system meaning they may or may not pull my number.

"Is she Black?"

"No, I met her in a group we belong to."

I was glad when the assistant apartment manager called me into the manager's office. She and the manager also thought I was too young, in my twenties.

"No, I'm closer to fifty years old."

"We wondered since this is a senior building, although we do accept some mature adults with disabilities."

The interview mostly consisted of signing a lot of papers.

"HUD will let us know in two to three weeks. So since you have to give the Supportive Living place thirty days' notice, September 1st would probably be your move-in date."

I told myself, 'all is as it should be', even though I am a little impatient that it took two weeks already for me to receive the certified letter, then another week because the assistant manager was on vacation. It could've been that, in that amount of time I would have had approval, and had given my 30 day notice by now. But heaven knows best; like why did I have to detour to the assisted living place first, and what was my purpose there?

She took me up on the elevator to the third floor to see a vacant apartment, which she explained would not be my apartment because mine would be a wheelchair accessible apartment. Basically all of the apartments there were the same size and layout. She opened the white folding closet door on the left. I was pleased at the length and tall height of the closet. Behind me, she showed me another closet that was for hanging coats. There was another door next to it and I was amazed that it was a continuation of the same long closet! The kitchen is a real kitchen! There are cabinets on two walls with upper and lower cabinets plus more on the breakfast island. Plenty countertops. A real refrigerator with a large freezer and large electric stove! The sink is not double, but it is large enough for a dishpan with space on the side to rinse dishes. In the large bedroom there is also a large long closet. I moved into the senior apartment building on August 31, 2005 and have been living here ever since.

My understanding of the reading was that the senior apartment building would provide my own independent space to heal (Auset). My health initially imposed the hexagram 60 self-limitations. Hexagram 7 (line 1) is similar to a disciplined army structure where everything needs to be in proper order.

Line 5 means punishment needs to be given out to someone who has transgressed against you. The Supportive Living director was inexperienced, as it was the first assisted living apartments designed for young adults with disabilities. His heart was right, but he used deception with us. Therefore he needed to be punished for his transgressions. I didn't do any punishing though.

Decisions Decisions

Getting Answers
to Life's Challenges

VOLUME 3

Sidelined

Haneefa Mateen

Contents

Introduction	231
PART ONE: HEALTH	232
Chapter 1: Geb Health	233
Chapter 2: Medical I Ching	238
Chapter 3: Would You Want to Live to be 100?	241
Chapter 4: What are Medical Specialists for?	244
Chapter 5: Prognosis	249
Chapter 6: Another Before My Time	262
PART TWO: LIFE USING A WHEELCHAIR	266
Chapter 7: Getting a Wheelchair	267
Chapter 8: Not for the Faint of Heart	272
Chapter 9: Trains	275
Chapter 10: Paratransit Services	278
Chapter 11: By Air	281
Chapter 12: Invisible	283

Chapter 13: Wheelchair Coming On!	286
Chapter 14: University	288
Chapter 15: University: Tarot Card Guidance	295
Chapter 16: University: Triquetra Spread	298
Chapter 17: University: Personal Reflections on the Meaning	301
Chapter 18: University: The Squeaky Wheel	308
Chapter 19: What if There is a Fire?	313
Chapter 20: Elevators Out	317
PART THREE: HEALING	325
Chapter 21: Other Aspects of Auset	326
Chapter 22: Be Careful What You Ask For	331
Chapter 23: Mother Mary in Africa	335
Chapter 24: Wisdom Gained	338

Introduction

More challenges tested what I vowed to bring back from my near death experience and Zimbabwe. However, I wasn't expecting this would mean acquiring a disability and using a wheelchair.

PART ONE: HEALTH

Chapter 1: Geb Health

Remember the first career reading that I did back in 1993? Metu Neter cards: Geb tem tchaas/Amen hetep. I Ching hexagram 40 Deliverance (lines 2, 3, 5, and 6) into hexagram 33 Retreat? Well, Geb represents our health or the health of a situation. In my case, Geb tem definitely was about to mean declining health, and a retreat from my career.

There was something about severe crushing, sharp ice pick stabbing, breathtaking chest pains and fatigue for the years 1995 through 1996, without doctors knowing what was wrong, would make anyone think they were going to die. It made me change my priorities in life. That's how I decided to go off to college and then to Africa. It would be a once in a lifetime deal. Just like my 87-year-old grandmother wanting to see the Western United States before she died. That was in 1992, and she was still living nearly two decades later. Therefore I do not regret my decision to go.

Prior to me going to Zimbabwe, I began to get up early in the morning and do grounding exercises with Tai Chi, and aligning my hara line from the book, *Light Emerging* and making my intention of being fully present in the Earth plane throughout the day. After all, how could I heal if I wasn't giving my body a live message?

Starting my morning aligning my hara line did help. This visualization seemed to make my whole day flow easily along with a positive mood. Definitely felt different on the days when I forgot or wasn't able to start my day that way. Similar happened if I stayed up during the night, I felt detached. Afraid to be fully present in the physical but I made my vow to do so anyway, after four years of religiously meditating twice a day and being a strict vegan had made me feel alone and spacey. I made this commitment to be more grounded after I realized that my health was probably falling apart, as well as the rest of my life, because I had gotten angry at my ex-husbands and roommates and told God that I didn't want to have anything anymore, because people used me for my money and my talents and frequently took away what I worked very hard to earn. Well, God answered my prayers. Now I, had to find a way to convince God to reverse my request.

Going to the School for International Training in Vermont and then on to Zimbabwe was a blessing, and I temporarily had some of my health restored. Although I no longer had the constant chest pains, there were a few warnings signs while I was on the college campus that all was not well. Occasionally I struggled to climb stairs and lost control of my bladder. In Zimbabwe, my menstrual bleeding was heavy, and I had terrible headaches which probably meant I was anemic.

Several months after being back in the United States, lab tests showed a different kind of anemia. My mean corpuscle volume (MCV) was high, indicating that my red blood cells were too large. Megaloblastic macrocytic anemia causes too few red blood cells, not enough oxygen, with symptoms of shortness of breath, tingling, burning and weakness in arms and legs with difficulty walking, high irregular heart rate with risk of heart failure, mood changes of depression, anxiety and confusion. I had all of these symptoms and had told the doctors that I had been a strict vegan for ten years. All of my blood work was usually just inside the border of the lowest normal range. Therefore, doctors frequently ignored my test results as not significant although I had severe symptoms affecting my daily functioning. Perhaps the reason other people who are vegan can get away without it affecting their health, is because they don't have celiac disease, gastritis, or Crohn's disease that I was later diagnosed with, that interferes with absorption of food like what happened to me.

Getting Medical Care

While I was homeless, I began to hate going to case managers, including Tim who was one of my favorite case managers, for making promises about how the system is going to help me. Built my dreams and hopes up only to have them torn down again and again. The case managers were excited about "money coming" to me, but that doesn't mean much to me without my health and ability to care for my needs. It was very difficult for me to even want anything anymore. Reality of being poor and homeless got shoved in my face day after day.

It felt like I was in a very desperate situation that I had not the faintest idea how to resolve myself, so I was forced to ask for help and depend on others. This perceived desperation made me impatient, although I had been patient with most previous life challenges. It's hard to have patience when appointments with doctors and Social Security offices are months apart.

They smile and say, "That's the way the system is. You just have to wait." Or, "it's only one month's wait. Usually it takes two or three months or even two years!"

But of course, I didn't want to hear that. I was in constant pain, exhausted and had depression because of the excessive waiting, and being unemployment with loss of friends and social status. My whole life was on hold.

The case managers seemed to not have done their homework. It was very hard to get a straight answer from anyone. They hadn't the faintest idea. Yet, while I waited for what may or may not happen from public benefits, they wanted me to continue pretending with them that everything was okay, and they were helping me. I had to sign their paperwork, so they get paid biweekly, while I waited over a year for money and medical benefits. Same with doctors, they didn't have to do anything for me, just treat me like a specimen so they can get their degrees and move on. Yet they wouldn't fill out the papers so I could get my medical card, so I too could move on.

As you can tell, I was very frustrated because without a medical card for a whole year, the doctors weren't able to do the necessary expensive tests like computerized tomography (CAT) scans or magnetic resonance images (MRIs) and blood tests to help them know what was wrong with me, to have an accurate diagnosis to give me medicine and treatment.

Tim did refer me to a disability lawyer after social security denied me three times during a year of me trying to go through the application process alone. The lawyer worked behind the scenes gathering my medical records, to put together a case. After a successful court hearing with a female judge, they approved me to receive Social Security disability income and benefits. I cried when I read the award letter because it described me in a way I wouldn't ever want to be.

Trying to get medical help so that I could get my life back became my main focus. I was angry that the pain and fatigue made me so tired that I could not think straight, which then made me irritable and forgetful. This made me feel irresponsible, lazy, and confused.

One day, I suddenly I realized I left my Social Security award letter with a case manager, whom I hoped kept it safe. I was feeling very trapped inside with the unpredictability of my illness and the weather. The weatherman forecasted "only a dusting of snow" but there was enough to shovel! I needed my Social Security award letter when I was to go to the doctor on the following Monday. I had to figure out how to get around in the snow, since walking was difficult for me and I didn't drive or have a car. I had planned a straight bus route, now I would have to take a detour. It would've been better if I had a bus pass then I wouldn't had to worry about how long my bus transfer card would last. I didn't have a bus pass because of the confusion about when my social security benefits would arrive.

I desperately needed groceries too. Some of my depression was from not eating enough, which then kept me awake at night, without sleep I was too tired to cook, or wash dishes and it became a vicious cycle. Public aid cut my food stamps and cash because my original Social Security award letter from the court decision made back in November stated that I would receive benefits through January. However, public aid only gave me cash for two months. I thought this would include getting a January check and food stamps, but it didn't. So there went my budget. Add snow to no money, and difficulty getting around, and you have a big feeling of being trapped with always having to wait.

Chapter 2: Medical I Ching

Destiny reading hexagram 34 (lines 3 and 6) into hexagram 38.

According to The Medical I Ching, hexagram 38 indicates sudden onset and rapid progress of diseases, but prognosis is fair for recovery in the end. Since there are contradictory symptoms, may experience negligence from medical doctors giving wrong diagnoses or prescriptions.

As you'll read in both my memoirs, doctors frequently misdiagnosed me resulting in me almost dying at least three times — first from an ectopic pregnancy, the other times from septic infections, probably from undiagnosed endometriosis, caught just in time. Each time I was in the hospital for several days before doctors decided to do emergency exploratory surgery because they didn't know what was wrong. After they told me what they found, I researched their diagnoses and found I had all the classic textbook symptoms! The doctors ignored my symptoms based on "nonsignificant" test results. Now, even Black women celebrities with money and good insurance say they weren't listened to and almost died during pregnancy and childbirth. More women began coming forward in 2021 and 2022, especially women of color, and telling their stories of having their pain ignored and misdiagnosed. Similar to the "me too movement", except that they're calling it "medical gaslighting." On social media and YouTube, you can hear the personal stories and read the hundreds of comments underneath.

Hexagram 34 described the earlier diseases I had with fevers, including complications of measles at five years old with pneumonia. Possible aggressive illnesses I'm not sure of because to me, perhaps because of delayed diagnoses, I thought my illnesses came on slowly. This gave doctors extra time to "save me." However, the neurologist did tell me that it was rare for even patients with multiple sclerosis's walking to decline so fast going from walker to wheelchair in four years. Muscle spasms are symptoms of neuromuscular diseases. Line 3 can have lung problems like I did with pneumonia. As I got older, I do 'catch cold in my lower back.' In high school, I had boils on my butt from sitting on those hard, wooden chairs. Line 6: My prognoses would be fair. Initially, doctors' prognoses were moderate to severe, but I recovered beyond their expectations. Headaches? Rarely, only whenever I had high fevers or anemia.

My lips and rosy cheeks are naturally red when I take my vitamins. Found out the hard way, that when my lips are lighter than my face, then I'm anemic. In 1999, I was having dinner with a friend but didn't have the appetite to eat. In the middle of the night, I got an awful pain in my lower belly. Afraid, remembering the other two times I had terrible belly pain, I called an ambulance to take me to the emergency room. There a white doctor examined me and checked the skin color "normal" box on the intake form. She later had a specialist reexamined me that was African American that wrote in my medical chart "skin color pale and grayish." After discharge she told me, "I'm glad the color came back in your face."

Friends noticed too and commented. I asked them, "But why didn't you tell me that before?"

I'd been going back-and-forth to doctors for two months for the cramping pain in my left back kidney area. They kept telling me my lab and x-ray results were normal. Later in the ER with terrible abdominal pain there were tiny kidney stones in my dark reddish infected urine. They kept me in the hospital for 10 days because even with IV antibiotics, the doctors had difficulty getting my fever down. They later discovered an abscess and tried a new noninvasive procedure to drain it. I improved soon after. One of the doctors told me, just before discharging me from the hospital, that he stopped the other doctors for doing major surgery on me because he was sure I would have died on the operating table. Now I faithfully drink my water and take my vitamins with iron in it.

Ever the practical one, it makes better sense to me, to solve the underlying problem than to try to cover it up. Lips dry and cracked? Drink more water. The rest of your body will thank you. Grateful that you also eat healthy nutritious foods, then your lips become naturally full and red. Perhaps men's attraction to young women with red lips is an unconscious wisdom for survival of both the woman and child throughout pregnancy and childbirth. When a woman is anemic, she is more likely to hemorrhage during childbirth. Now with lip gloss and lipstick men don't know what they're getting.

Chapter 3: Would You Want to Live to be 100?

In the book, *Love, Medicine and Miracles,* Dr.Bernie Siegel asked, "Would you want to live to be 100 years old?" When I thought about the question in 1989 and again in 1999 along with the street corner Jehovah Witnesses asking, "Wouldn't you want to live forever" my response was, why would anyone want to live forever? Especially in this mess of a world we've made!

Later I read, *Return of the Rishi,* by Deepak Chopra M. D. where he wrote that spontaneous remissions are possible with the desire of the whole person to recover completely because the body has to obey when both the doctor and the patient believes deep in their hearts that the patient can get well. Not just with restored health but also happiness. I would like the happiness, but at this point in my life I don't know if I wanted to live to be 100 or to recover completely. I did seek out answers after a doctor told me I almost died in the hospital in September 1999. I was so happy to be alive that I was silly. Then I wondered why I was so happy to be alive after wanting to die inside all year after losing my friends, my health, income, status, independence, home, etc. My life situation hadn't changed. Medical records gave me the impression that there was a strong chance that I might have ovarian cancer. I had to wait two months to get appointments and get retested. In the meantime I agonized and did some real soul-searching. This led me back to Dr. Bernie's Siegel's other question, "If you only have one day or two weeks, six months, a year to live, how would you spend it? Certainly, you wouldn't waste it trying to please others and doing things you hate."

In one way, I feel as if I wasted a whole year and a lot of mental and physical energy worrying about my health, the healthcare system and services for the poor indigent people. It was one constant struggle. I wasn't happy most of 1999 and perhaps it's because it was easier to focus on my health than the pain of comparing the previous two years when I was in college and Africa. There I felt the happiest I ever remember being in my whole life. I was also the healthiest. Perhaps I couldn't imagine or dream of happiness and all I experienced while I was away as being possible upon return to the United States. All I remember is the pain and loneliness I had before I left.

For two decades, I struggled alone with being the first Black woman in the Air National Guard kitchen, the only Black nurse on staff, the only Black student in class, the only Black patient in therapy groups, the only one in my immediate family to complete college and become a professional. First in my family to get a divorce not only once, but twice. Having had a near death experience I saw and related to the world differently. Only one meant total self-sufficient emotionally because no one I knew understood what I was going through, and if they did they didn't say. Only and first adds up to lonely.

If I could actually choose, to be healthy again, maybe I would. When I learned to meditate, I made my own inner peace and joy. But I longed deeply for companionship and understanding from others. I cried and prayed to not be so lonely.

To eventually choose to begin knocking down self-imposed barriers to possibilities of living in a supportive community with others, maybe even have a family or a mate. It would require a lot of effort.

Chapter 4: What are Medical Specialists for?

After the standard wait of two years, Social Security gave me a monthly check and Medicare benefits, then I was able to go to better hospitals and specialists. When I moved out to the suburbs my doctor's appointments and hospital care were unbelievably better. Patients were seen by the doctor within a few minutes of arrival. This was a big difference from receiving health care at Cook County hospital, or Loretto hospital with full waiting rooms and ever changing medical student doctors every time I went, sitting all day waiting to get registered, to see the doctor, for the lab tests and X-rays, then more hours to have my prescriptions filled.

A couple of my friends, and also older family members who would tell me going to Cook County Hospital and other teaching hospitals was the best, because they had up-to-date medical science. I didn't find this to be true, especially with the disrespect poor people "of color" received. Perhaps true for elders who remember a time when they spent three days in waiting rooms at Cook County hospital, while I complained of only six hours or more. Researching now as I write this book, the history of Cook County Hospital, I read that indeed it was previously the best in the United States as it implemented the new law that doctors had to have standardized training and take an exam to become doctors. Cook County hospital pioneered the first blood banks and specialized surgeries. Considering that in the 1800s hospitals didn't even exist, if you were lucky doctors made house calls, but even then medication and treatments were very few, so basically health care was limited to somebody sitting next to your bed holding your hand until you expired. This puts what the elders were trying to tell me into perspective. But back in the early 2000s, I thought I was receiving inferior care.

I grew up only knowing of having a family doctor. Therefore, I didn't know there were specialists. While I was in the hospital in 2003, after a kidney stone and endoscopies for digestive problems, the doctors brought in an infectious disease doctor, because they were wondering how come I had partial paralysis and was using a wheelchair. She asked me, "What countries have you traveled to?"

"Zimbabwe in 1997, Jamaica 1996, and Korea while in the Air Force in 1980."

"Have you been to wooded areas in the United States?"

"Yes, the college in Vermont and I frequency went camping outside in tents in the Midwest."

"We will test you for Lyme's disease, and Dengue Fever from Jamaica's mosquitoes and other diseases."

When the tests results came back, she told me, " I have to send another blood sample, on ice all the way to Texas. I spoke to a specialist there, because it's a possibility that you may have brucellosis. Brucellosis is rare in United States because we vaccinate our farm animals. It does still exist with livestock along our southern borders."

Maybe it was from trying to milk the cow in the Zimbabwe village. I didn't get symptoms immediately. It started with extreme fatigue and sleeping day and night after I returned to college in the United States. I was so tired that I will wake up take one spoonful of food, that my classmates brought to me, and fall right back to sleep. Gradually, during the next year I began to lose the use of my legs and then my arms. But it's been four years since I was in Zimbabwe.

She called me a week later excited, "I never had a patient with brucellosis before. You're my first patient with it! You're lucky to be alive. Although brucellosis is endemic in Africa if you had stayed there you probably would've died. We can treat you. These will be strong antibiotics, so we will have to monitor you closely."

I took the antibiotic for six weeks and then she sent another blood sample to the doctor in Texas and gratefully the results were negative.

I thought the infectious disease doctor was to be my new doctor. When I made another appointment with her for an unrelated minor ailment, she asked me, "Why don't you go back to the other doctor you had when you were in the hospital? She's your primary care doctor."

After the infectious disease doctor diagnosed me with brucellosis, she also referred me to the neurologist who finally gave me an additional diagnosis of spinocerebellar degeneration. He, the infectious disease doctor, and my primary care doctor were true medical detectives.

However, there can be too many other specialists with few of them communicating with each other. In 2007, A Filipino doctor who worked as a home care nurse thought I had Raynaud's Syndrome and recommended to my primary care doctor that I go to a rheumatologist specialist. He looked at my fingertips and nail beds with a small microscope and told me I did indeed have Raynaud's Syndrome. He prescribed a calcium channel blocker. When I told my cardiologist, she changed my medication to the same. With this new knowledge about how much trouble spasms of tiny capillaries can make, it occurred to me almost all my pains were from spasms: coronary artery spasms, mesentery artery spasms, urethra spasm urinary retention, interstitial cystitis with crampy bladder spasms backing urine up into my kidneys. If my specialists had talked to each other they might have figured this out amongst themselves.

Raynaud's syndrome is vasospasms or constriction of the arteries and capillaries, so the fingers turn pale white, then bluish from the lack of oxygen, then red as the fingers warm up. Rinsing my hands or food items in cold water would make my fingers throb. Drinking cold water would also give me chest pains and headaches. I hated having to dig, to get food out of the freezer. My fingers felt sore for hours, sometimes days afterwards. Raynaud's syndrome can similarly affect the feet.

I remember feeling miserable after walking five long street blocks to school when I was 10 and 11 years old. Sometimes, I would go to the school nurse. Coming from the upper mid-Atlantic states to the southern Midwest then moving to an upper Midwest state with below zero temperatures and windchill, I wasn't used to the cold. Most of the time I was without mittens and no thermal underwear. It seemed like it would take hours for me to warm up. One day I saw an index card on the nurse's desk with my name on it and the word "hypochondriac." I wondered what it meant. It may have helped if she had known about Raynaud's syndrome. But maybe not. My family was poor and probably couldn't have done anything about it anyway.

This new neurologist told me my symptoms would be like multiple sclerosis, but I didn't have multiple sclerosis. One of MS symptoms is intolerance to temperature extremes. Initially, this was predominantly with the heat outside in the summer or inside a hot room. It wasn't until 2015, that I read in a *Momentum* magazine article that people with MS can also have cold intolerance and Raynaud's phenomenon. Because neuromuscular diseases affect the autonomic nervous system, there's difficulty regulating internal body temperature to automatically sweat when too hot or shiver when we are too cold. For me, being too hot or too cold is extremely painful, and causes my arms and legs to weaken.

Chapter 5: Prognosis

It was unusually hot outside. I went inside the bank, and after standing in line for a while, when I got up to the teller's window, I had difficulty using my hands. I had to ask him to take my state ID out of my wallet for me. Usually I would be all right after being in the cold grocery store. Afterwards, on the way home and after I arrived home, I had difficulty breathing so I called my neurologist and he told me to go to the emergency room. Then they could transfer me to one of the hospitals he was affiliated with later, if needed. They admitted me to the hospital overnight, and then transferred me in the morning to one of his suburban hospitals. Problem was they didn't give me any medications during the evening or night.

    This happened on Friday of Memorial Day weekend. In the hospital bed, I was surprised that I had difficulty turning and sitting up on my own. The nurses' aides had to give me complete bed baths and diaper changes. A headache started that got progressively worse each day, that made me dizzy and nauseated anytime I moved my eyes —to try to read or write, even to look down at my lunch plate, then up to the TV screen. It felt like both of my eyes kept sliding to the left. After that I ate with my eyes closed and I stopped watching TV. It was hard to focus. It was difficult to dial phone numbers while shifting from the blurred words in my pocket telephone book, and then back to the phone. Eventually I remembered that I could just ask the operator to dial the number for me.

The nurse called my neurologist. He arrived wearing a Hawaiian floral shirt and shorts. I told him about the bad headache and problems with my vision. He gently said, "I will order an MRI. Sorry this is happening, to be honest I was expecting you to be bedridden by now."

He came again early the next morning and told me, "You've had a small stroke. An occipital stroke. I'm shocked myself." He did another neurological exam on me, then said, "I will order an MRA of your carotid arteries. It is similar to an MRI but uses different software. I will start you on Plavix or Lipitor."

I asked him, "When did I have the stroke?"

"I don't know, maybe Tuesday."

He started me on physical therapy, there Diana stood me in between the parallel bars, but it felt like my feet were stuck to the floor! My feet were close together and not moving. This was the first time since my diagnosis in 2003, that I was unable to stand up or control my legs. She was holding me up with the gait waist belt. This really scared me.

She taught me how to sit up and lie down since my back and arms were weak.

She said, "It doesn't look like your eyes are moving back-and-forth, just closed. You should open your eyes while reading, writing, looking down and turning your head. In time your eyes will accommodate."

I reluctantly replied, "Even maintaining eye contact with conversations makes me feel nauseated."

She would purposely talk to me squatting down to my level, or on whichever side bothered me at the time, all while encouraging me to keep my eyes open.

Each day in the hospital, my writing was improving, especially with my left hand. But I'm right-handed and because it was faster, I would try using my right hand but it made me dizzy and sick with a headache. I told my neurologist. He explained, "You had a right-sided stroke. With your eyes, it is not just your left eye. They keep writing 'left eye' in your chart. But is the left side of your left eye, and the left side of the right eye. Remember when you were in grade school, and you used a piece of cardboard while reading so that you only saw one line at a time? That may help you now."

Then he went on and on about Monet and Van Gogh and their visual difficulties. I wanted to scream. I don't want to do abstract painting! I'm not ready for that. Was he trying to quell my enthusiasm? He did not believe I will recover my eyesight or adapt? Aren't I standing after not being able to stand last week?

I told him, "I feel grateful that my condition was not worse."

"He said, "Like a glass half full."

I said, "No. Glad that something better may come of this."

He asked, "Are you able to transfer yourself from the wheelchair to the the bed, and toilet and back again?"

I said, "Yes, I am doing that mostly by myself. But they don't want me to do it alone yet."

He said, "Well, you should be able to go home in a couple of days."

I said, "The physical therapists were talking about me having acute care rehab."

He replied, "I have to look at your chart. It would be good if they can get you walking. But if they only get you transferring, at least you're no worse than when you came here."

I knew I needed to do more than be able to only transfer. I needed to get back to standing and walking at least a short distance, like I was doing before I came to the hospital. I felt like crying but waited until he left.

Intensive Rehabilitation

My neurologist signed me up for intensive physical and occupational therapy. They also did a speech therapy assessment. Respiratory therapy monitored my breathing and bipap machine throughout the night because they said my breathing was too shallow. The transfer papers from the emergency room had a diagnosis of 'generalized weakness with respiratory distress and diminished breath sounds.'

A few nights later, I was lying in a hospital bed, most of my body hurt. Muscle soreness after exercise is to be expected but, in addition I had burning pain from my hips down to my toes, and from my shoulders to my fingertips. I remembered previously feeling like my whole body was on fire daily. Any part of my body that I used burned. When I lived at my aunt's house, I started using my wheelchair more often, and taking the baclofen for muscle spasms, most of the burning pain went away. Now the burning pain is back.

The good news is, the physical therapist told me, "I believe that you won't be needing the wheelchair. You should be able to walk. We can teach you how to walk properly."

She guided my legs, especially my hips. This was exciting news.

Occupational therapist had me opening and closing buttons and snaps. My hands would stop working about halfway through these exercises. She said my fine motor skills were okay. She made the task harder as she gave me instructions to remember to not look down while I was trying to concentrate on tasks with my hands. I felt frustrated and wanted to quit.

My challenge is writing and reading. Most of my clothes don't have buttons.

They reported I was progressing well in physical therapy. Early one morning a different occupational therapist came and surprised me with a walker. I used it to walk to the toilet and back to my bed. He also helped me pull my shorts and paper panties up, which felt weird. Although I needed the practice, I would have rather had a female. The walker did help me stand longer. My knees were still bent, and I struggled to keep my balance. Later at 11:30 AM, in the gym the physical therapist also had me walking with the walker.

Preparing to go home, the physical therapist asked me, "Is there anything else I could help you with?"

I told her, "Walking without a walker would be nice, because a walker would get in the way in my small kitchen, also holding onto the walker hurts my hands. She had me walk around the hemibar holding on with only one hand. I did better once I learned the foot pattern, and she showed me how to lead with the right hand. I asked her, "What do I do when I start with the right foot."

She said "It stands on its own. I would be more worried about you using a cane and especially without anything because your left foot drags and you may trip. May need AFO braces."

She walked and walked me, around the parallel bars, to the car and back in the morning. That afternoon, she had me walk to the mat, then the long way from the mat table to the door, into the hallway so I can get the feel of walking on carpet and then finally walked me back to my chair. I felt like I was going to faint, flushed with the sweater I had on, but had no way to take it off while I was holding onto the walker. I no longer felt my legs. I stopped to rest saying that I needed to get my legs, left arm, and my head back. I tried walking some more, but there wasn't much improvement. She offered to bring me my wheelchair, instead I refused it as I slowly walked to my wheelchair. Why the heroics on my part, the determination to finish like the requirement to finish everything on my plate?

The good news, which is what gave me the energy to overdo the walking in physical therapy and occupational therapy is that the social worker called to make arrangements for me to go home next week. I wanted to show that I'm really ready to go home!

It will go down in my medical record how many yards I walked in physical therapy, but I will decline all that extra walking from here on out. By pushing my limits, am I given the wrong impression as to how patients with MS or similar symptoms are to be rehabbed? Some doctors advise that those with MS pace themselves so that they don't get overheated which causes the muscles to have temporary paralysis or weakness. There were only minimal variations in the exercise routines of all of us patients in the gym, although most of the other patients had strokes. One of the physical therapy students, said to me while very close to my face, "It will only make you stronger."

Is not quality as important, if not more important, than quantity? That morning, the male physical therapist student commented on how I don't pick up my feet when I'm tired. Later I told the female student that I did the twenty repetitions today without resting in between, so that they could all see what happens to my legs when I do too many repetitions. I also couldn't even feel my legs. None of this was written in my chart, instead only what exercises were done. At least some of the pain was mentioned. However, my decrease in walking distance wasn't from the pain. Didn't they hear or understand anything I said?

The Psychologist

Dr. Zogota, knocked on my door at lunchtime. It was strange to me to have a psychotherapist come to my room. I usually go to their office. I guess it's similar to doctors coming in. He came in and sat in the reclining chair. His hair was shoulder length. He said, "The nurse said you wanted to talk to me."

   I said, "I don't know if she told you the reason I want to talk to you. I haven't been able to talk to anyone about the progressive nature of the disease I've been diagnosed with. My sister is in denial, as she is with most serious topics. I did try to talk to my brother too, about my Living Will when I was having problems breathing. My neurologist told me soon after I came into the hospital, that he expected my condition to have declined by now to being bedridden, not be able to walk, talk, feed myself, do anything. It's only been three years since he diagnosed me with spinocerebellar degeneration. I've been doing well for three years, but now this happened. He initially told me it would be a "graduate decline." I live alone and haven't had any noticeable decline of the use of my arms and legs, may have even done better this past year. Now this! May be time to talk about it."

   Dr. Zogota let me talk and talk, only saying at the beginning, "You can eat your lunch." But I knew I couldn't talk and eat at the same time. For safety, since I choke easily, as well as conscious of time and memory lapses, I said, "I'll wait. It's a cold plate anyway. Chicken salad, red grapes, and strawberries. Oh, except for a small bowl of rice and a small bowl of canned green beans."

I began by saying, "I didn't let myself think or feel about what is happening to me since I've been in the hospital. At first, I was shocked, everything seemed surreal. But last week, I started to get some clarity. I was able to write more in my journal without getting the terrible headache, nausea, and my writing started to flow."

"How are you able to write better? Was it emotionally, physically or your thinking?"

I stuttered, beginning then pausing, "Yes, physically because I would feel very sick, dizzy and nauseous when I tried to write. Journaling, although difficult, helped me emotionally to open up. I felt a little better here when you asked me about my occupations and hobbies, but it also made me feel sad because I couldn't do them anymore. My thinking improved too because I was better able to finish my sentences and thoughts."

I tried to look at my journal for excerpts to read to him the differences in my clarity, but had difficulty finding the pages.

He surprised me by commenting, "You only wrote a page and a half."

I thought 'How did he know that? Then I realized that he was watching as I turned the pages. Some days I only wrote one or two sentences.

"Yes, in the beginning most of the time I couldn't finish sentences."

I decided to stop looking for the specific pages, and just tell him what I wanted to talk to him about. He listened in silence as I told him what I had told the nurse, adding more to explain.

Last week, he ended his initial routine new patient assessment visit by saying, "I'd like to come back and talk to you some more. I'd like to talk about some of your irritation with staff."

I was comforted and relieved that he understood how annoying it was for staff to repeatedly ask me the same questions over and over. It didn't matter — the regular daily staff plus all the new students, doctors and rehab therapists. Although they were all trained to ask me, 'Do you need anything,' it didn't seem like they were understanding me when I tried to explain how too much physical therapy exercises gave me more spasms and pain.

He had also told me last week, "You are difficult to read because of your smile."

To me he is even harder to read because he kept a straight face. Today, waiting for his response, I went on and ate my lunch, not wanting my rice and green beans to get colder, I asked him, "Aren't you going to say anything?" I was actually worried that he wouldn't say much. But he said a lot.

"You seem calm as you tell me all this."

"I was surprised myself at how peaceful and calm I've been this week. Considering what I went through over the past three weeks."

"I get the feeling that you've been through worse things in your life than having a neuromuscular disease like MS."

"Well, I wondered this morning why I felt so calm. I was thinking maybe it is because I've been through dealing with this already when I started going to my therapist in 2004 to deal with losses. In 1999, I lost my physical health, income, status in a community, career, family and friends. I was homeless. But there are other kinds of losses. I used to belong to an online MS support group where members talked about losing function, grieving then adapting only to have yet another loss, grieving then struggling to adapt some more. This has gone on and on and on, where I barely do much of what I used to do, so that I don't know who I am anymore. Like I don't feel I have an identity. Some religious spiritual beliefs promote giving up one's identity. But it's an awful feeling. In therapy over the past year, I felt fuller, like the void had been filling up. I've done much more in life than I told you, traveled and more. I've wondered if I never do anything else, would I be okay?"

"Has anyone on your health care team told you, you could die in a year? I thought people with MS . . ."

"No. People with MS have almost the same life expectancy as the general population. But there are different types of MS. Some people with MS you wouldn't even know they have it. Others that can be in wheelchairs or bedridden, is rarer. My neurologist told me that even experienced neurologists would only see one or two cases of primary progressive MS throughout their whole career. Primary progressive MS is what he initially diagnosed me with. I have a young friend in her 20's who was bedridden in five years and can't communicate. She could live another 40 to 50 years. I don't want to do that to my family."

Dr. Zogota was silent, but his shift in his seat showed his discomfort and perhaps agreement with me. "You have a very complex personality."

I laughed and said, "Why? You won't find me in a textbook?"

"I won't find any pathology."

"I would be curious what psychology tests would show now. I took some tests in 1990."

"What did the test show?"

"Well, three things. (Blushing). I only remember one."

"What was that one?"

"Delusions of grandeur." (I didn't tell him that the reason why I only remember delusions of grandeur is because it was a Black woman psychologist who did the testing. She didn't consider it pathological, because most Black patients had a higher score for delusions of grandeur on the MMPI Personality assessment. I, of course, didn't know the MMPI back then or what it was for. It is probably because we have to survive, in spite of so much discrimination, oppression, having to overcompensate and succeed with anything that we do. Not bragging, just a normal way of life for us).

"There must've been a lot going well in your life then."

"No, things are not going well at all. I wish I had the test results for comparison to, if I took the test now. The results would be like night and day. I went away to college and traveled. I've grown even more since I've been using a wheelchair. I've had to learn to speak up, to advocate, blossom and become more sociable.

"What did you do before? You're kind of young to be here."

"I was a nurse, an artist." I didn't tell him the many other things I've done in my life.

"You're a unique person. Most patients give up. They don't have the intelligence, goals, or the creativity that you have. I don't know what to tell you. I can't sugarcoat it. I think you will do fine as long as you don't put off putting your affairs in order."

Previously, I expressed frustration with financial challenges to getting appropriate adaptive equipment that would help me be more independent. The state wouldn't pay for the equipment unless I was going to work. So I was trying to save up to purchase it myself. But I had to move twice last year. I did buy a computer, so that I could use Dragon Naturally Speaking voice recognition dictation voice-to-text computer software, to type for me. Dr. Zogota chatted a little about the Dragon Naturally Speaking, and I gave him some advice for using it himself to help with all the paperwork and charting he has to do.

He wished me well and said, "I'll be looking for your book."

Results

I stayed five weeks total in the hospital. Mother Dear flew in to visit me. My cousin came several times since she lived nearby. Staying extra weeks in the rehabilitation hospital had me worried about my apartment. I gave my cousin my keys to my apartment, to bring my checkbook so I could pay rent because I remember back in 1999, when I was in the hospital followed by a recovery residence, I was told that I would lose my transitional housing with the homeless agency if I stayed away longer than thirty days. Amazingly and gratefully when I called and talked to my current apartment manager, she assured me that, "Don't worry about paying your rent while you are there. Just get well. This is your home now."

A month after coming home, I read about the MS hug. An MS hug is often the beginning of an MS exacerbation. The tight sensation around my ribs that wouldn't let me take a deep breath. Then I got weaker, where I had difficulty even sitting up or turning over in bed. Also, what my neurologist initially diagnosed me with — progressive relapsing MS —starts out gradually worsening, but later has acute attacks. But when I showed him this information, he argued that all neurological diseases have relapses whenever there is an infection. He did consider giving me IV steroids while I was in the hospital but changed his mind.

I think it is also possible that I may have had a TIA (transient ischemic attack) temporary brief mini stroke, although the neurologist told me that he had mistakenly thought another patient's MRI was mine, and therefore I didn't have a stroke.

What if it was actually my MRI pictures, but I had recovered from the stroke before follow-up MRI's were done?

Chapter 6: Another Before My Time

In 2003, soon after I was diagnosed with brucellosis, there was an article in a nursing magazine about Florence Nightingale suffering from depression and went on and on about her having depression, even Bipolar Disorder. Florence Nightingale also had brucellosis. Crimean fever is what brucellosis was called back in the 1800's. She probably acquired brucellosis in ways similar to how I did from milking an unvaccinated cow and eating unpasteurized milk in the form of yogurt while I was Zimbabwe. In addition, I helped hold a baby goat for an injection. Assumptions were made in the article as to psychological reasons why she took to her bed, even after almost dying of the high fevers. Her being in a war, nursing wounded soldiers, along with speculating that she was grieving because her mother died could be traumatizing and depressing.

More recent articles defended her symptoms as being physical not psychological. Back in the 1800s doctors diagnosed her with neurasthenia psychosomatic or hysteria. One doctor said she was lazy and didn't want to work! How could a doctor say she had mental illness when she didn't really ever stop working in spite of the awful pain that I know all too well. Brucellosis is very difficult to diagnose in humans. It can affect the nervous system, joints, heart, and digestive system.

CHAPTER 6: ANOTHER BEFORE MY TIME

Symptoms come and go, so that is why she was able to still be productive. However, because she was productive, described with "superhuman effort" often pushing herself to work 20 hours a day when she could, the other days she would be very sick, therefore, a doctor decided that she had bipolar! He assumed these were manic episodes.

Florence Nightingale was unable to walk for six years, and although she was mostly bedridden this is when she did the most writing and correspondence with officials to establish nursing as a profession when she was only in her 30s. She promoted supportive services and employment for other nurses. Since she was good in mathematics and statistics, she was able to include diagrams and research in her manuals. Florence Nightingale founded the first nursing textbook, the first nursing training school, and the field of public health. She lived to be 90 years old.

Same with me, when I had chest pains and was beginning to have difficulty walking, not admitting they did not know what was wrong with me, the doctors sent me to a psychiatrist. It wasn't until four years later, after three previous neurologists, that a new neurologist that the infectious disease doctor referred me to, did more MRI's and added the diagnosis of spinocerebellar degeneration.

Florence Nightingale wasn't the only one experiencing war traumas or Brucellosis. Why me out of my half a dozen siblings, was I the only one in my family who was diagnosed with spinocerebellar degeneration that is usually a hereditary degenerative neuromuscular disease. And of my classmates, the only one who came back with brucellosis? I'm was probably more cautious with food, activities, and hand washing than they were!

Florence Nightingale was given credit for revolutionizing hospital care by promoting the necessity of fresh air, good food, and clean water for drinking and sanitation and personal hygiene that decreased infections and therefore unnecessary deaths of soldiers. Often having to sneak in to care for the soldiers at night after the male officer doctors would go to bed. Doctors back then didn't want women nurses.

Well, in the process of doing recent online research, looking for Florence Nightingale's birthdate to see what personality traits we have in common, I was stopped in my tracks by a photo of an African American woman, Mary Jane Grant Seacole, who also did nursing. Born fifteen years earlier than Florence Nightingale, she actually did much more than nursing. Mary Seacole was a doctoress, herbalist and businesswoman from Jamaica who had experience saving many lives from tropical diseases, even worked alongside military doctors before the Crimean War, yet was denied by the British War Office to serve as a nurse because she was Black. Florence Nightingale also would not allow Mary Seacole to join her nurses although Mary Seacole was light complexion being of mixed heritage. They did talk and sometimes met together, therefore it is possible that Mary Seacole taught Florence Nightingale about hygiene and sanitation that she had already been using for years prior. Mary Seacole's personal history and contributions to the world are fascinating. Her accomplishments are astounding for any person, especially women, then and now. She wrote her own autobiography, *Wonderful Adventures of Miss Seacole in Many Lands* (1857) and she traveled independently with her own money, that she made herself as a doctor and business woman, providing many different services. She owned hotels and stores. Her story goes on and on in Wikipedia for each decade of her life. Mary Seacole was fearless. A true heroine on and off the battlefield.

I also tend to be fearless, although I do less traveling now when using a wheelchair. Whatever needs to be done, wherever I am divinely guided to go, I go, problem-solving and getting it done in spite of criticism.

PART TWO: LIFE USING A WHEELCHAIR

Chapter 7: Getting a Wheelchair

Emotionally it was difficult to think of what it was like to go from walking miles to being totally exhausted after walking two blocks. Other than taking a bus for long distances, I previously walked almost everywhere because I never had a car. In Zimbabwe I walked two hours over rough terrain up and down hills to and two hours back from villages. Approximately six months after I returned to the United States I began having difficulty walking up the huge mound in the middle of the streets. You are probably thinking, "Huh, what mounds? Well, I too never noticed the gradual incline and declines on either side of the streets where cars are usually parked before neither. A taxi driver observing me one day said, "You look like you are trying to climb a mountain." Soon after, climbing stairs became almost impossible and then impossible.

Used to doing at least twenty activities a day, I learned to be grateful for accomplishing only one or two tasks a day. This was very humbling, but also terrifying for me to have to depend on other people for my physical needs. My legs would collapse with little warning. With reluctance, after reading an article about a doctor with multiple sclerosis who gave in and started to use a wheelchair saw it actually gave him more freedom and ability to do more activities because he had less fatigue. I too, discovered with using an electric power wheelchair I had less pain and exhaustion. Gave me my independence back.

My first wheelchair, a Golden Alante was delivered within two weeks, ten days before Christmas in 2001. The wheelchair technician had me practice driving it in the apartment building's wide hallway. He told me not to worry about accidentally scraping the walls because the landlord couldn't sue me for it. Then he left. Left me in the doorway of my small efficiency studio apartment to figure out how to get the wheelchair all the way inside without breaking my furniture or me. Frustrated, I cried. He hadn't shown me how to turn, go sideways or backwards. Being me, I kept at it until I parked it with minimal damage. Taught myself how to drive the wheelchair from then on out.

The most useful information the wheelchair technician told me was to let my wheelchair push open doors for me instead of with my arms. I didn't remember the reason why, because he told me a lot that day. I wish I had heeded his warning because over time I badly injured my left shoulder. Our arms aren't really designed to repeatedly be in a backwards position as we hold the door open long enough to drive the wheelchair forward. Now, I ask for help. It's weird though, I knock on doors, and from across the room I hear, "It's open."

I knock again.

"It's open!"

They come to the door, don't see me and walk away. Or puzzled say, "The door is not locked." Or opened gratefully with a smile, "Oh, come on in."

Insurances didn't give us a choice in wheelchairs. A wheelchair technician from a medical supply company came out to your home, measured your height, width and depth, and noted whether you are right-handed, left-handed, or no-handed. Maybe they ask you what color you prefer. Then he returned in a couple of months with a wheelchair. I wish it was like going to a car dealership where we could test drive a variety of brands and styles. Some wheelchairs have front wheel drive meaning the largest wheel is in the front. Rear wheel drive is when the largest wheel is in the back. Whether a wheelchair is a front wheel or rear wheel drive, believe me this makes a huge difference in steering a wheelchair. When I received my Permobil in 2003, it had rear wheel drive, it was like learning how to maneuver a wheelchair for the first time.

Usually insurances will only pay for a new wheelchair after you had it for five years. Heaven blessed me otherwise. I went to the Abilities Expo where they have educational workshops, entertainment, and vendors selling different types of wheelchairs, equipment, accessible vans, and assistive technology. This is where I learned about Dragon Naturally Speaking software that allows you to talk and it types for you. What drew my attention though, was a a beautiful blue bathtub apparatus that would lower me down into the tub and when finished bathing, rises to the top of the bathtub and sits me up. The last time I'd been in a bathtub was in 2001 when my legs suddenly wouldn't move. I didn't know then that any time my body was overheated I would get paralyzed. My helper struggled for a long time to try different ways to get me out. She did eventually. But that was too scary to even think about ever trying again.

I scheduled an appointment for the dealer to come out to my home to measure the bathtub and me. He asked me, "What's your diagnosis for why you are using a wheelchair?"

"Multiple sclerosis." (A previous neurologist wrote possible multiple sclerosis on a physical therapy prescription).

"That's the wrong wheelchair for a progressive disease. How long have you had this wheelchair?"

"Two years."

"Well, usually you can only get a new wheelchair after you had it for five years, but they gave you the wrong prescription. With smaller wheelchair companies they are going to give you the cheapest wheelchair because insurances only pay up to $5000. If the wheelchair cost more, then the company takes a loss. In addition, the company basically just gave you a wheelchair out of a box on their shelves. A one size fits most. It didn't even make sense for them to measure you."

He made the arrangements and returned in a few months with a huge Permobil power wheelchair. At least he took plenty time to show me how to drive it, how to go backwards which I simply avoided until then, and how to get out of tight spaces.

"Pull forward as you turn." He repeated this several times until I got it. I've been grateful to him ever since.

Besides my new wheelchair being bigger, and not designed to take apart like the Golden Alanté, it had several advantages. Customized to fit my body, it had a seat cushion, side supports to keep me from leaning or falling forward, leg side supports to prevent my thighs from embarrassingly gaping open, it tilted and reclined to relieve pressure on my butt, decreased backaches, with a shock absorber suspension system underneath for a more comfortable ride. The Permobil wheelchair is a European import, built sturdy like their cars. Unlike my Golden Alanté, that probably was designed for home use only, had multiple major repairs within the first six months of having it: the back of the chair broke, and later both the front motors had to be replaced. It seemed every time I went over just a crack in the sidewalk something broke. Although I was gentle and cautious, same as I am with the rest of my life, it would break. To this day, I still tense up and get an automatic startle reflex whenever I accidentally go over a larger crack in the sidewalk. In contrast, the Permobil wheelchair requires very little maintenance. For the price tag of $18,000 versus $5000 that's how it should be!

Now by law, we are required to get fitted in a hospital physical therapy department by a rehabilitation assistive technology professional or occupational therapist. Some rehabilitation hospitals do have several different style wheelchairs to test drive along with expert supervision. So far, I've not been that lucky, because of course it's what everyone would prefer so it takes too long to get an appointment. A compromise was having an assistive technology professional from a wheelchair company evaluate me in the presence of a rehabilitation medical doctor. Again, I never saw what my newest wheelchair would be until it was brought to my home.

Chapter 8: Not for the Faint of Heart

The old buses back in the early 2000s, had hydraulic lifts that would break down whenever the weather temperature was too hot or too cold, shutting down the whole hydraulic system, that meant the bus couldn't go anywhere. Therefore, bus drivers regularly passed up people in wheelchairs waiting at the bus stops. The newer buses now have long flip-out ramps that come out after the side of the bus kneels down lower. Because of the ability of the bus to lower still depends on hydraulics, occasionally when it's really hot in the summer the new buses break down too. Twice this happened to me when I was on a 147 express bus when it sputtered and stopped on DuSable Lakeshore Drive. All the other passengers could get off the bus and transfer to other buses that came along, except me because since the whole electrical system was down, the driver couldn't let the ramp out. In addition, there was no sidewalk to put the ramp on. The angle would have been too steep. I had to wait on the bus, with the driver until the supervisor and later the roadside assistance came.

Another time the bus ahead of us on DuSable Lake Shore Drive had a small fire, stopping all southbound shoulder traffic. Fireman came to help get me off the bus. One fireman on either side and another standing in front of me kept me and my wheelchair from tipping forward while going down the steep wheelchair ramp onto the shoulder of Lake Shore Drive. Then the firemen safely guided me onto inner Lake Shore Drive near Belmont Avenue where I could catch a bus to the university downtown.

    I'm glad the firemen let me stay in my wheelchair because I don't like to be carried. I was dropped a few times prior to getting a wheelchair. Usually by men who wanted to be heroes and carry me on stairs by themselves. Sweating while carrying me up the stairs, then hours later they tended to struggle as they got tired near the bottom of the stairs, dropping me on my back on the sharp edge of a stair.

    My most terrifying incident in my wheelchair was when I had asked the bus driver to get the bus as close to the curb as possible to put the full length of the ramp on the sidewalk. She had a jeering attitude a couple of times before, as if she had a grudge against anyone with a disability. This time I was begging her before she got to the stop, but she didn't. For some reason or another my new wheelchair I received in 2014 tipped dangerously forward on steep declines and the new curb cuts. Sometimes when I took a peek out the bus's door and saw the ramp was going to be too steep when the drivers put it down, I would ride to the next bus stop and hopefully it would be better placed. But I underestimated this time, plus with the driver's attitude there was no guarantee that she would park the bus any better further down the street. So I ventured out the bus door. Teetering in the middle of the ramp, I could go neither backwards into the bus nor go forward, without my wheelchair threatening to dump me face first onto the sidewalk with over 300 pounds of machinery on top of me. The bus driver didn't get out of her seat nor say anything to help. There was a small crowd of people waiting to get on the bus. They just stood there. Most were older people but there was a good looking muscular young man near the front of the crowd. Time stood still, until I gained enough clarity of mind to call out to him. He came over and up the ramp, held onto the front of my wheelchair supporting and guiding it down safely onto the sidewalk. I hugged and thanked him as I sobbed with relief. He gratefully hugged back. And I continued on my way. I was so shook up, I rode myself the rest of the way home rather than get on another bus. I reported the driver to the transit authorities, perhaps those who witnessed the incident did too because now all of the bus drivers pull in close to the curb and let the ramps down fully onto the sidewalks.

Chapter 9: Trains

I had not experienced problems while on the elevated nor subway trains in Chicago until recently. At the Clark and State station, there were sounds of fighting in the subway, yelling, screaming, cursing, glass breaking. The train engineer, who drives the train, told us we will be at a standstill waiting for the police. Meanwhile the power was cut to the train. I guess there was risk of someone being pushed onto the tracks. We had dimmed lights, but it meant the train couldn't go anywhere. He left the doors open allowing more and more people to squeeze into the train. No one seemed to care about COVID and social distancing. They just wanted to get home. Later the engineer told everyone to get off the train and go upstairs to take other transportation but told me to stay. He got off the train a few times to tell the police that gathered on that platform what he had witnessed, which was different from what the woman who was causing the trouble was telling the police. Allegedly, she was randomly spraying people with mace.

Imagine what it was like for everyone to evacuate the train, including the train engineer, and leave you alone on the train in your wheelchair. I couldn't get off the train because the platform was higher than the train doorway. Someone, usually station attendants or the train engineer will bring the yellow gap filler ramp. Luckily, after a half hour, the electrical power was restored, and the train continued in route without further incidents.

The second time this happened, I was on the Orange Line train at Midway Airport station. As the train pulled out it kept starting, stopping, and mildly jerking. The train engineer stopped the train, then walked through the train to the other end and drove the train back into the Midway Airport station. She told everyone to get off the train. They did, but then she closed the train doors and left me. I saw two cleaning staff on the platform, so I knocked on the train door. They were talking to a middle-aged man wearing all navy blue. As he came closer, I saw he had a pin on his sweater similar to airline pilot wings. He was another train engineer. He calmly came over, opened the door, and with the gap filler ramp got me off the train.

He asked me, "Do you want to get on the other train? We are about to depart now."

I nodded and said, "Yes."

It all happened so fast. Somehow, I deep breathed and didn't panic. What could have been a wheelchair user's worst nightmare, didn't sink in until a few days later, as I realized my fellow Americans were in such a hurry that they did not look back to see if I needed help. This scene played over and over in my mind. I decided then that it really wasn't safe for me to take the train anymore for a while. Not until the COVID pandemic, staff, food and housing shortages decrease so that homeless people or not so desperate to have a warm place to stay that they're hoping to be arrested and jailed. They stay in elevators overnight, urinating, sometimes defecating and breaking elevators so people with disabilities can't take the train. My empathy goes out to them, In the meantime, it is best for me to take the paratransit vans, hopefully to get a straight ride to my destination and back home safely.

Chapter 10: Paratransit Services

When there is snow, rain, heat or cold I have to take special paratransit vans or taxicabs that have a ramp and a large space for people in wheelchairs. Paratransit service provides "door-to-door" transportation instead of having to wait on bus stops. Sounds great, but it is "a shared ride." We have to call the day before our trip to schedule a ride for the next day. It's best to call as close to 6:00 AM to get the pickup times you want. Otherwise the reservationists will tell you there are no times available within that hour.

Taxicabs were promoted as allowing us to take spontaneous trips, like anybody else, and be the only passenger in the taxicab, instead of riding in a paratransit van full of other passengers. Initially, we could purchase taxi vouchers for $5 to cover a $13 trip. The catch was that the vouchers expired in six months. While people who walk could get a taxi right away, those of us using wheelchairs couldn't call any of the taxicab companies directly. Instead, we had to call a central citywide phone number and they would send us a taxicab. We didn't get to choose the cab company. They might send us a Yellow, Flash, or Blue Ribbon taxicab. There were fewer wheelchair accessible taxicabs, only fifty for all of Chicago, so it could take an hour or more for the taxicab to come. Sometimes I would go with a friend or helper who could push me in my little transport wheelchair, then a cab would come in five minutes. Occasionally I took a taxi home from the university at night and told the dispatcher I'd pay cash instead of a voucher, and the drivers came right away.

Later, I temporarily stopped using taxis when it took me three hours for a taxicab to come get me from the grocery store. Due to this gross inconvenience, I was losing money since there were no refunds on the taxicab vouchers. I only kept a few vouchers for emergencies. Over the years, there were improvements when more independent taxi companies were added. Fares became $3 for a $15 destination, and we now use a debit type card instead of handwritten paper carbon copy vouchers. During the COVID pandemic fares were free up to $30.

Some good that came out of the COVID pandemic shut down, was initially only one passenger was in the regular Pace minivans. Plus, they started occasionally sending taxis for me at the paratransit price of $3.25. How now I wish that Pace would give me a taxi regularly! After the worst of the two years of COVID pandemic was over, Pace returned to squeezing as many passengers as possible into mid-size buses. It has taken two to three hours to get to doctor appointments, university, work or other activities and longer to arrive home. You could try to plan scheduling a much earlier pickup time and still arrive late.

The main problem is the many add-ons. Some days, the closer I got to my home, the dispatcher adds other passenger pick-ups and drop-offs to the route, making the driver go west and south of my home three times only for the customers to not be there. Drivers have taken me past my apartment building to drop off someone who got into the van after I did. If I'm coming from far south to go far north, the drivers should really be taking the expressways either I-55 or I-94 into DuSable Lake Shore Drive cutting the travel time to an hour, maybe an hour and a half during rush hour. That many passengers shouldn't ever be put on my route home or to work in the morning, especially when they are that far away from my destination.

It is wonderful when Pace surprises me with a taxi ride. the taxi drivers will call and tell me their estimated time of arrival and if they may be late. Even if "late," I don't mind because I know they will still get me there on time. Another benefit, as with other paratransit rides, the varied conversations during long commutes are precious as we learn from each other.

I like my independence and freedom to go and return when I choose. In the spring, I bust loose. Inhaling the smell of flowers and budding trees, wheeling myself along the way. If you are wondering where I escaped to, you'll find me gleefully shopping anywhere or in a city park.

Folks suggest I get my own car or van. Sounds like a good idea to drive myself wherever I need to go. However, price of a wheelchair accessible van starts at $80,000 to $100,000 and that price is for a basic van similar to the paratransit van where someone else chauffeurs me around. A customized modified van with hand controls since our legs wouldn't be able to step on the gas or the brakes, costs more. I'd need special mirrors since I don't have peripheral vision in my left eye. Plus, the cost of special driving lessons may be only partially paid by some insurances for rehabilitation physical therapist specialists. Not to mention having to move to a warmer climate, so as to not have to find somebody to shovel me out from wherever I'm parked!

Chapter 11: By Air

The airport crew broke my wheelchair. This was despite me putting simple instructions in large font on a large card on the back of the wheelchair. I wondered why I was waiting a long time for them to bring my power wheelchair to the plane's door. Waited so long that the plane had to leave. After waiting awhile in the waiting area, down the hallway was coming a man with my wheelchair. The top of the chair was folded in half, kissing the seat. I yelled, "Oh, no!"

I was relieved when he opened it up and helped me into my wheelchair. But then he said, "Ma'am, you need to go to the claim's department."

He didn't tell me the United Airlines claim's department was all the way on the other side of O'Hara Airport! Up and down several elevators, through the long hallway and beside the airport pedestrian walkways that are similar to escalators except it moves flat along the floor for over a mile. We were trying to hurry because I had a scheduled paratransit ride home. Down another elevator to the baggage area was the United Airlines claim's department. The clerk explained that United Airlines does not pay for a replacement of wheelchairs, they only will do repairs. They will send a wheelchair repairperson to my home in the next day or two. We made it home, but soon after, the upper part of my wheelchair seat suddenly fell completely backwards! What if that had happened while we were going through the long underground tunnel with no one to ask for help if I were injured?

The wheelchair mechanic came the next day. He put metal rods on each side to hold the back straight up. Luckily, I still had the Golden Alante for an emergency wheelchair. I told him that the batteries were low. He brought and installed two new batteries the next day. This was good however, I still needed my Permobil wheelchair for outside my home. Remember, the Golden Alanté wheelchair tended to break even when going over a small crack in the sidewalk. However the straight up position on the back of my Permobil wheelchair gave me severe backaches. So I prayed often to make it through the day.

Chapter 12: Invisible

A couple of weeks later, I'm at my therapist Monica's office trying to explain my frustration with waiting to get my wheelchair fixed or a new wheelchair, plus the whole messed up air travel experience. How I really needed a personal assistant when I go to conferences, because I could barely move the first two days after I traveled. Packing before I even get there tired me out. Previously, before I became disabled, I would start packing two weeks ahead of time. As I thought of items, I would throw them in an open suitcase. And then followed up with a list I checked off. For years, I was not a last minute person. The past two times I traveled, I packed a couple of days before. And then I forgot to bring some important medical equipment and had to suffer the consequences. Most people didn't know how much I had to push myself up and beyond both my physical and emotional capabilities the whole time that I was away at the conference.

Monica asked, "Are there organizations for professional people with disabilities? Where you won't feel so lonely? Who have to struggle the way you do? Who may have tips for traveling?"

Well, there is the Progress Center for Independent Living where most of the staff has a disability. I really wanted to say, 'Sure I know a lot of people with disabilities, who hardly go anywhere because their homes have stairs, they were not given adequate electric wheelchairs and the constant challenges are too difficult. Emotionally, it gets tempting to give up. Therefore when I do go out, I feel lonely. There are two extremes: either young men who use the small racer type wheelchairs who can drive their own cars, and then there are people who have to depend on someone to do almost everything for them.

Even at the conference for rehabilitation psychologists, the psychologists with disabilities were ignored at a social event that was scheduled in the hotel's restaurant bar. The waitress told me, "The ramp has been broken since November. This is February. They put out extra tables in the hallway for you who use wheelchairs."

She led me to the empty tables and asked, "Would you like to order a drink or food?"

I responded, "Not now. Putting extra tables here does not solve the problem. This is supposed to be a social! Why are they over there, and I am stuck out here?"

It was then that I noticed another young woman sitting on her scooter at a table with a young man. I don't know how long she been sitting there. It was 9 PM, the social was supposed to have started at 7 PM. I'd been talking to someone else about a technology games exhibit and lost track of time. Caroline introduced herself and her husband to me. And said, "Yes, this is the women's rehabilitation psychology group and we've wondered why they didn't come down here to join me. It is as if I am invisible."

Monica said, "You all didn't ask them to come down?"

I said, "Why should we? They're supposed to be rehabilitation psychologists. Caroline probably didn't ask them because earlier the wheelchair transportation company didn't come to get her from the airport. They had to call a colleague to come and get them with a regular vehicle which meant having to take her scooter apart and putting it back together again. So she arrived to the conference late. She was probably too tired to fight yet another battle. And why should we be the ones to always go the extra mile?"

I did network with other people with disabilities there, and they are all working professionals. But I was the only African American using a wheelchair. Previously a mentor advised me that I would have to go up to people and network. And I did, I'm not shy, I reached out each day I was at the conference. It didn't help that the reception area was so small I could barely move anywhere in the room in my wheelchair. And what do you do when you're the only dark complexion person in conference rooms of 200 people? Again, why should I have to be the one to always have to go the extra mile?

Chapter 13: Wheelchair Coming On!

"Wheelchair coming on!" The driver yells to other passengers on the bus.

Paratransit van drivers regularly say, "I have to go and pick up another wheelchair."

Rarely would they ever have to go to an address to just bring out a wheelchair. I've tried gently correcting the drivers by saying, "Oh, you are going to go get someone else who uses a wheelchair. What is their name?"

They may respond with the name of a person as if I know them. Point well taken. May even apologize. However, most of the time this goes right over the driver's head. It is difficult to repeatedly hear that instead of looking forward to welcoming another customer, some drivers and dispatchers refer to us as an object or worse an inconvenience.

***

The Art Institute of Chicago hosted the Bisa Butler quilt exhibit during the summer of 2021. Two older black women

CHAPTER 13: WHEELCHAIR COMING ON!

standing ahead of us were talking about quilting. I asked them, "Are there Black quilter groups in Chicago? Where?"

Turning to my friend, instead of me she said, "There is one on the Southside. You can look it up online for her. Just go to the park district website."

As I started to show her, on my cellphone the pictures of quilts I made, she turned and walked away.

This slight was forgiven soon after, as a middle-aged Black security guard saw we were looking at an old black and white photo next to a quilt. He came over next to me, smiling, looking at me directly and excitedly told me, "A young woman came in and told me that that was an old picture of her mother, that Bisa Butler used the photo to design the large colorful quilt next to it!"

He acknowledged me as a person and an elder with grey hair. I returned the favor by excited telling him, "You witnessed and are yourself now a part of history as your picture was taken with the artist Bisa Butler and the now famous daughter!"

In my own family recently one of my brothers told me, "I didn't come visit you before because you were boring."

Huh? What did he mean? I am the same me. The only difference is now I have more confidence and do walk more around my apartment. I have always done creative projects, cooked, went out, worked and traveled. Then I remembered, perhaps is because he and my other siblings and cousins went out to clubs, casinos etc. without even inviting me. They always assumed that I would stay home with my grandmother. To me going out to clubs is boring. And how most of my family sits around and watches TV when visiting or they're not at work is boring too.

Chapter 14: University

No Seat at the Table

The ethics class teacher announced that we were moving to a larger classroom. The other students didn't know I emailed the teacher with the request, "Could the extra chairs and tables be moved out of the entrance to our classroom by Thursday?" I ccd the person in charge of ADA accessibility in the student service department, and also the program deans just in case our classroom teacher was not on campus the days before class.

For months, the extra tables from the university group activity room were lining the walls of the hallways. Bravely, I navigated through this obstacle challenge plus the students passing through or socializing sitting on or standing by the tables. But now the overflow of tables were pushed into adjacent classrooms.

Later, the teacher emailed me that she was not authorized to move the furniture. She also sent an email to the deans and student services department, who assigned us classroom 1311A. Our ethics teacher sent us students an email the morning of our class.

I arrived ten minutes early to get a "good seat" I parked my wheelchair at a table "desk" but then I saw there were only 11 chairs, with possibly space for 12 students. We would have 15 students if everyone came. I moved my wheelchair to the outside corner of the tables to allow for one more chair. My large Permobil motorized wheelchair can't fit under most tables anyway.

The teacher came in and quietly asked me, "Do you have enough table space."

Not wanting to draw any more attention, I replied, I'm okay but there are only 12 seats."

She spilled her coffee as she tried to squeeze past my wheelchair. She exclaimed, "This room is not any bigger than the other one! I'm going to find another classroom," as she left.

She returned quickly and said, "We are moving to room 1311D." All my classmates got up and went out of the classroom except for the teacher and myself, as we waited for a student dropping things as she tried to quickly gather her belongings. "Sorry," she said, "I'm trying to get out of your way so you can get past."

I said, "You're okay. Take your time. It's more important to be safe."

As I was the last person out of the room, no one thought to save a space for me. The student who fumbled with her belongings arrived at the first available chair at the same time as I did. She again thought of me and moved to another seat. The teacher got to observe all of this.

I sent her an email thanking the teacher for the room change, explaining that I usually get to class early in order to push the furniture out of the way so my wheelchair will fit. In the other classroom there was no space for me to push the extra chairs out of the way or move the tables further in so my wheelchair would fit, and students could get past. The teacher could see for herself why I needed to be the first person into the classroom not the last. Perhaps it is because when empty, the new classroom looked deceptively larger. But here again, were extra chairs stacked up behind me in the walkway, making it frustrating, to try to back up to position my wheelchair as it frequently bumped into the chairs. For four years, I've become accustomed to arriving early to classrooms to push the tables towards the center of the room to widen the walkway. Otherwise students rushing out at break time and at the end of class don't think to push their chairs in, and this made it difficult for me to get in, if I arrived on time or late. When students are already in their seats, I then have backpacks, purses, and coats on the floor to contend with.

Way back when I was in elementary school, the teachers would tell little children "Stand up and push your chairs in" before they dismissed the class. Perhaps they thought of liabilities and got tired of kissing foreheads, knees, and telephones when they had to report injuries to the principal and the parents. Ironically, since this was an ethics class, we were studying laws to protect the rights of clients, and to do no harm. What about us graduate students? Does the university care about us or the faculty? How can we even care about clients, when we have become so selfish just to get grades, and survive somehow in the rest of our lives? With our actions on automatic pilot how can we think ethically about other people? We forget about other people because we're forced to forget about our Self.

On my way home, I thought of my role in this situation. In an effort to not draw attention to myself in classrooms among my peers and teachers, I may have spoiled everyone by trying to do the problem-solving all by myself. Could I have yelled, "Save a seat for me" as my classmates rushed in the room?" Did I appear to be passive? Have I become too passive as I sit by waiting? I don't even go out at break time because I have to push all the chairs in to get past them. In addition, it would take me longer to get down the elevator and return in time. Not to mention having to get past people's chairs again if I'm late. Last semester, teachers and students did ask me if I wanted anything, before they went downstairs. One teacher even offered to pay for a snack or drink. But I have a gluten-free diet. Most food items in the vending machines or food court are sandwiches or pasta. Drinks would be okay, but I couldn't tell them, although I wore a diaper with extra pads I don't want to wet my pants all the way home as the Chicago potholes in the streets make the van ride shake all the pee out of me!

If I continue to move the furniture myself, and tell people "No thank you" when they offer to help, they'll think I don't need any help. But how to get a balance between not wanting people to assume I'm helpless and therefore a burden, and my over proving that I'm independent enough? My sore shoulder won't allow me to keep yanking doors open and pulling chairs out of the way. My new wheelchair doesn't seem to be as strong as my old wheelchair was for pushing heavy furniture like the classroom tables out of the way. Now I have to be concerned about protecting my new wheelchair. The economy has affected us all, as insurances are reluctant to pay for repairs and companies have downsized, or gone out of business all together. Understaffed, the wheelchair company had me wait weeks for even major repairs. Previously they came the same day or the next day or at least the same week.

Similarly, the university downsized their employees. There used to be an employee who made sure the classroom furniture and supplies were set up early each morning. There were written notices in each classroom to not move furniture into other classrooms. When I thanked my teacher for moving the class to a larger room, I added the simple statement that there used to be an employee to move the furniture. I was trying to be tactful, and gently pointing out that moving us to a larger room will not solve the wheelchair accessibility problem, because anyone could dump extra furniture in the new classroom too at any time.

By ethical standards, psychologist cannot discriminate by denying therapy to clients with disabilities simply because their offices are not accessible. The teacher did ask me loudly, "Haneefa, do you have enough space at the table?" In other classrooms, she asked me, "Haneefa, you have anything to write on" since I would use my lap to write on when there was no room at the tables for me at all. Perhaps that was her way of drawing my peers' attention to the situation that I needed to be included. These are "teachable moment," but is it my responsibility to always teach? And to always problem solve? Classroom teachers could be the role model as to what to do in these situations. We are all learning.

In the crowded classroom, a student had us move out-of-the-way while she moved another table into place so there would be enough seats. But still there was not enough room for me. If I had been standing or sat on the floor people probably would have been uncomfortable and said, "No, we will move over so we can all sit down and fit at the tables. Years ago, beginning when I was a teenager, family and other people always protested, "Why don't you have a seat," when I was the only one standing. I often stood because sitting in chairs caused me excruciating back pain. Now in classrooms it may be possible if I lower my new wheelchair to fit under the desk but when my wheelchair is not tilted upwards and back, I get backaches.

Spiritually, I wondered what to do to improve my situation and have places accessible for me and others who use wheelchairs. What does it mean to not have a place at the table?" Even when I do have a seat at the table I'm still set apart because I can't break bread together. Aware that my wheelchair sets me apart in my home too, I now sit on the futon couch with my guest for at least a little while. But there is no space for a table in my home.

With Fen Sui, red-colored accents along with loveseats or pairs of chairs are recommended to attract guests and mates to a home. The few chair seats that I do have, and every other surface is full already! Mostly full of textbooks and papers. Since reading about Fen Sui, I've made more of an effort to make space before anyone comes, and to keep the recliner in my bedroom and the spare wheelchair in the living room clear at all times. But when it really comes down to the underlying feeling and reality, there's no space in my apartment for anyone to feel welcome! Not even myself! Although friends have tried to help organize and rearrange it as they are usually used to doing, they don't understand that most homes are traditionally arranged for people who only sit around watching television or playing video games. I have to squeeze in storage of my textbooks and craft supplies while still having room to maneuver my wheelchair.

Meanwhile, symbolically, there's no room in my life for me neither, as the graduate school doctoral program demanded all of my thinking space twenty-four/seven. This year, I admit I don't have energy and patience to extend my remaining reserve to family and friends. And I'm sure they could feel that although I was physically present, my mind was far away analyzing and planning for the next deadline. Much as I wanted to be with my grandmother in Philadelphia there was no space for her or I at her apartment. Family members forget, same as at the university that I do need help, because I tend to push myself to be as independent as possible. This can be physically exhausting.

Chapter 15: University: Tarot Card Guidance

The Church of the Spirit had a summer workshop series on recognizing and working with spirit in daily life. There was a workshop, "Tarot as a Tool for Spiritual Unfoldment." I previously avoided tarot because I assumed tarot cards were used for fortune telling by psychics. Plus, the amount of cards in a deck seemed complicated and scary to me. It was suggested we bring a deck of Rider-Wait cards with us to the workshop.

   Dr. Kenneth James, a medium and Jungian analyst psychologist led the workshop and explained that although Spiritualists are advised to seek direct communication through a medium or personally, tarot cards can be used to enhance our connections to spirit. Using one's own intuition is best, while getting a feel for the card in your hand and the immediate message while looking at the colors and symbols on the card. He discouraged the use of tarot books for interpretation, except for perhaps one book, *Holistic Tarot: An Integrative Approach to Using Tarot for Personal Growth*. He gave a quick overview of basic meanings of the minor and major arcana as well as the suits of cups, wands, swords and pentacles. Then instructed us to silently ask a question of spirit, then to pull from our own deck three cards, and lay them out on the table in front of each of us.

Love? That's the question that came to my mind. Most of the time I don't think about love or seeking a relationship. Curious and amused, I followed Dr. James' instructions. I turned over the Overview (right side card) IX Swords, Challenge (middle card) IX Hermit, and then last the Action (left side card, reversed) IV Emperor. When I saw the Hermit card, I put my head down and sobbed a little. It's difficult to have a close relationship with people, alone up on top of a mountains by yourself. The same characteristics as a Saturday born person, a loner. The pictures on the other cards also described me very well, including my overall and current challenges. At home, I read the interpretations:

Overview: IX Swords. Lots of feelings of loss. Picture of a woman sitting, in a dark room on a bed, looking depressed. May tend to blame myself for what happened by thinking I could have prevented it. However, what happened was unavoidable and not in my control for reasons I don't understand now. True, sometimes I have a surreal feeling of being unsure of what is real or not. I have had a lot of losses of family and friends that had me feeling I could have done more, and now has me hesitant to get really close to new people.

Challenge: IX Hermit. The Hermit represents wisdom, guidance, and mentoring. I need to be open to advice from those who are wiser than me. Tend to be nonviolence, compassionate, and have gift of prophesy. Hermits take a solitary path to acquire wisdom. That's nice, I like doing artistic crafts and reading but too many solitary activities can be lonely as I tend to frequently leave other people out.

Action: IV Emperor. Represents authorities, dominance, superiority, fire yang energy, iron will in my career situations. Since I am a woman, the card may represent a father figure, which is true because it was my first impression of the man on the card. My fathers made me afraid of authority.

In the reversed position (card was upside down), indicates I need to be assertive, authoritative, and take leadership in solving the problem. In other situations, I may need to be less harsh. If in conflict, which I was at the university, I am justified in my beliefs, not to be blamed and will later achieve success. But I do long for better fairness and cooperation in higher education. Stressing over trying to survive a doctoral program didn't leave time nor energy to even think about love. Nor socializing. The author wrote that there is a possibility of overthrowing tyrants and a new world order in this lifetime. My lifetime? And soon? That would be great!

Chapter 16: University: Triquetra Spread

I did a tarot card reading regarding delays in obtaining a practicum required for clinical training. When I read the tarot books' interpretation, the insight that was already coming to me, was validated. These cards were verifying what I was already seeing or intuiting that I had a question about but wasn't sure of.

Soon afterwards, I requested a private mediumship consultation at the Church of the Spirit with Dr. Ken James. An awesome reading so accurate and filled with connection energy that I forgot to record it. Although he didn't know my question or even that I was studying to be a psychologist, the messages that he brought through from spirit described my challenges at the university.

Later, I excitedly told Dr. Ken James that in the *Holistic Tarot* book, I discovered a section on using the Triquetra spread, that is used when previous tarot card consultations indicate ongoing problems. It helps give guidance on what inner growth, changes and divine interventions are needed to improve the situation. Simply, doing the Triquetra reading also has a spiritual component of being a prayer that energetically opens the way internally and externally. The interpretation of the cards I previously pulled with my eyes closed from the tarot card deck was similar to his mediumship message for me.

Signifier Card: Queen of Swords. Note: I chose the Queen of Swords as my signifier card because in a situation at the university I needed to confront an African American teacher who seemed to make it harder for African American students. He had a history of not making clear his expectations for written assignments for all the students in the courses he taught. Perhaps he had been there too long and didn't realize he had simplified his instructions too much. Plus, as he was the teacher who interviewed me and denied my admission to the doctoral program twenty years ago, when I was up walking but a little wobbly.

This was a required diversity class that showed us mostly videos about slavery, portrayal of "negros" in the old movies, and a few videos about the other three "people of color" groups in the United States — the Native Americans, Asian Americans, and Latino Americans. Each student had to make a list of all the stereotypes we had about each of these "minority" groups. Except that we were not allowed to list stereotypes we had about white people! Yet, African American students had to list stereotypes about other African Americans.

Card 1 Hangman XII Self-Sacrifice. Card 1 is the traits to focus on first and master the qualities. Advice: Need to yield to the greater good. You are tasked with the grave responsibility of sacrificing yourself for others. The mob has hung you because they do not approve of your beliefs or what you have done. But you are right, so you must trust yourself. You have wisdom, enlightenment, divine knowledge with what is good. Your different perspective offends the masses and so they prosecute you. But you do not need their approval. Hang in there. Also you have gained spiritual growth and innate prophesizing ability. You must forgive those who have condemned you. Must make a sacrifice for the greater good of the world.

Card 2 The Emperor: IV Authority. Card 2 is the traits you can master with the support of others and must ask for help with. Advice: You must wield great authority. Be commanding. Be demanding. Be a leader. Strong leadership skills are crucial to resolving your problems.

Card 3: The High Priestess II Intuition. Card 3 points out an important trait but is the most elusive to you. Therefore you must devote extra willpower to it. Advice: You have very good intuition. Use it. In making decisions involving the issue, go with the gut instinct. Represents spirituality, psychic energy and intuition, keeper of science, wisdom and knowledge. You must activate your intuition to retrieve this powerful unconscious knowledge, memory, and ability to encode, store and retrieve your experiences. Keep sensitive information secret for now and do not tell others yet. But be prepared to advance if needed at any moment, and appear calm and serene. An accomplished woman who strives to excel in a male-dominated institution. Using the command of personal femininity over yang or male dominant setting.

Chapter 17: University: Personal Reflections on the Meaning

I'd been living the depressed mood of the Nine of Swords since the fall semester. I've since read that the Queen of Swords is able to bear her sorrows, a lot of sorrows, and courageously speaks up, so I now know this was a good choice for the signifier card. Although I've pulled the Nine of Swords twice previously and I knew that it says it's not my fault, I would still question myself. Automatic ruminating, which I had not done before, especially at night caused insomnia. Questioned myself, asking if I did the right thing or said the right things. The teacher demanded honesty yet took issue with my honest sharing and advocating in my written assignments in the diversity class. How could I have written my papers differently? Why did I stay in the program anyway and be the victim? I lost my appetite. Some days I didn't feel like doing anything. Like how much more could I endure?

Interestingly, I pulled these cards for the Triquetra spread a few days before I was to meet with the two co-teachers for the diversity class. The tarot reading helped me to cope and know what to do with the meeting. I did end up having to take a leadership role in order to keep the meeting focused on specific goals, such as asking them to give me feedback and guidelines for revising my paper in writing (The Emperor). They wanted me to share more of my personal history which I had refrained from doing in the diversity training class with my peers during group because there are some students who gossip. I would have shared some more with the teachers at the meeting, except they kept insisting on their own assumptions and I saw they would not have understood. Under pressure, I started to get whiny and then remembered the High Priestess card advice not to share my secrets, to stay calm/serene, to take the lead and be demanding.

A couple of weeks later, I received notice that I was to have remediation. I had remediation before, that held me back a year from my therapy practicum. Instead I was assigned to do clinical training in the university counseling center. I did well there, enjoyed having clients and supportive classmates and teachers, learning how to administer the MMPI, PIA, and other brief diagnostic questionnaires. My written reports were fine, versus the other teacher who sent me there for remediation after grading a previous report that had so many red ink marks that you could barely see what I typed! I quietly put it in my file drawer at home and didn't ever look at it again. What good was all those red marks without explanations of how to make corrections?

Now I am sentenced me to eight sessions of biweekly remediation. That was my punishment (Hangman card). The dreaded remediation that was every diversity student's worst fear. We trembled through each class carefully choosing each word — oral and written. Since the multicultural diversity class was psychological torture for all the students we could not imagine what remediation would be like, nor having to repeat the class!

I appealed to the two deans and was still sentenced to remediation. They assigned me to one-on-one sessions with a South Asian diversity teacher. He was nice enough, mostly giving me reflective questions to answer about my experience in the diversity class as well as, a Black older woman who used a wheelchair, while he waited for the African American teacher to tell him the reason and goals for the remediation. Halfway through we still didn't know. He stalled on asking the initial teachers because he, like the other teachers, did not agree but were afraid to confront his colleagues (hence as Dr. James' spirit message in April predicted, there would be a split).

The way the diversity class was structured and with the threat of having to repeat the class or remediation was an unjust practice that I spoke up against. Students before me should have never gone through and that no other students after me should never go through this (Hangman card). What was tricky was, I mostly just knew it was wrong, because of what one of the teacher's underlying attitude was but could not explain it easily in words (hence the tarot advice to trust my intuition anyway).

Answering the assigned questions was cathartic allowing me to get my anger out on paper. He also asked for suggestions for improvements, which he later told me was implemented into the curriculum.

Another wonderful side of this is that although I had to go through this emotional pain, Spirit provided guidance and support along the way, both from other people and with scholarly journal articles, books, and videos to share with the teachers to support my points (Card 2). The hardest was learning how to ask for help. From childhood, I'd became over independent (Queen of Swords). Now all of my childhood defense mechanisms that were no longer needed were being challenged for me to heal and let go. My core feelings of abandonment and isolation now made me desperate to be heard and acknowledged. I was not allowed to be angry and resentful as a child, or as a woman, so initially I turned the anger and fear inward onto myself as depression. Having to feel the anger and resentment now, as the Nine of Swords advised was painful, and made it difficult to forgive the teachers (Hangman card).

Much of what the teachers did was from ignorance, not knowing what to do with a student who used a wheelchair, who was also older with rich life experiences, honest, and was culturally aware. Intellectually, I could rationalize their behavior but emotionally it was hard. In previous years at the predominantly white university, I fought silently with much inner conflict trying to hold onto who I was inside. Culturally, spiritually, and as a woman I valued relationships, emotions, interdependence, and intuition. The too many left-brain competitive activities of graduate school often had me feel cut off from myself and the world. So eventually, I reached a bursting point where I had to speak up and share of my culture when appropriate. Gratefully that semester, my other teachers were very supportive and encouraged me to share. So I regained my confidence over the long process. But over proving and defending myself had become a habit that, yes it was time to let go of, and ask or demand that others take up their responsibilities in changing the educational environment.

Personally I think it was the university's strategy to protect the university from losing accreditation because they weren't supposed to be enrolling more students than there were available clinical training sites. Black and older students were less likely to get chosen. In addition, the state's lack of adequate funding closed down many of the mental health clinics and agencies in the inner cities.

When I finally got a therapy practicum in a far away suburb, there were potential clients that were allowed to refuse to have a Black therapist. Unfair because Black patients don't have the luxury of being able to choose the skin complexion color of their medical doctors, nurses or therapists since colleges make sure they don't enroll, maintain, or graduate enough Black professionals. We are not dumb. We excel in most of what we do.

***

A friend called me and said "I just pulled the Seven of Swords from the African American tarot cards deck. I'm confused. When I look at the card, I see a man throwing the swords. The African-American card interpretation is about deception."

I read the interpretation from the *Holistic Tarot* book. What caught my attention was when the Nine of Swords card is reversed which I hope is happening for me now, then I would be in the healing stage as the emotional pain from a sense of loss is decreasing. I was beginning to see the overall situation. In time, I would be starting to hope that the worst is almost over.

"Wait a minute. I thought you said Seven of Swords."

"No, I meant the Nine of Swords. The African American tarot deck shows a man with a sword on both sides and on his back as he's pulling a sword out. But I don't understand these little pictures of African Americans at all. This one shows a man chasing someone out of his store who may have stolen something."

I said, "I thought that little picture is in the left corner of the cards was to represent famous Black people."

She said, "I don't know. It may be a famous person. I don't get it."

I said, "I do. I've been living the Nine of Swords. Yesterday I was crying and depressed same as I have been for two months."

She said, "You have?"

"Yes, I have been, although I know that it says it's not my fault. I still go there and feel guilty. Last week, my therapist reminded me of that, even though I didn't say I was blaming myself. She knew. I just automatically go to question myself whether I did the right thing or said the right thing. I like the African American cards better. They fight back. Not just sit on the bed in the dark, depressed, with the window blinds closed. Even the man chasing after the other person is fighting back! Thank you very much for sharing that. You made my day!"

She said, "I did?"

I said, "Yes, you did. I don't know how the card applies to your life, but it certainly has been my life for most of 2015. Similar to with my I Ching and solstice readings. I rarely know how the readings will play out. I don't know what they mean until later."

The next day I called my sister on my cell phone, while I was in the paratransit van on my way to the university. I said, "Remember I got the Queen of Swords last year at the beginning of 2015. I didn't know what it meant at the time. Now after rereading it this week I get it. She's a bad ass queen. She is able to bear her sorrows."

She said "What?"

I said, "All in all I feel better this morning. I have more energy. But the worry and instant replay like scratched records had crept in from time to time."

After I hung up the phone, I felt a tap on my shoulder. The young man's tap, sitting in the seat behind me in the van, broke through my thoughts.

"You'll be all right."

I wholeheartedly told him, "Thank you. That means a lot to me."

He could feel my worry. He understood.

Chapter 18: University: The Squeaky Wheel

Later in the day when I met with the assistant clinical training director, I found myself getting agitated. I had told myself I would be calm as I gently told him, "People are all just trying to stay afloat. Some practicum supervisors are worried that they won't be able to give me enough hours. They suggested that renewing my CRC or other counseling license may help."

He said, "So they can bill insurances."

I nodded as I continued, "My classmates have therapy practicums in the northern or far west suburbs because they have cars. I don't have transportation. I have to look at reality for what it is. I started asking for help last year and I'm asking again now, because we need to come up with strategies on how to do this. I can't do this by myself, although I'm sure tried. You saw me on Tuesday and commented on how bundled up I was, and asked me about the big bag of salt I was carrying for melting the ice. Now I have to carry a shovel and an ice pick with me. No one has shoveled out the bus stops. I talked to the security guards here at the entrance to the building leasing our university. One of the security guards told me, "It's the city's job to shovel the outer sidewalks."

Perhaps they are protesting because the mayor raised the property taxes. In all the years that I've been coming here, they've shoveled the sidewalks. To get on the bus to get here, I had to make a way through the hardened snow. This is my reality, as is with other people who have disabilities. I have friends neglected in nursing homes because the governor is holding back the budget and hasn't paid Medicaid bills in almost two years. The governor before him delayed payments six months out. Since 2008, with the Great Recession people lost their jobs and/or health insurance coverage. Therefore, a lot of local community mental health centers and hospitals were forced to close. So where am I to get my clinical training?"

The assistant clinical director of training's face was without smiles this whole time that I'm talking. None of his usual jokes or inserting music album lyrics and release dates. This made me angry because I felt he was still trying to push me to do more to get a practicum, as if I wasn't doing enough. I surprised myself and said while raising my voice a little, "I've been here too long. I'm starting to feel like a child gone wild and crazy."

I meant to say, "I feel like a neglected child that is left to run wild."

What I didn't know, as he walked me across the hall to fill out some forms, is that the new administrative assistant hadn't sent notices to my personal emails with updates to keep me informed of the practicum process due dates and forms. This was January, one important form was due back in October. She might have sent it to my campus email, but I was probably buried too deep in class assignments, and partially immobilized with depression and emotional pain from the diversity class and having to do an unfair remediation.

The next week it snowed again. From home, I called the management company office requesting that they shovel. The person who answered the phone said, "Another person in another department handles that. And he doesn't get in until 8:30 AM."

I gave her my name, phone number and emphasized that I use a wheelchair. A few minutes later, on the website I saw the contact emails for the property manager, so I wrote him the following:

"Will you see that the sidewalks are shoveled all the way out to the curb? For those of us that use wheelchairs, walkers, canes, etc. we need to be able to get out from vehicles onto the sidewalks. And the buses and special paratransit vans need to be able to let down the ramp flat onto the sidewalk. The area around the bus shelter needs to have a clear wide path."

As an afterthought, I ccd the assistant clinical training director, who responded immediately. He forwarded the email to the student services department. When I arrived to school at 10:30 AM every inch of the sidewalk was cleared along with the entire plaza area, which at 12 degrees air temperature no one would be sitting outside anyway. However hundreds of people cross the plaza to get to the main entrance of the building because the Metra Millennium station is located in the lower levels. To say I was immensely impressed is an understatement.

Unfortunately, the path to getting me an internship was not cleared as fast. In fact, even with some faculty teachers trying to help from behind the scenes, others added more storms and obstacles. I was on my own, as most staff gave up trying because the few usual avenues they attempted went nowhere. The problem is that often you don't find out that your request didn't go anywhere until weeks later! Welcome to what the world is like for people with disabilities.

An abrupt realization came to me, I would have to constantly tell everyone what using a wheelchair and otherwise having a disability is like. As other people with disabilities will testify, we explain but people conveniently forget. Every moment would have to be a "teachable moment." My therapist introduced me to the terms "teachable moments" and "picking one's battles." However, all the burden becomes on me to decide when it is a teachable moment, and when it is a battle worth fighting at that particular moment. All the consequences are also all on me for whatever of these decisions I make. Doesn't the power differential matter with me being the student, and them being the teachers who decide my grades and my fate based on how much I cooperate and don't make waves?

Therefore, should I have been the "squeaky wheel" sooner as my academic advisor told me.

He told me to, "You have to bug the training department every two weeks because it's the squeaky wheel that gets results."

What was I to do when they had me bogged down with irrelevant stupid aggravations that took up most of my time? When the training department staff changed almost every year? Yet, the deans were the same. And they always ask, "How may I help you?" Really?

I did go to them again and again, but as with customer service phone calls, their replies and recommendations are prepared scripts that they tell to everyone. Or put you on hold, sometimes indefinitely, so after a while you just hang up. Somehow, even in person they see, but don't see that I am in front of them in a wheelchair. Especially when upon arrival, they tell me, "Have a seat, I'll be with you in a minute."

Thus, if I didn't squeak enough it was my fault? I understand the concrete barriers such as stairs and walls, but I don't know if I'll ever understand the human attitudinal barriers.

After a while, I couldn't care about graduate school anymore. Certainly not to put all my energies into it. In order to survive, I began to develop my interests and sense of belonging elsewhere. I submerged myself into Black community activities, developed my spiritual abilities, and designed knitted winter accessories.

The knitting served two purposes for me: one) a sense of accomplishment in doing something right, contrary to the University making me feel "all wrong" with their unpredictable expectations, and two) by making complicated knitting patterns my mind was occupied in a positive way instead of being obsessed twenty-four seven with the constant replays of what the teachers said, or what I could've said, or what I did say and then regretted.

Did I even want to be a psychologist when my teachers treated students and each other in such uncaring ways? After all, aren't psychologists supposed to study and understand human behavior so as to empathetically help others? Would I be pressured just to graduate or have a job in this profession to behave the same way? Do we ignore the realities of everyday life and pretend we are safe as long as we are high up inside the ivory tower of academia? I refuse to numb myself and go back to being a zombie, alive but a walking dead inside. Almost 30 years ago when my abusive husband took almost everything away from me: my family, friends, job, home and then when my cupboards and bank account were bare he moved on. On the verge of losing my soul too, I vowed then not to let anyone try to steal my soul. The shock of this memory and its similarity to the abusive situation at the university woke me up to my aliveness. Being alive meant being awakened to the painful truth of what was happening around me and to me.

Chapter 19: What if There is a Fire?

We were in a staffing meeting, on the fourth floor, when the alarms sounded. I listened for the number of bells to try to determine what type of danger or drill. Our supervisor was leading the staff meeting and asked us which alarm it was. He said, "Fire alarm. Do you know what to do?"

He then directed us to evacuate. I stopped my wheelchair at the entrance to the main stairs, watching everyone go down the stairs except the supervisor and me.

"Where is the fire marshal?" I asked.

"Do you know what to do?"

I started to say, 'In all the drills I've been in I was told to wait in my wheelchair at the top of the stairs.'

Previously, in preparation for a possible fire in my apartment building, I called 311 and asked what to do. They didn't know, instead recommended I call my local fire department. For a month, I searched for their number that used to always be in the front of the large white and yellow phone books, now not even online. Finally I asked some firemen at the Access Chicago Disability Expo at Navy Pier and they gave me a card with a fire department number on it. I called and she told me, "The firemen know where your apartment is, just stay there and they will come and get you."

I asked, "What if I'm visiting in another apartment, or in another area of the building?"

She repeated, "The fireman will know what to do."

While I was thinking about an answer for my supervisor, two male staff members appeared beside me. They were both tall and well-built. One older and stocky, the other young. The young one said he was an EMT. I asked him, "Then you know how to do the fireman's carry?"

He said, "Yes."

"With two people? It's easier with two people."

He told the older man to reach under me with first one arm and then the other, he did the same as they lifted me from my wheelchair. They slowly carried me down the stairs. There was heavy smoke on the second floor. We continued down the stairs with my knees up and gaped open, my back leaning backwards. I didn't feel like the men would drop me, it was just uncomfortable. Another man came and supported my back. When we got to the lobby they asked for a chair and sat me down on it. When the fireman came down to give the "all clear," one of the staff told me someone would bring my wheelchair down. From the lobby I saw the elevator door open and someone was calling my name, almost cussing as he struggled to steer the wheelchair to turn it in the direction he wanted, to get it out of the elevator doorway. I yelled, "Use two fingers. Just two fingers! Use a gentle touch!"

I was glad it was my old wheelchair. The older man didn't say anything much throughout our ordeal. I wondered if he thought I was being ungrateful and rude when I had asked earlier where the floor marshal was. And later commented that we took too long to get out of the building. We would have gotten burned up if it was a real fire. The EMT then said if it had been a real fire, he would have just slung me over his shoulder. I walked sideways from the chair to my power wheelchair with them holding me under my arms on both sides.

Later, the administrative assistant told me she called and looked for men to come and get me down the stairs. I expressed my gratitude. Other staff during the following week approached me and told me they were glad someone brought me downstairs, and others said they would have carried me down themselves. I felt loved and cared for by these responses.

It was an unsettling feeling to have almost everyone leave me on the fourth floor. I know it was a minor fire. But still! So much for the previous instructions I received in the Michigan Plaza building fire drill, where I had to wait at the top of the stairs for what was described to me, would be a soon to come, young, handsome, muscular firefighter. It was just in our imaginations. The drill was over soon, and no one had to carry me down thirteen flights of stairs of a downtown high-rise building. It's difficult emotionally to get past memories of September 11, 2001 and stories of people in wheelchairs left behind or a few heroically carried down.

When I arrived home that evening, I checked YouTube videos and saw that the "fireman's carry" is when the victim is slung over a fireman's shoulder. Years ago, one of my friends invited me to her house for Thanksgiving. She and a woman neighbor carried me very smoothly up and down her front stairs. The carry technique that they used is the "two person lift." According to the video, even a victim that's lying on the floor can be assisted into a standing position, to then sit on the two rescuers' linked arms. This would have given me a more secure ride.

Asking my apartment building manager and a security guard about their procedure for a fire wasn't much better. They laughed and said, "There are sprinklers in each apartment. If there were a fire, then there would be water flooding everywhere. You don't have to worry."

Well, I could take some consolation that maybe I wouldn't get burned up in the fire, but the water from the sprinklers would short out the electrical circuits on my wheelchair.

Chapter 20: Elevators Out

It happened. Time to go home and the elevators that were working two hours earlier, decided to stop working again. One was stuck in the basement and the other on the third floor. Emily did all the usual tricks to try to get the elevators to move. She went down to the third floor and pushed and pulled on the elevator door to get the door to close. It wouldn't budge.

My phone rang, "Ms Mateen, your ride is outside. They will only wait five minutes."

"Give me time to get downstairs. I'm on the fifth floor."

"We can only give you five minutes."

"They are 35 minutes late, and they can't wait five minutes for me! I've waited three hours or more for them on other days."

"Tell them to wait for you! Tell them we've got to have time to get down the stairs. We will need more than five minutes."

Emily led the way to the stairwell.

"We need to do the firemen carry. Two people can do it."

"I can't do all that. We'll help you. Josh you get in the front of her. I'll get in back of you on the side. Dr. Mateen, you hold onto the railing here. Come on we'll help you."

As I stood there, in my mind I'm starting to panic. What if this was a fire? Here we go again. People assume that since I can walk some that I can go up and down stairs. Even when I explain to my family and friends they still don't understand.

This is why previously I've hid that I could stand up and walk. Even at the expense of my own self-humiliation as I allowed people to do for me what I could do for myself. Obviously, I've made a mistake that could one day cost my life, just so that I could be myself, my authentic self. People could respect me for being me, not a wheelchair.

A therapist coworker used a walker for walking long distances. However at the clinic she would go without her walker to get her clients from the waiting room. From then on, I did the same. I sat in a regular chair after parking my wheelchair in a corner of the large office room. I got better respect from other coworkers and clients. Although I would suffer after walking too much during the day, with awful pain in my back, and from my knees down to my toes at night, I was determined to graduate. But this is so wrong! Plenty people can't get up and walk, and like me they can do plenty more, and are very intelligent.

***

Memories of when I allowed well-meaning family members to convince me to go up and downstairs anyway. They were harder to get it in their heads that I couldn't do stairs because family are the ones who have seen me walk the most in houses where floors are flat and smooth. They too have told me, "You can do it. We'll help you get up the stairs."

And they did. However, my rotator cuff in my left shoulder was severely injured although two people were lifting and moving my legs up the stairs, because I was literally pulling myself along the side railings. People don't know that the same problem with the muscles in my legs being partially paralyzed, also happened to my upper arms. That was in an emergency situation, so I did it. Another time I didn't want to get embarrassed, or embarrass my sister and brother, or delay the small crowd of people waiting, and thought I was stronger, so I allowed my brother to intimidate me into climbing the stairs. I get severe back pain each time I try, going downstairs too, that lasts for days afterwards. Later my brother told me, with his head down and a sad look in his eyes that he had to struggle to hold my back up from behind. It was then that I understood while I could move my legs better, I lacked core upper body strength control to hold myself upright.

"Let's go, Dr. Mateen. They are going to leave you."

I took one shaky step down. This was another emergency situation. Whatever has needed to be done I've done it. Pushed myself to just do it in the moment. Looking down the steep stairs to the landing, I remember thinking many times in the past that in an emergency my legs would just automatically work. I've been practicing walking longer and longer at the office and walking heel-to-toe forward instead of sideways. At home doing my Qigong exercises, which to my surprise was strengthening my core, so that for example I have been able to stand longer at my kitchen sink washing and rinsing dishes with less sharp pains in my upper back. I still had to pace myself because having my hands in moderately warm water would make all of my muscles weak. Same if the room was too hot or too cold. Here we were standing at the top of the stairs in a cold hallway on the fifth floor. It was much shorter flights of stairs that I tried to navigate years ago. How could I do five or more flights of stairs going down?

I got my answer for sure, as I decided not to do it, I turned and struggled to lift my leg up the one step. We walked the short hallway back into the office.

A coworker looking out the window said, "The van pulled off already."

The rest of my coworkers gathered around me in the large office waiting room. Everyone talking all at once, in a dazed atmosphere of confusion. We put our heads together to come up with solutions.

I felt helpless. None of the solutions seem to make sense. They've waited with me before, as Pace paratransit would almost strand me if I hadn't been able to keep calling Pace on my cell phone. Learned the hard way that if I didn't schedule my ride home before 3:00 PM, the drivers could be three or more hours late to get me from the office, not to mention the other two hours ride to my home as they picked up and dropped off and picked up and dropped off other passengers along the way. Drivers have "no showed me" gone off leaving me, without giving me the courtesy call to let me know they were there and give me time to come down from the fifth floor. Dispatch would then say they didn't have any rides available for several hours.

If someone else gave me a ride home, I would have to leave my wheelchair at the office. Up until now, I haven't had to do that. I've been practicing my walking just in case, thinking maybe it would be okay if I had to. But why did it have to happen on Wednesday? The office was closed on Thursdays. On a hybrid schedule, I wasn't due back to work until Monday. How would I get to the grocery store or other places outside to take care of business? Even if I ordered groceries, ever since the COVID pandemic whoever delivers food leaves the bags downstairs in the lobby. They are doing construction on the first floor of my building. Management staff is rarely in the office.

But I still had to get downstairs to go home. Calling the fire department was a suggestion. But what if the firemen came right away, since the firehouse was only a few blocks away? Still didn't know how long I would have to wait for a ride home. Would the firemen carry my over 300 pound wheelchair down five flights of stairs? If not, was the new sidewalk to my building flat enough so I could walk across, to the elevators, and to my apartment when I got there?

So many questions and possibilities. Instead of continuing to guess, I decided to call and find out what our options were with the fire department.

I called 311 because this was a non-emergency call. No one answered. It was 4:30 in the afternoon the staff probably went home. So I called 911 immediately saying, "This is a non-emergency call. The elevators are not working. I need help getting downstairs."

"To where?"

Puzzled, I said, "Downstairs to the first floor."

"We only take people downstairs to go to medical appointments."

This I didn't understand. Many of my friends who use wheelchairs have fallen in their homes, and often called the fire department to help them get off the floor and positioned back into their wheelchair or bed. I've never had to call the fire department for help before. So I didn't know their procedures.

A coworker grabbed my phone and said loudly, "She uses a wheelchair. The elevators are not working. She needs to get down to the first floor. The first floor!"

The call-taker transferred the call. A deep husky voice said, "Have the door open for us."

Neither one of them allowed me to explain or get more information from them. So much for that idea. Within ten minutes, my phone rang, "We're downstairs. The doors are locked, how do we get in?"

Two firemen arrived with their special seat. It reminded me of the ultrathin transport aisle chairs used on airplanes. I'm thin, but I can't imagine how anyone bigger than I am, fits on the seat and be comfortable. The firemen looked at me, and looked at my motorized wheelchair, scratched their heads and then said, "No, we can't carry that down."

One fireman came by me, asking me my name and birthdate. If my coworkers didn't know my age, now they do. "How do you spell it" as he tried to write it on his blue exam gloves. I said, "Here give me the pen. It will be easier for me to just write it."

Unknown to me, outside in the hallway were several other firemen trying to fix the elevator. We heard a loud, "Hurray." It would be great if they have the elevators fixed and this saga over with. But then disappointment as the elevator still didn't move.

To my relief, four fireman helped carry me down the stairs. Two firemen in front holding handles on each side and two firemen in the back holding handles on each side of the special seat. As I waited while they position themselves, I told myself not to think about the times that I've almost been dropped. Trusting that it will be fine since there were now four men carrying me instead of one or two. They only rested very briefly when setting the chair down on each landing to make the turn to go down the next flight of stairs. They didn't moan and groan. We were downstairs quickly.

The same fireman stayed by my side the whole time. This was comforting. In the building entrance lobby downstairs, near tears I told him, "I'm remembering all the times I didn't have the patience to wait for in line for slow crowded elevators. I would simply run up the stairs two steps at a time as if it was no thing!"

I didn't realize how shook up I was until I tried to do simple things while sitting downstairs waiting for a ride home. Like recalling people's names and forgetting I already had other information in my phone but asking others. It was difficult for me to concentrate. Grateful that my boss sat next to me, and other coworkers stayed past their usual work hours. It would be days later, after the shock gradually were off, that I realize how traumatic, re-traumatizing the whole event was. How terrifying having to totally depend on others, was triggering for me. I still didn't know how to fully trust and accept help.

Hadn't even remembered that I hadn't taken my muscle spasm medicine baclofen since very early in the morning. I thought my legs were stiff as I walked on the sidewalk to the car because I had been sitting for an hour waiting in the cold hallway lobby.

And of course, during the night my mind kept going over what happened. Maybe all of this happened because a couple years ago I prayed for complete healing. Heaven graciously conspired to gradually have me without my wheelchairs. My current power chair needs new batteries, and the armrest is dangling when it should be giving my left arm and shoulder support thus reducing shoulder pain. Actually it's time for a whole new wheelchair but may be too expensive for me to afford. Do I even want a $30,000 wheelchair if I'm being shown that I may not need it anymore?

My portable fold-up, fit in the trunk of a car travel electric wheelchair got broken during the move while my apartment was been remodeled. Now I don't have a backup wheelchair. The movers left boxes stacked everywhere so I couldn't use a wheelchair in my apartment anyway. Therefore I had to do more walking.

Plus, recently I've had nightmares of unconsciously walking away from my wheelchair at large conference events, and then having to walk to find where I left it hours later when it was time for me to go home. Other nightmares of being on public city buses and being distracted while talking to someone else. Jumping off the bus at an unknown bus stop, only realizing later after the bus pulled off that I left my wheelchair with my jacket, purse, everything. Dream interpretation books indicate wallets and purses symbolize personal identity.

Since the COVID pandemic, we've all had ongoing multiple crises which kind of force us to let go of our old identities, and ways of thinking and doing. I've certainly changed a lot so I was hoping that leaving behind my wheelchair was just symbolic. Just in case this becomes real, I started strapping my heavy fanny pack to my waist.

Here in the daytime, I actually walked away from my wheelchair. It was no longer a just a dream. Left it at the office. Calmly not thinking about how people have broken my wheelchairs in the past. I had to fully trust that all would be well. Because yes my wheelchair has become an almost invisible extension of myself. Very much a part of my identity after twenty years.

PART THREE: HEALING

Chapter 21: Other Aspects of Auset

During the Ausar Auset Society Church's meditations to achieve a goal, including spiritual growth goals during the solstices, we were instructed to start with Auset at the bottom of the Tree of Life and go up, one-by-one for each deity to Ausar near the top. Doing the Auset meditations, with seeing ourselves being held and breastfed by Mother, was intended to take us back to memories that our habits and childhood conditioning originated from. Allowing the memories to surface, along with the feelings to help us release and heal the past, so we could move forward in our lives.

Until reviewing my life now, as I write this second book, it hadn't occurred to me that my multiple years of receiving counseling and psychotherapy was probably a continuation of the Auset healing that began in Zimbabwe. There they nurtured and cared for me similar to how families determine every need and give instructions to a young child. In a foreign country, not knowing the language nor culture, what else could I do? Heaven knew that otherwise I would have resisted this care, and I did resist when I returned to the United States and became ill and unemployed.

Special Prayers and Miracles from Great Mother Auset Yemeja Azna

I learned of the power of Great Mother Azna in 2004, when I was reading Silvia Browne's books about being a psychic medium, interpreting dreams, where she vaguely mentioned choosing from a list of archetype type categories that she titles "life themes" that we each agreed to before we are born. I wanted to know more about the life themes and came upon her book, *Mother God: The Feminine Principle to Our Creator*.

Although I knew about the mother deity personas of Auset and Yemeja since 1991, and did rituals with Auset's mantras and meditations, somehow I had not thought to pray to Her directly. When you think about it, unless you had an abusive mother, more often you went to your mother when you wanted something or when you were in trouble. Your father was more likely to say, "No." Or be too busy. There are many stories about people when they were about to die called out to their mothers first and then to God. So why not me?

I followed the instructions in the book, *Mother God*, for petitioning Great Mother Azna to say aloud specifically what I wanted, including a timeframe of when, then ask for a sign. Answers can be subtle and come from different sources such as new ideas and opportunities. Great Mother Azna tends to send flowers to acknowledge that She heard your prayers. The flowers She sent me were red geraniums, and a small houseplant of tiny red roses. Usually soon afterwards your wish is granted. In brief relaxation meditations, She shows me a garden of red roses in bright, vivid colors, while giving me a warm feeling of peace and love. Later that day I receive an answer to my prayers. But sometimes it takes much longer. Long enough for me to have forgotten my request and when I made it.

I reserve special tough requests for Great Mother. Simply my choice, She fixes small problems too, but since She is known for granting miracles, miracles is what I ask for. I talk to Her aloud. I prayed a lot to Great Mother while trying to survive the Supportive Living situation. Eventually, of course, I got brave enough to want full healing.

When I got tired of having to wear three different incontinence products — a diaper, pull-up, and thick pad all together, and these still weren't enough to hold my urine — I cried out to Great Mother for help. I had to change them at least six times a day when I was away from home. Incontinence supply companies shipped a month's worth of supplies in large boxes that filled my closet, lower bookshelves, nightstand, behind and underneath my bed. Space where I could have put my clothes and craft items. I had no bladder control, especially when I was too cold or too hot. Could not drink carbonated sodas or coffee without the floodgates opening, peeing non-stop. Honestly, I don't know how other people get away with drinking that stuff all day. The physical therapist had me doing Kegel exercises, which she applauded since I did them well, yet became disappointed because when I was trying to get up from the physical therapy mat, out came my urine. The problem was during changing positions from lying or sitting to standing is my brain couldn't tell my legs what to do and my bladder perineum muscles how to tightly close, and do both at the same time. Medically I shouldn't have been able to move my legs at all to transfer to the wheelchair, or to walk. I had to mentally will my legs to move.

First, Great Mother made me allergic to the absorbent gel inside the pads causing me to break out in rashes and blisters. Then I stopped urinating as frequently at night, noticing my bed would be dry in the morning. With time, I was making it to the toilet on time without even a dribble. The only time I had accidents was when I was like a kid that doesn't want to stop whatever I was doing.

The next miracle I asked of Great Mother was to not have to use a ventilator at night to breath. My neurologist diagnosed me with both central sleep apnea and obstructive sleep apnea. Central sleep apnea is when the brain forgets to tell the diaphragm breathing muscles to breathe. I was gasping for air whenever I started to nod off to sleep and through the night. So instead of a continuous positive air pressure (CPAP) machine for snoring, I had a variable positive air pressure (VPAP) machine that was set at a specified rate and rhythm to breath for me whenever I stopped breathing. During the Great Recession's early years many companies closed, including respiratory supply companies. In addition, some specialists at hospitals stopped taking patients who had Medicare insurance. My primary care doctor did what she could to get me supplies, however without respiratory therapists and pulmonologists who specialized in neuromuscular diseases, there was no one to reset my VPAP machine as my condition changed. If I gained or lost weight the mask no longer fits, and neither did the rhythm match my breathing rate anymore. It was as if I was fighting against the machine plus the cold air hurting my nose and the back of my throat was incredibly painful. So gradually, I ditched using the VPAP machine. And I did alright without it.

It took years for me to get brave enough to ask Great Mother for my arms and legs to be healed. This would mean a huge change in lifestyle and thinking. All of my requests were answered gradually over time. When the airline broke the back of my wheelchair, severe back pain kept me from sitting in it for long periods, so I had to get up and move to relieve the pain. My apartment kitchen was too small to turn my wheelchair around in, so I had to stand and hold on to the kitchen counter. Initially I was tired and dizzy but gradually could stand longer and longer enough to prepare meals. Gradually my back and knees didn't hurt so much during the day from trying to walk, and took less revenge at night. I had less stomach troubles with constipation, as being upright allowed gravity and exercise to aid proper digestion. One day, I will return for another bone density test that will show my bones are healthier too.

Chapter 22: Be Careful What You Ask For

There is a saying, "be careful what you ask for because you just might get it!" Let me tell you the story of a friend who been praying and praying, including doing rituals to Osun to lose weight. Soon afterwards, her rent was raised. Police put a boot lock on the wheel of her car because of her daughter's old unpaid parking tickets. This meant she had to walk to the grocery store three blocks away and walk to the bus stops, instead of drive. Then her credit card accounts were closed, which stopped her from using her credit cards to eat out or order restaurant home deliveries. She was angry, feeling unfairly inconvenienced, and got mad at God because she believed that it must be evil things happening to her! Hey, her prayers were answered. Quick, fast and in a hurry. What more did she want?

We get comfortable in our routines, make resolutions to change but excuses and events get in the way, and/or we often don't know what is truly involved in order for our prayers to be answered. So our spirit guides force the issue by giving us real life experiences to teach us what we need to know in order to have what we want. Perhaps they get tired of us nagging them and say, "Here, here take it! Are you really sure that's what you want?"

Some of us don't know when we are receiving a gift or will try to give it back. Ungrateful, we would rather return to old routines and continued crises.

Prayers are answered, but sometimes it may not seem like it because although the Bible says, "ask and you shall receive," people don't always listen and follow guidance given to them from spirit. Results may be delayed because a person is not using their gifts and talents the person was born with and are not on their own destiny path. Instead, they are trying to follow someone else's expectations. When you are on your own destiny path, life flows synchronistically with all the items and people available to help you.

Another important reason prayers may not seem to be answered, is when you are being prepared to be able to receive, or to carry out the duties of the role or job you were praying for. You want to get married or find the ideal companion. But do you even know what love, or a healthy relationship is? Most people don't know what love is, because we weren't taught in our families, schools, nor communities. Learning love is a process that occurs over a lifetime. Each encounter with another person or being, is an opportunity to accept and learn about love. Sometimes we have to experience what love is not, in order to desire and learn what real love is. The same with careers and personal talents.

We have choices, when we are at a crossroads. I like to call these situations "life detours" and use the analogy of being on a highway. With ongoing construction at different times of our lives, we are forced to or have the opportunity to take a different road. You may discover that this different side-road is even faster. You might find what you have been needing or wanting along the way. You meet people who may share stories, information and directions that provide answers or a different way of relating. Perhaps you will experience new beauty and fun.

Or you may come to a dead-end road and have to figure out how to turn around, and get back on your journey. Some people choose to stay on the highway with the construction or poor road conditions because either other options were not available, or they were determined to take risks, or they were half asleep and missed the warning signs. Sometimes they may end up stuck in a rut, but eventually get out. This may seem to take some extra frustrating time, but when you look back on your life years later, you'll see you were still traveling in the direction of your initial personal goals or destination. Each detour scenario gives you a different perspective on your life. Therefore acquiring more strength, knowledge, and self-esteem along with your new abilities to now understand and accept your prayers being answered.

Overtime I added to my aligning my hara line morning prayer ritual. After reading, *Mystical Traveler,* also by Silvia Browne, I say, 'I align my I Am' with divine rays and allow divine rays to flow through my rays. I also allow Great Mother's rays to flow through my rays." To this I later added, "I remember, love, respect, and honor you Great Mother. As above, so below, restoring balance to the world. Bringing back true love, peace, harmony, and unity. I'm open to assisting, and experiencing you Great Mother, the yin in all that is. Including experiencing the yin in those who have chosen male or yang energy bodies. Bringing back our acceptance of our emotions which is our connection to all that is as One. My heart is opened to being love, experiencing love, learning love, sharing as well as receiving true love. I ask that all that is — everywhere — has plenty of safe and healthy food, safe and healthy resources, and most importantly safe and healthy environments filled with divine true love, peace, harmony and unity within each of us and within all that is."

When I do this morning prayer, my whole day flows smoothly with love and caring, as other people also offer their presence or help.

Our emotions and intuition are the foundation of healthy relationships as we feel and know what our loved ones and others are feeling and thinking. There was a time, before colonization when it was not possible to lie to ourselves or to others. We were energetically connected to each other as One and telepathy was natural. Emotions give us the passionate energy to follow through on creative ideas, to fulfill our true potential individually and most importantly together as a universe. Father God has been hiding away from us for a long time, afraid of His emotions and true unconditional loving intimate relationships, He pushed Mother God and Her emotions away. Well, She now has the courage to step forth and make Her presence known. Restoring balance to the world.

Chapter 23: Mother Mary in Africa

What further had me fall completely in love with Great Mother was reading the book, *Our Lady of Kibeho: Mary Speaks to the World from the Heart of Africa.* Mother Mary, also known as the Virgin Mary, appeared as spirit apparitions that only a few Catholic school children could see. She was real to them. They would spontaneously go into trance with their eyes looking upwards and relay Mother Mary's messages. Most of the messages were given through songs that were about the need to repent, love and care for each other. Starting months apart, this happened first to one of the girls and then later another girl. The school, church, and other officials didn't believe them, and initially bullied and punished the girls. However, as word got out the children drew crowds of people who witnessed the holy visitations and experienced the overwhelming peace, joy, love and miracles as the public also received healing of their illnesses or injuries, and given whatever else they asked for. All Mother Mary required was that they pray with a rosary, and most importantly love each other, forgive themselves and their neighbors by not holding even a tiny bit of animosity in their hearts. Villagers fed and cared for those who made the pilgrimage from other cities and countries. The messages and miracles continued for several years during the 12 years before the genocide in Rwanda. The genocide happened because some people didn't heed Mother Mary's patient warnings and later very descriptive visions of pools of blood warnings of what could happen, if they did not purge their hearts of malice.

In her later book, *Left to Tell,* Immaculee Ilibagiza tells stories of surviving the actual genocide. It was her silent prayers to Mother Mary that saved her. The intense energy of love, along with her silent prayers confused the would-be killers, because they were expecting her to be afraid. It was as if she temporally became invisible to them. Thereafter, Mother Mary led Immaculee to places of safety, comforted her in the loss of her family, helped her form new relationships and careers.

One Sunday, as I meditated with Great Mother at the Church of the Spirit, beyond my half closed eyes I saw a large light blue glow in the middle of the front of the church. Later during the service, I noticed many women were wearing turquoise blue that day. I wondered if there were and are many other sightings of the Mother, and why She was reminding me of Her presence so often and strongly. What message is She needing to get through our thick heads?

In my brief exposure to Christianity as a child, in the Bible and multiple readings of the Quran although there is the story of the Virgin Mary giving birth to Jesus, afterwards the emphasis is only on his life, and his ability to perform miracles. His mother's ability to manifest miracles was omitted. He acquired some awesome genes and had a great role-model. People prayed to him and the Father, but I hadn't heard of people praying to the Virgin Mary. I knew Catholics had Saints and that there were many statues of the Virgin Mary, but I have not studied Catholicism.

Over the centuries, Mother Mary appeared to many children and people who did not know of her or had no religious exposure at all. She brings warnings and comfort. Unfortunately, leaders who wanted to keep "power," publicly accused the children of lying so that wars and other wrongdoing could continue. I believe Immaculee Ilibagiza's incredible stories are true because I witnessed Great Mother's miracles in my own life before I read her books. I'm very grateful for Great Mother healing me.

Chapter 24: Wisdom Gained

Having a disability taught me a lot. It helped me think outside of the box because I had to compensate and solve problems and tasks in a completely different way than I had learned coming up, from most people I knew. If I don't try new ways now, I would be like many of my friends with disabilities stuck in their homes. And I was determined not to go into a nursing home.

The reason I can walk at all is because I walk sideways, like a crab. I moved my legs forward stiffly from my hips, since I have difficulty lifting my knees to pull up the rest of my lower legs. Proximal weakness, meaning the quadriceps muscles in my thighs struggled do their job. For me, trying to walk forward had me tripping over my own feet, almost falling. I catch myself by jerking upright hurting my back. Walking devices — such as canes and walkers — are made for people to walk forward like everybody else. Well, me being different shouldn't be a surprise. What's beautiful is that I did teach myself to walk. Although sideways, it's walking! I can get across a room quickly, so quickly that people don't notice that I'm walking sideways. Walking backwards is also easier, except I can't see where I'm going. If my head could turn 360 degrees, then I'd be alright!

In the rest of my life I've also learned to compensate, adapt, and be okay with doing things very different than other people.

What does it matter how a task is done as long as the goal is accomplished?

You May be Wondering . . .

What do I believe in? Over my lifetime, I've noticed it doesn't matter what belief or religion I've explored, the universe still provides for me with guidance and abundance. Has shown me miracles in the midst of crises, therefore ever increasing my faith. Faith may be the key to healing — faith that life can be better. Of course I've also done my part to improve and maintain my health. It makes better sense to be aware of your body, mind and spirit as well as the effect of the environment. What does your body need in order to be in balanced harmony? What has illnesses and crises taught you, that has given you a better quality of life with increasing inner satisfaction?

Much of what we learn in life is from experience. In regards to religions, holy books, and rules, I'm gaining a deeper understanding of their initial intent and meaning. The natural innocence of young children, indigenous and gnostic beliefs before the major religions forced dominance over truth and peace. Personally, I prefer to say, Great Mystery, Great Spirit, Pure Love, and or maybe Infinite Intelligence within all instead of "God" because no one knows for sure how the universe functions. So why argue? We could all do our part as humans co-creators to have healthy and safe environments for all.

Decisions Decisions

Getting Answers to Life's Challenges

VOLUME 4

FULFILLING A DESTINY

Haneefa Mateen

Contents

Introduction	343
Chapter 1: Destiny Progress	344
Chapter 2: Rethinking Education	352
Chapter 3: A Difficult to Understand Spiritual Reading:	357
Chapter 4: Oshun's Blessings	363
Chapter 5: Sekert (Oya's) Influences on My Destiny	368
Chapter 6: Healing the Past	373
Chapter 7: The Beautiful Ninety-Nine Names of Allah: Wazifa Card Set	376
Chapter 8: Facing Death and Loss	390
Chapter 9: A Friend Responds Through a Medium Message	395
Chapter 10: Ochosi Revisited	405
Chapter 11: Getting Rid of Clutter	415

Chapter 12: Spiritual Transformation	420
Chapter 13: Career Path	424
Chapter 14: Another Tough Assignment	431
Chapter 15: Applying Accumulated Wisdom to How I Provide Psychotherapy	436
Chapter 16: Work on What Has Been Spoiled	440
Conclusion	443
Books and Articles	445
Author's Bio	451

Introduction

By the end of this book, hopefully we will have both gained wisdom about the meaning of a long life.

With time I understood the difference between being spiritual and being religious. Of course like other people, I use both. Religion, as I've learned prayers and rituals from different religions and cultures. Spirituality is the peace, calm, satisfaction, sense of purpose and connection to self and the universe. Religion is the beliefs, practices, rules and rituals often taught to us by society that we do together with other people that is often done at a place of worship.

Religions and holy scriptures threaten human beings with damnation and going to hell for our transgressions, yet doesn't tell or show us <u>how</u> to stay out of hell. Just, "don't do this or don't do that," with contradictory messages of "we were born in sin," "confess and you'll be forgiven," and don't let the devil tempt you." To be honest, I've tried and tried to understand the Bible and Quran translated into old English, with stories I can't relate to our current days and times. Religious leaders arguing over the meanings.

The use of oracles and other forms of divination can show each of us, as well as our communities how to stay out of unnecessary hell in both this life (and the next). This is what I learned.

Chapter 1: Destiny Progress

After saying a prayer asking for guidance in 1991, the first question I asked was about my destiny. I pulled the Het-Heru Hetep card. From the Ausar Auset Church classes and books, I learned that with a Het-Heru destiny, that throughout my life I should strive to be joyful, to experience pleasure in healthy balanced ways, be sociable, harmonious with others and nature, and appreciate the beauty in all. Further, I'm to be aware of how I use my imagination in my thoughts and daydreaming fantasies as these could come true in life. Strong inner joy and pleasure raises the life-force which will inspire and motivate me towards passionately fulfilling my goals. Best to decrease tendencies to be timid, seeking too much pleasure, wanting to feel good all the time by daydreaming or using intoxicating drugs, alcohol, sex and other addictions to avoid unpleasant tasks and responsibilities. Careers to consider are all kinds of artists: dancers, musicians, singers, writers, entertainers, make-up artists, fashion designers, interior decorators, drawers, painters, graphic designers, and animators. Het Heru is also known as Osun in the Yoruba traditions.

At 66 years old, let us together see how far I have come in fulfilling my destiny. Hopefully, you have already read earlier stories of my younger years and how I got to where I am now. You can help me judge my progress as an outsider looking in.

Could be near the end of my incarceration as my parents lived to their 60's and 70's, or I could be halfway since my grandmother lived to be 106-years-old. This timeframe is of course is in terms of a Western idea of a chronological lifetime. Some people are done with their true destinies at much younger ages. From what you've read of my divined destiny goals, let's review how have I done.

Het Heru Hetep (Oshun)
Relationships

Well...while the creative aspects of Het Heru are flourishing ...I've probably failed in the romantic relationship love area of my life. Or at least need to hurry up and put my concentration in that direction.

Sex? Sometimes behind closed eyes, recently, I imagined what it would be like to have someone lying beside me holding me close. What if television dramas and movies were true about heterosexual intercourse being exciting, painless, enjoyable, nurturing, caring, beneficial and healing? Get so hot down there that you gotta have it right then and there. He wants you and you want him. Then my mind slides down memory lane. He's bigger, stronger, dominating. He takes up most of the bed. He has to have the television on loud all night, with the windows open in the wintertime. Whatever he's seen and expects, has to be performed on him regardless of what I may want? Or that he's been with someone else and may or may not be honest enough to say, "Honey, you need to go get checked at the Board of Health."

"What for? I feel fine. I had my annual physical already."

Too young to understand. Now I'm older. Perhaps older and wiser. But who cares about wiser?

The song, "I want to thank you" by Alicia Meyers, came into my head recently upon awakening. I'm hoping it is a sign that my desire for a companion is answered. I liked this song decades ago, but at that time I turned it into a praise song to God. Now I'm hoping that the lyrics, "I want to thank you, heavenly Father for shining your light on me. You sent me someone who really loves me and not just my body. It took a long time for it to happen. I prayed a long time for it to happen, but I knew those nights I prayed, that you would send me someone who is real and not someone for play" will come true for me. Appreciated for who we are. Not just our bodies or what our bodies can do for someone else.

I'm hoping that the COVID pandemic crisis has taught us all too well that people are precious. Since being shut in, I've craved and prayed for someone, or that a group of people comes into my life, who have also been doing their emotional growth, maturing, now ready to have someone else along for the journey, able to appreciate, respect and value themselves and others.

A year ago, I kept hearing the song lyric, "I am getting married in the morning" so often that it was annoying! No one has showed up yet, at least that I've recognized. Maybe they tried, and I wasn't paying attention. A companion, a true companion is what my heart desires. Marriage is the furthest from my mind, I've been there and done that twice. Sex is something I don't have to have. I had sex in my marriages only because society taught me that that's what I was supposed to do. So I'm not sure what the message means. Perhaps, my heart needs to open and trust more. And I could read more romance novels instead of only nonfiction books!

In regards to I Ching hexagrams 8 and 45 guidance for moving to Chicago, it took time, fifteen long years of living here for me to find and gather together with people of like mind, mostly after my having to heal first, then being introduced to the Church of the Spirit, and later becoming a psychologist.

Beauty

Winter solstice 2021 *Sacred Path Card Workbook* spiritual guidance reading asked the question, "Have you been neglecting your appearance?" Yes.

Well. . .well...does being at home in my jogging suit or pajamas during the COVID pandemic shutdown give me an excuse? I was getting dressed everyday wearing a different color top and sometimes different color trousers, but then that meant my laundry was piling up. My helper was only coming once a month. After getting pain in my abdominal hernia from lifting, I decided not to be the superwoman, to instead compromise, and be more like everybody else.

A monumental question is, "Whose idea of beauty?" By extension, how should my appearance be? What do I do with comments like, "I like it when you let your hair down." "You have beautiful white hair. You should show it more often?"

I could possibly think about doing that. But again, isn't my hair beautiful no matter what hairstyle? Why do I only get compliments during the winter when my hair naturally straightens out?

At my age, my hair is too thin to style it like I used to. With a receding hairline, you can't see much of my hair on Zoom unless I sit sideways, which I do occasionally. It is really strange though, that I get these comments when I am the only dark complexion person in the room. Often don't compliment the other women's (or men's) hair, so why not comment on my skin instead of my almost nonexistent hair? Ah ha, duh because I'm also the only one with naturally gray hair!

Recently, I saw a "Red Table Talk" video on the increasing popularity of African American women shaving their hair bald. Jada Pinkett Smith and her daughter Willow, and the rest of the women are absolutely beautiful! Having a bald head or a low-cut brings out our natural facial features. They talked about feeling free.

Freedom. I know some of that freedom of just being able to shower, grease up, and go. In the past, I used to cut my hair every 10 years, usually because I'd grown tired of having a full head of hair down to my shoulders. It was so thick it took 12 hours to dry naturally. I couldn't tolerate the hot heat of a dryer, so I combed and braided my hair immediately after shampooing it and let it dry. Therefore, I only washed my hair once a week. The rest of the days, I let it down if I chose to, and then braided it in small braids before bed at night. That was a lot of work.

Many people don't know or think about how much damage perms and weaves do to African American hair and scalp. Neither did I know weaves did long term damage, until I saw the "Red Table Talk" video. African American women are shaving their hair because harsh hair treatments are causing alopecia bald spots where the hair doesn't grow back. India Arie sang about women without hair after chemotherapy in her hit single, "I Am Not My Hair" in 2006. The main lyric words are, "I am not my hair. I am not my skin. I am the soul that lives within." I'm really, really, really wishing that we could accept each other for the natural beauty we all have inside and out.

When I was younger, I dreamed of designing and styling my hair in big bold ways similar to the models' hairstyles on the fashion show runways. It's wonderful that my hair is now growing down my back, since I don't comb it everyday like I used to do, when I went out to the university or to work. Gray hair is brittle, sheds, and breaks off easier, so I try not to stress my hair too much. I will be learning new ways to style my hair, especially since I can't find gray bobby pins to match my hair color. Paying $12 for a small package of thirty gray hair pins that still showed in my hair was ridiculous, but I had given in to a friend's teasing. However, now that I am aware of my nearing the end of my destiny, I want to be able to check that dream goal off of my bucket list. So while other people are going bald, I am letting my hair grow longer.

Recently people, male, female, old and young approach me and tell me how beautiful my silver-gray hair is, and how pretty, smooth, young and glowing my face looks. Asked me, "What do you use?"

Nothing, other than being calmer, with less worries, and therefore less wrinkles the only change has been hopefully a deeper sleep and natural vitamins with more iron. Just water on my face folks, same as I've done since I was a teenager.

Creativity: The Artist

So far with what I've written and reviewed of my life, there is a lot of warrior and counseling energy but not much about creativity. So how has creativity been at my core, my strength that keeps me going?

Probably I would not be me if I wasn't doing some kind of art. Even during times when I've felt too busy and overwhelmed to do art, such as in graduate school, someone will inevitably ask me to do an art project or will need a problem solved. Yet somehow, I find the time. Knitted baby clothes for my adopted daughter's firstborn. Mittens for children and people who were homeless. Custom make African American dolls because since my childhood, there are still very few dolls that look like us. Quickly learned how to quilt after I got tired of being cold at night with much too short, acrylic fake fleece blankets. Out of necessity with a sense of urgency, I wrote books. Creatively cook with whatever I have or can find at the farmers' market because of the COVID pandemic high cost of food. The list goes on.

Why make everyone one else rich but us, if we can make it ourselves? I've felt that way since I was a teenager. Buying jeans with someone else's initials or logo, and calling them designer jeans didn't make sense to me. Am I not a designer too? I embroidered butterflies on the back pockets. Also sewed my own jeans to fit my long torso and crotch with a small but bigger African American butt than store bought jeans. Otherwise to sit in women's jeans for more than an hour was painful torture.

I'm still the Amateur archetype in that I enjoy making art, but only sold a few of my creations, some are stashed away or I give my art away or sell it at low prices. My creativity, however, had taken the place of socializing with my family, friends, and community. So has years of university education. I heard of perpetual students, but I had not intended to become one! When I was younger, I thought college was stupid because the money that people spend on college is a down payment or the entire price for buying a house or financing a business. My conscience really bothered me while I was in the doctoral program. Scholarships, and student loans with stipends each semester were given freely without considering one's credit history. Yet, African Americans aren't given loans for businesses and for owning homes in their communities. I felt guilty for having this privilege just because I could excel in school.

Chapter 2: Rethinking Education

North American feminists say they are concerned about how we can help the women in Afghanistan. The Taliban are reported to be taking away education and jobs from girls and women. But have we considered what is education? How many years should education be? How much of the education that we have, do we actually use? How does the education in the United States help us survive? Are we taught survival skills in school? When starving can we eat the textbooks that we bought? Or the computers and smart phones that we can't really afford?

Water is a primary necessity, more essential than education. But why is it the women's responsibility to haul heavy water? How did this come to be? Boys and men go to school and then to work, usually to do migrant work in near by or foreign countries. Education for only a chosen few, and of these, only a few are hired. How did it come to be that we think that working in someone else's factory sweat shop, office, store, home, or school is required for survival? Previously, everyone including men would simply walk to the stream, river, or gather snow for their own drink of water. No one owned the land. Anyone could eat freely of the wild fruits and vegetables.

But colonizers came in and took the land from the people. With modern day slaveowners or rebel gangs forcing people to grow inedible crops like cotton, poppies for opium, coca for cocaine, etc., then too much edible crops are also exported to other countries for them to get rich and fat, while your own family barely eats and is paid subsistence wages, therefore you are forced to continue working in the fields to survive. Sharecropping. Your soil ruined, eroded, dried and cracked from excessive commercial farming. Then the rain stops as there is no water going up to come down as rain, and rivers and lakes are redirected for a hydroelectric power for the rich people and the cities. So called "developed countries" make sure other countries stay poor.

What happens to relationships and families when our focus is predominantly on education and careers? When the child is "smarter" than the parents, but doesn't know own culture? Or how to survive. Education and careers separate families and communities, as children and the breadwinner go off to faraway places to get the best that's offered. "Brain drain" is when the young educated go off to other countries or other areas for employment, depriving their own communities of the experts and professionals that their parents sacrificed and risked investment in. Too often, young adults don't return to live in their home communities.

I haven't returned to my home community after going away to college the first time, as I unexpectedly continued on to graduate school. Honestly I didn't know what a master' degree was. Certainly didn't know what a PhD was. I knew about a master's in nursing. That was about it. In order to be a nurse practitioner you have to have a master's degree, and now there are nurses with PhD's. I hadn't planned to go onto a doctorate degree. It just happened. And of course, with the amount of assignments for two years at the master's level, I wasn't thinking about more school.

But I was online one day and typed in Argosy University because I had brochures from when I applied there in 1998 a little after I came back from Zimbabwe. I looked over the website and needed more information, but instead the website didn't give it to me. A chat box came up. So I typed in my phone number, and was startled by my home phone ringing as soon as I put in the last number. I ended up talking to one of the admission's staff. She was a great salesperson and told me I only had two weeks to get all of my application materials in. This meant rushing to order and pick up my transcripts.

Of course, yes, I did an I Ching reading first. This reading is similar to when I inquired about going to the Argosy University in 1998 and got Hexagram 42 Increase (Maat) (lines 1 and 6) into hexagram 8 Union. Amen Hetep. It's furthers one to do something great and to sacrifice your own life to help others. Must work on one's own flaws first by getting spiritual help. By living a spiritual life, you will receive abundance, and the strength and energy to carry out one's new increased responsibilities. Warned that if you don't share with others then you may incur more crises and disasters in your life.

From 1999, I was given time almost 10 years — of hexagram 33 Retreat from employment — to work on my flaws, heal my own traumas, and gain confidence before I could counsel others. After this personal growth, was I now ready to attend Argosy University?

I asked again in 2010 and received Hexagram 19 Approach that describes an idealistic situation favorable in the beginning with people coming together, those in a higher position helping people in the lower positions. However, this is time limited as I found out the hard way. After the first year there was very little support from the administrators of the university. Hexagram 19 advised it was best that I reach out for help but it is also important to find the right person. I needed this encouragement because I wasn't good at asking for help, but after that first year of graduate school I was forced to ask for help. Line 6 of hexagram 19 is guidance about coming into the world with a weakened body and the need to heal the body before can go out in the world to work. Hexagram 19 is the complement of Hexagram 33 Retreat. There is return after retreating and now was the time to return.

Metu Neter: Ausar tem maat/ Amen tu maat is about the need for me being unified and calm within, and with others. Taking neither gain nor loss to heart. This aspiration was sorely tested.

While I was in Philadelphia visiting my family at my grandmother's house, I had my admission's interview over the phone. Two hours later they told me I was accepted, and I could start either in January or in the fall. I just took these synchronous events as a sign from heaven.

The other reason I continued on to the clinical psychology doctoral program was because although everyone in the master's level counseling program had the same required counseling courses, the rehabilitation counseling classes was mostly about how to help people get jobs. For those who had intellectual disabilities, and were in special education classes in high schools, as they became adults, we helped them transition to the workshops and set them up with job coaches. This had little to do with therapeutic counseling. Ever since 1990, when I first went to therapy myself, I have wanted to help people who had experienced trauma to heal.

What put the nail in the coffin, as far as me being a rehabilitation counselor was that my vocational counselor started sending me email after email with want ads for working at McDonald's and Burger King. Seems there is some kind of rule that if you get rehabilitation services then you need to at least work a job for 90 days before the Department of Human Services Office of Rehabilitation Services can get paid. So she didn't care where I worked. I would never do that to a client who uses a wheelchair! Like could you see me flipping burgers in a wheelchair? Where would I ever fit in a McDonald's kitchen? Now that I think about it, I'd be in the way, while they are running back-and-forth with the french fries and burgers. Plus that, I had graduated with a master's degree. That's an insult on top of insult. I know there are plenty of people who have graduated from college who are flipping hamburgers because they have to pay their rent. But still! Did she ever try to match me up with at least some of my skills? Like for an office job? No! Maybe I could've worked as a cashier taking the money. Maybe as a manager. But managers always end up pitching in if an employee is absent. They would have to flip burgers, mop floors and clean toilets, load stock, and whatever else was needed. Or maybe refer me to a job at the corporate office?

Chapter 3: A Difficult to Understand Spiritual Reading:

Didn't See it Coming

Initially, my winter solstice reading for 2018 was confusing to me.

   Metu Neter cards: Het Heru tem maat/ Maat tem maat
   I Ching: Hexagram 30
   Sacred Path card: 10 West Shield Intersection/Goals
   Sacred Contract Archetype: The Addict

Why did it change from an open Het Heru tu maat at the summer solstice to a closed Het Heru tem maat? I thought in terms of spending. I had no other income except the school loan stipend. Yet I spent and lived as if I still have extra money. It may be Maat tem because more people are asking me for my money and my time. I give and then worry that I gave too much. Some people don't or won't do for themselves.

  I was exhausted after eight years of grueling graduate school life. So for the beginning of 2019, I needed to take time to rest and to get clarity. I do have more than others in terms of "money" because I save, and my only expensive addiction is buying ebooks. Everyone has an addiction, which is defined as anything you keep doing despite the negative consequences, you have wanted to change but has been difficult to change, although you have tried. I also share of my time, clarity and intellect. So how do I know when to share and will not to share? I witnessed people who are used to demanding that other people do almost everything for them. Refusing to follow guidance given to them repeatedly over and over again. Want other people to do the hard work and sacrifices. Stuck in likes and dislikes from childhood.

On the contrary, I have constantly sacrificed my likes and dislikes in order to achieve, which was mostly driven by my desire to heal emotionally and spiritually. Ambition got me a higher education, and previously good paying jobs. But judged by other's standards, I lack material wealth. Yet heaven blesses me with a flow of abundance. What I need just comes, including in the form of money.

But then I started feeling lazy. I didn't feel like pushing myself to do anything. I was recovering from a year of fear, that shook and undermined my confidence in all areas of my life because I'd been rejected again and again for internship clinical training. Exhausted. Het Heru can be lazy and extravagant. Yet the Sacred Path card: 10 West Shield Intersection/Goals was advising me that I needed to retreat, rest, have time alone to care for my own health and spirituality. This is the opposite of my usual workaholism. Recent astrological interpretations from the Mercury retrograde, full moons and eclipses explained that everyone was tired, exhausted from the struggles of the hard life lessons of 2018. Most people were begging to rest. There was hope that the new year would bring in lighter loads and freedom. The main lesson of 2018 was to learn who we each really are, our authentic self, and awareness of our true heart's desire.

The winter solstice reading of 2018 challenge of Het Herut tem maat/ Maat tem maat was reminding me not to get depressed and discouraged with the many delays in getting a clinical psychology internship. I finally received approval from my chairperson in August for my clinical research project (CRP) that is similar to a written dissertation. Great, however, the bindery relocated without telling me until two months later, and then announced it would require more time for them to get the printing machines set up and to print my CRP.

On the evening of March 1, 2019, I heard a knock and thud against my apartment front door. Outside was a large box. Inside the box were three beautiful hardcover copies of my CRP! Early as possible Monday morning, excitedly cherishing my success, I rushed a copy to the Dean and assistant dean of the clinical psychology program, for the last signatures of approval. They gave me lots of congratulations for finally obtaining an internship and finishing my CRP.

I took the other copy to the librarian, so she could put it on the back room shelves filled with the other CRP's from many previous years. She mumbled something about, "I don't know what will happen to the students' CRP's if there's no physical campus or program anymore."

And she didn't know what happened to the email for my digital copy of my CRP to be taken to the registrar for final sign off on my transcripts. I sent her the email again, and then rush down to the register's office.

Four days afterwards, on March 7, 2019, my cell phone email chimed with an email from my academic advisor. This was a surprise because he's usually slow to respond to my emails. I had invited him to my presentation at the upcoming ABPSI convention. He wrote that he wasn't going there this year. But then he also wrote: "Not sure if you are in the loop with what was announced today regarding the school, and Friday being the last day of operation. If you have not, please make sure you get copies of all your records. The National Register is offering the opportunity to bank, meaning to store your credentials and items for free. This will allow you to keep a record for the future."

I reread my academic advisor's email. I wondered if I understood it correctly. That the next day would be the last day of Argosy university? All across the United States, Argosy university campuses abruptly closed due to bankruptcy.

I was lucky that I read his email while I was waiting for my psychotherapist that morning, so I could cope with what that could possibly mean. Afterwards, I went up to campus. Everyone was supportive in spite of being in shock and the surreal feeling of the situation.

On Friday, reality set in as I saw empty library bookshelves and empty shelves in the teachers' offices. Boxes, books, litter in the library and the hallways. There were less people on campus than yesterday. Some students I hadn't seen in years. I wandered the halls, frustrated. I ate lunch with two of them. We shared information and strategies on what to do next.

The next day I cried and sobbed as reality began to personally sink in. I went on and went to the Association of Black Psychologists Chicago Chapter meeting, where they had written "ARGOSY STUDENTS" on the agenda. I'm glad I went because otherwise I would have stayed home isolating myself against being around people who would have asked me how I was doing. ABPSI sent emails inviting Argosy students to come in, and they had Argosy University alumni there for support and to validate our experiences at the university. Someone also thought to grab as many bound copies of CRP's by people she knew as possible. I did not think about grabbing mine while I was on campus although I took a few library books I was interested in. The meeting also had lively discussions of relevant current topics that lightened my mood.

Maat is also optimism and faith. How do I manage to have faith and optimism with so many disappointments and delays?

Het Heru did show up in surprising ways. First with creativity, as I started knitting shoes again. One order was for a red and blue pair with only instructions size 8 narrow, high top style, with no preference for either red or blue. So it was left up to me how to pattern the red and blue yarn. I also excitedly began designing and sewing my clothes again, which I hadn't done in 30 years. It was enjoyable with true pleasure and excitement. Somewhat bordering on addiction. Sewing is mostly what I thought about. I would even forget to eat and frequently stayed up late. Here again with Het Heru, I didn't know if I was spending too much money on fabric and sewing supplies.

I hoped it was okay. Years in graduate school was mostly T-shirts and jeans, without much attention to fashion or appearance. So now I get to dress up.

But sewing at times was also frustrating. I'd forgotten how to sew after so many years. I put my pants together completely wrong. I had to take it all apart and do it the right way. My confidence was shaken, and I began to doubt my abilities in other areas of my life. I finally got brave enough to make a list of what I still wanted to achieve, what were my dreams and goals. With Het Heru energy, her imaginings can become real, and actually manifest in everyday life. Both positive and negative imaginings will manifest. Angel numbers also reminded me to stay positive and to write my goals. This encouragement gave me such a welcome change from my previous apathy and fear of the future.

Surely as I Ching Hexagram 30, line 3 predicted something good is coming to an end to be replaced by something better, with small miracles along the way and synchronicities, I did somehow believe much better is happening and is in the making. I was distressed the prior two years, because I hadn't matched for an internship. In a few months, I began an internship with all I wanted for clinical training: health psychology, integrative spirituality, and working with children. Who would've known?

Chapter 4: Oshun's Blessings

After I paid $50 for a spiritual reading from a Cuban condomble priestess to tell me, "You already know what I know, so I can't tell you what to do," I wondered what I did know that she and a prior Ifa priest said I knew. Well that was almost 25 years ago and I'm beginning to understand what it is that I may know that they know. This is only because I have begun to listen more, pay attention to the subtle messages that we all get and to follow that guidance. In addition, like a babalou is trained in using the Ifa for 20 years before being considered a babalou, I have been using the I Ching and Metu Neter for 20 years but without a teacher. Experience taught me as I've simply been shown how the readings manifest and describe situations accurately. Note that 50, 25, and 20 are all multiples of five — Osun's number.

Many synchronistic spiritual connections to people and events occur at the Association of Black Psychologists conferences. Perhaps because there are so many high energy powerful spiritual people there. Let me explain:

I'm reminded of a past ABPsi convention where I was looking for the location of the silent art auction. On the way when I turned into the vendor area, I was surprised to find behind me a table full of tall beautiful African dolls, each unique. The man selling them said, "A woman in Senegal makes them. Earlier a woman saw the dolls, picked up one of the dolls and yelled and cried out. As I observed her, I told her, "Nothing like this has happened before. Later I gave her the doll free of charge."

Hearing him tell me this, I was curious. I said, "I want a doll but not for free." Aware of him observing me, cautiously I went to select a doll. At first, I saw a light peach colored eyelet lace dress on a smaller doll. But her face was not that attractive to me. As I looked up and was about to move on past her to the other dolls on the table, there was another doll that seemed to be looking at me. I couldn't see her dress, only her head. I went over and picked her up. My right index finger traced along each side of the braids with cowrie shells that outlined her face. Then immediately down her back to her ample buttocks. Then up over her shoulder lightly tracing her smaller breasts. Tears came to my eyes in the process. My femininity! Osun is giving me back my sexuality and womanhood! I grabbed her up, holding her close to me.

"This is another one." He told another man as he nodded towards me. He went away for a little while and returned with a small credit card machine and asked slowly, pausing in between each word, "What numbers do you want me to put in here?"

I said, "Five zero. $50 for Osun. Can I have her for $50?"

Silently I thought, if I had $500, I would give it to him. I've seen similar size dolls that didn't have as much detail, costing $300. The price on the tag was $70.

He held his head down as he slowly punched in the numbers.

The other man who was short and round said, "The other woman who chose the doll is a priest. You're a priest too. I knew it the first day when I saw you and saw the circle of braids on the top of your head. Are you a priest?

I said, "Yes, somewhat. Perhaps a closet priest."

He nodded and said, "You could be trained in Africa."

I asked him, "Are you a priest? Do you do Ifa readings?"

He said gruffly, "Yes I'm a priest. I'm a well-known priest."

I ducked a little, mostly from him feeling insulted, but I wasn't ashamed to have not heard of him. And even if I did, I've not been impressed by people's titles. There were many famous people at the conference and I really didn't know what I was supposed to do with them. Do I curtsy and bow as I did in Zimbabwe? Or do I prostrate myself prone on the floor?

He said, " I don't usually do readings, but I will make an exception for you. If you come back at 10 AM tomorrow I will do it for you. What did the doctors tell you was wrong with you? Why are you in a wheelchair?"

I said, "The doctor said it was multiple sclerosis at first but the next month after looking at my MRIs changed it to spinocerebellar degeneration."

He said, "I can consult with other doctors and priests in Africa."

I said, "How much does a reading cost?" I still had my Visa card in my hand. I hoped it wasn't a lot.

He said, "I would have to do a reading to see how much to charge. Wait here."

He came back, stood by the side of a table and threw several coins on the carpeted floor. I saw nichols, dimes, and pennies. The other man reached down and retrieved a stray coin and told him, "Here's another coin."

It was a dime. The priest added it to the other coins and threw them again.

He picked up the coins and turned to me saying, "You have to be honest with me. You have to tell me the truth. Tomorrow you have to tell me the truth."

I said, "I'm usually honest. This year, Ochosi has been working with me, making me aware of when I haven't been honest and of my own unconscious injustices towards other people."

He said, "I know."

Later the other man said, "Tomorrow you have to be honest, tell him the truth, tell him everything. Remember God will be speaking through him. Listen to what he says. It is not the man, as you know him, speaking. It is God speaking through him."

The next day, I waited and waited for the priest starting at 10 AM. I missed some of the conference sessions because of it. I asked the other man if he had seen him. He told me to just go and he will find me when he comes. I checked back later in the afternoon. The priest came and said, "The young woman never came and brought me the cowrie shells for me to do the Ifa reading."

He talked on and on about her. But I doubt that he intended to do the Ifa reading for me after the coins he threw on the floor yesterday told him the truth. He was probably the one who wasn't being honest. When he threw the coins on the carpeted floor of the hotel, he immediately understood its meaning and without an explanation walked away. I went home and did my own I Ching reading. No, to allowing him to help. The main point here is respect for the divine guidance is above our own personal opinions. Osun was initially the only Orisha shown the secret of how to throw the Ifa cowrie shells to divine the future.

I brought the doll home and placed her on the nightstand by my bed. When my Nigerian personal assistant saw her, she put her hand on her chest and wide eyed briefly stepped backwards. "Nana Yeye Osha! Nana Yeye Osha!" she said.

"What's wrong? What's a Nana Yeye Osha?"

"That doll looks just like the wise women who you see in the streets that people give money to. You see what she has in her hand?" She pointed to the large woven straw spiral disc in the doll's right hand. "That's how you know."

"Oh! That's how come the priest told me the doll was special and that I was a priestess too."

Chapter 5: Sekert (Oya's) Influences on My Destiny

Het Heru's personality traits are the opposite of Sekert's traits. I was born on a Saturday. Sekert is also Saturn energy expressed as introverted, a loner, serious, celibate, enjoys solitude, being organized and on time, saves money and can be miserly, with austere or minimal furnishing and clothes, often serious and practical.

Het Heru is outgoing, friendly, social, freely sexual, having to be around people, partying, spending money on beautiful clothing, makeup, hair, home, car and fun. This has made striving to be more like Het Heru challenging.

The day on which you were born describes more of your personality than your astrological sun sign. It is how people actually see you and how you operate in the world. You can go on the internet to find what day of the week you were born on. Simply type in your full birthdate then "day of the week."

Summer Solstice 2021 reading:

Metu Neter cards: Sekert tem tchaas/ Uatchet tu tchaas. I Ching Hexagram 11 Peace and Harmony (lines 3, 4, and 5) into Hexagram 58. Sacred Path card: 13 Coral Nurturing.

CHAPTER 5: SEKERT (OYA'S) INFLUENCES ON MY DESTINY

Sekert tem tchaas reminds me of my attempts of trying to adjust to being an elder. Sekert is the elder, the old crone. During the months between June and December 2021, I was too busy, too Sekert hyperfocused on whatever task I was doing. Rushing to make little Black dolls and other miniature houses, churches, furniture and scenes in preparation for the Association of Black Psychologists' psychoeducation program, "Family Friendly Suicide Prevention" the first week in December.

The Sekert personality is able to sit still for long hours, patiently concentrating on detailed tasks, sacrificing other needs to meet deadlines of a long-term goal. Tasks that would be too tedious, boring and tiring for most people. One day, I did ask myself, why was I pushing myself through this? It was actually starting to get boring, monotonous and sometimes felt too difficult to problem-solve how to sew tiny doll clothes or insert tiny parts of prefabricated miniature houses when my old hands have a slight tremor and I can barely see closeup items. Hasn't what I've done already enough? Do I have to be such a perfectionist? The next day, my enthusiasm returned as I recommitted myself to finishing. Woke up with ideas on how to repair mistakes or easier ways to do projects. Friends and family also cheered me on by telling what I was making was amazing. One of my sisters told me the dolls have healing energy.

The older we get, hopefully with experience, we have learned that there are often solutions to problems, instead of giving up when make a mistake or are in a crisis. Mistakes or crises often are not as huge or hopeless as our minds think. Just a tiny change can make a great improvement.

Loneliness is a pervasive disease spread globally as a by-product of capitalism and "success." In the United States, the public schools, religions and families often don't teach relationship skills. We need neighborhoods that care about and support everyone, with adults to role-model healthy relationships, problem solving, and show respect for elders and their wisdom. It is a great loss to society when we don't honor our elders and learn from and apply their wisdom.

Uatchet along with Sekert is our unseen Ancestors helping us. Over those past few months, I had more insights, integration of memories, synchronicities, serendipities, and remembered more deep nighttime dreams. This also reflects Sekert and our Ancestors' ability to manifest our daytime dreams, goals, desires and needs.

Sekert is also our destiny and tries to bring us back around to getting back on track. Lately, I noticed I started saying in conversations with others that I was checking items off of my "bucket list." Usually I don't like that term because I'm not that old or ill, but the COVID pandemic reminds me daily that I could be gone any day, and same with people and organizations I know. It is not promised that any of us will wake up tomorrow. Sekert is our awareness and preparation for death and rebirth throughout our lives. Each life transition, even a positive change such as graduation, wedding, pregnancy, births, job promotion, moving to a new neighborhood or city means a small death of leaving behind the old to embrace a desired new adventure. We struggle initially with new situations and are tempted to leave. Sometimes we do leave. Yet, reminiscing doesn't bring us back to how we used to be before a major change. COVID pandemic forced a lot of changes within us, and the environmental around us.

Is it possible that our bucket list begins in childhood? When I was a teenager, I was making several different kinds of dolls. I cut and wrapped copper wire with old cotton brown stockings to make doll bodies. Designed the custom-made dolls for relatives based on their interests. For example, I made a bendable beautifully costumed skater and a ballerina. Made a poster size flute player with brightly colored felt on a burlap background. Later I sewed assorted shades of tans and brown dolls made with Raggedy Ann and Andy sewing patterns. I was spurred on by the fact that multicultural brown skin dolls were rare when I was a child.

I have also wanted to illustrate children's books ever since I was a little bitty girl. At age fourteen, I entered a popular drawing contest in magazines, and won ten dollars. My foster parents bought me a Jon Nagy drawing kit. Hours and hours I spent teaching myself how to draw faces. I would fill up a whole sheet of paper with just eyes, another with noses, and one with all mouths.

As an adult, I came to Chicago to the School of the Art Institute intending to learn book illustration and computer animation for non-violent video games. Most of my elective classes were figure drawing. Unfortunately, admission to computer classes were based on seniority, so the classes were always filled by the time my turn came to register for classes. Just before I dropped out of art school a senior student advised me to just buy the computer software and teach myself, because that's what he had to do anyway. Computer software cost in the upper hundreds and thousands of dollars at that time. So as much as I tried over the years that didn't happen. I bought some cheap basic computer software but didn't have the time to use it.

Now with new technology, videos and animation is available to the general public, it is cheaper, quicker and easier than 20 years ago, when artists had to use hundreds of hand drawn storyboards to make a movie. You can make a GIF of yourself with just one click. However, life has its detours so fifty years later, life brought me back around to making bendable dolls, and requests for children's books and videos about our ancestors' unseen role in our lives. Sekert influenced by Saturn is slow, real slow, with careers that take off running much later in life. But how slow is slow!

Turning Points

You may remember that with my very first Native American card reading with the Medicine Woman Cards, in 1994, I was advised to made a list of what major events happened every seventh year of my life up to the age of thirty-five years. I went off to college and to Zimbabwe soon afterwards, then returned to the United States to become homeless. Thereafter I was surviving crises, or making life changes that seemed to come faster, and faster than seven years, as I focused on healing. I forgot about turning points, until 2022 while writing this book. To my amazement, looking back I see that major decisions and changes in my life did indeed mostly occur every seventh year:

42 years old: Lived in Zimbabwe

43 years old: Homeless

45 years old: First wheelchair

49 years old: Briefly stayed in an assisted living facility until I got my own apartment

52 years old: Began graduate school master's program

54 years old: Began graduate school doctoral program

64 years old: COVID pandemic. Graduated from doctoral program.

Chapter 6: Healing the Past

Full healing requires attention to all areas of our lives, **physically** (healthy food, sleep, exercise, safe homes and neighborhoods) **emotionally** (all feelings are acknowledged. Be valued and accepted by others in relationships and the community) **mentally** (be able to think clearly, using your skills and talents) and **spiritually** (having faith, a reason for living, peace, harmony and morality).

But how far back in the past do we have to go to heal? Do we ever really die? What if we lived other lifetimes in other cultures, with different genders and skin complexions? Can it really be healed?

A friend introduced me to the *Past Life Cards*. I decided to buy my own deck, and use the cards to get guidance on what would help me heal my Muslim childhood trauma issues, that I was working through with a Muslim therapist.

Past: Egypt. The past life that triggered the situation inquiring about.

May have had a significant past life in Egypt. When a stubborn negative pattern refuses to heal, its roots may be from from a past lifetime. May have an interest in Egyptian culture, spirituality, astronomy, astrology. Or could have feelings of avoiding traveling to the area because of unconscious memories past life traumas from there.

Current: **Trust and Faith.** What you need to know, and to work on right now.

Being able to have faith and trust in the universe, people, and yourself affects your peace and joy in life. May have experienced betrayal in a past life and therefore have difficult trusting other people. The other two cards also influence how much faith you have.

Future: **Communal Living**. What your immediate future could be like if follow the guidance.

Probably lived in a convent, monastery or tribe where your basic needs were provided. Everyone contributed collectively to the community. In your current life you are bothered by an individualistic monetary system and living alone. Have to find a balance between individual and group needs and reach out for help.

My Immediate Impressions and Reflections

First, the photos on the cards are so meaningfully related to my known past history, and current life situation. The Egypt card has a photo of the pyramids. The upside-down middle card has a photo of a statue of an angel. And the last card has a photo of the Anasazi Native American stone dwellings built into the side of a mountain. In my present lifetime my outer appearance is an African American with Native American heritage. A Native American medicine man told me to check out my African culture because it is similar to the Native American culture. I was led to a group of women who practiced traditional African culture, however soon afterwards, I became a member of the Ausar Auset Society Church that is based on Ancient Kamitic now called Egypt's spiritual beliefs. Yet, I never had an interest in visiting Egypt or the pyramids as many

African Americans have excitedly done or wish to do. Nor has reading scholarly books on Kamitic history interested me. I did gain passion for studying astrology, but only as it helps us understand ourselves. Not interested in interpreting the stars nor predicting the future. I'm content with letting someone else calculate and read astrology charts.

I lost my trust and faith during this current lifetime's childhood and into young adulthood as my cruel fathers and second husband used religion to abuse us. They had been converted to Islam. Abuse happens in all major religions because people are people, but also conquerors used religions to try to destroy advanced civilized cultures. Indigenous spiritual practices were forbidden, hidden, corrupted, and fragmented into multiple unrecognizable pieces. Angels were once indigenous deities, therefore it makes sense that the middle past life card Trust and Faith is upside down. And central to both African and Native American cultures is communal living. Previously, I had past life memories of being a male chief of a tribe and watching my people leave while I stayed to do what I could to carry on the traditions. Yes, at my core is a deep, deep longing for communal living. I resent that the Romans and later Arab Muslims invaded Egypt and northern Africa, and that American society forced us to live separately and be competitive, instead of with cooperation and trusting each other. Not even sure if we know how by now.

Chapter 7: The Beautiful Ninety-Nine Names of Allah: Wazifa Card Set

And at last, but not least, making peace with my Muslim upbringing, by finding the beauty in Islam, in the meaning of the ninety-nine attributes of Allah. As a child, I remember seeing a list of the ninety-nine Names of Allah in the back of English translations of the Quran. It took me a while to find it in recent publications, in fact I didn't find a list until the end of the final draft of this book. This was worth the wait, as I found it, and more while reading the book, *Physicians of the Heart: A Sufi View of the Ninety-Names of Allah*, it immediately brought tears of joy to my eyes. The authors sum up and describe very well our deep internal longing that is usually difficult to put into words. Especially difficult for those who have had near death or other spiritual experiences to describe, and more so for other people who haven't, but struggle with emotional pain and addictions. The deep, deep longing for connection to the universe and each individual's unique purpose in life. The book, *Physicians of the Heart* has the best explanation I've seen.

The authors wrote from a different Islamic perspective than I've known. Not religious, instead a gentle psychological, mystical, spiritual perspective. All these years, I didn't know that the Quran was actually mostly sounds of words of power similar to mantras, and the Hadiths had stories of the Prophet Muhammad's mystical experiences. I had given up on ever understanding the Quran even in English. Perhaps earlier even if I was told this, I probably would not have understood until after I had my near death experience in 1982. The authors of, *Physicians of the Heart*, help us all to see and feel that Allah is the essence of pure Love and much more, within and around us. Not a huge man sitting in the sky full of wrath for our sins.

Initially, my goal for studying the list of ninety-nine Names of Allah was to show how Arabic names were perhaps based on multiple "deities," similar to ancient African stories of the different attributes of one God. Further, I wondered if other people also noticed how their birth name's meaning affects their own destiny as their life unfolds. Learning more and more about the meaning of my own name helped me to understand myself better. To my delight, in the book, Physicians of the Heart, I found where my name Haneefa came from. It is based on the Arabic word haneefah referring back to Abraham tradition of believing in the ability to obtain the inner state of unified consciousness of oneness. During my near death experience, I experienced the oneness with total love, peace, acceptance and understanding. When I returned to my body in earthly life, I longed to feel that incredible love and peace again.

The book, *Physicians of the Heart,* is so named because Sufi healers use the special encoded sounds of the Arabic words of the ninety-nine Names of Allah to heal mental and physical ailments. Most mental disorders are actually spiritual dis-eases of not being connected to the universe and community as one. Each of the Names of Allah invoke and awakens a specific energy the patient needs, for example Ar-Rahman unconditional love and connection, or Al-Jabbar for inner power and strength.

I believe and know the healing potential of sounds of power because I've experienced this myself. For nine years after my near death experience, I prayed pleading for understanding and for what to do with my new way of thinking, seeing, and relating to the world. My prayers didn't begin to be answered until I came to Ausar Auset Society Church where they introduced me to how to have an inner sense of peace through meditation, mantras, rituals, yoga, and better mental and physical health with homeopathy, Ayurvedic and Chinese medicine. These practices helped me integrate and start to make sense of my spiritual and psychic experiences.

An Ausar Auset Society Church priest gave me another name, the Khamitic name AkhiaNeter-t that means, "God is my joy," based on my Metu Neter card Het Heru destiny reading. West Africans and other Africans have a tradition of having naming ceremonies a week after an infant's birth where insight into the baby's destiny is obtained during a ritual, then announced to the gathered community. This is the true meaning of "it takes a village to raise a child." The community learns the child's potential strengths as well as weaknesses to be able to guide the child throughout life. From birth each person is taught to be responsible for their personal growth as well as the whole community's ongoing growth. This is also a Native American tradition, and we acquire more names throughout life as others observe and appreciate our individual talents. When you hear other people say your name, they are invoking energies to assist you. Hopefully, your parents chose names that have meaning.

The ecstasy of connecting to Allah or Oneness is similar to having the overwhelming love, peace and acceptance of a near death experience. Some dreams also give another glimpse of the afterlife or between lives and different dimensions.

I had another natural ecstasy experience in my earthly life when I performed a Het Heru ritual in 1995. On a Friday, dressed in a blessed tie-dyed green and yellow dress, I went down to a river in a small rural town. It was a partly sunny and warm summer day. Singing the Het Heru mantra I offered Het Heru five nectarines, because I couldn't find peaches. I put the nectarines in the water one by one. As I deep breathed and looked at the water, I imagined myself in the river flowing gently over, under, even squeezing around large boulders in the rough waters. To my surprise, I was filled with contagious joy and peace for weeks afterwards.

Similar aftereffects happened when I went another time to a large city river. I again imagined myself flowing with the water. The difference was I didn't have the peaches to offer and it was a cloudy, dreary day and my depressed mood matched the dark weather. Yet, afterwards I still experienced inner joy. These rituals were done alone. Could you imagine the power of a group ritual for Het Heru and other deities' energies?

Physicians of the Heart explains how invoking any of the specific ninety-nine Names of Allah restores hope and endless possibilities of being able to transcend beyond our present way of how we think about ourselves. Similar to Yoruba Ifa deity characteristics, the authors acknowledge and include the dualities of the natural opposites of virtues. Helping us go beyond the woundedness of shame, worthlessness, and loneliness. Seeking a better life and relief from suffering, we are shown the possibilities of changing and growing spiritually. With the healing practice of invoking of specific names of attributes of Allah it is possible to change our thoughts, moods and behavior. Therefore taking responsibility for our actions to improve the world.

Several of the healing attributes would be useful, making it difficult to choose just one of the ninety-nine Names of Allah. Gratefully, the authors of *Physicians of the Heart* designed the *Wazifa Card Set,* so we can pick a card from the deck, and gain understanding. Then go to their website for the correct pronunciation for chanting.

Ninety Nine Names of Allah

The following is a list of the ninety-nine Names of Allah in the order the authors of *Physicians of the Heart* has them in chapter 5, and also on the Wazifa cards with brief descriptions. For the initial purpose of getting to know more about how one's destiny may be related to one's given name, I've summarized the descriptions into a few words. But please read the book, *Physicians of the Heart* for much richer, deeper meanings and healing of which is the original intent of the book.

1). **Rahman**: Unconditional pure Love. 2). **Rahim**: Loving Mercy. 3). **Malik**: Embraced, held, loved. 4). **Quddus**: Purifying, letting go. 5). **Salam**: Peaceful. 6). **Mu'min**: True Faith. 7. **Muhaimin**: Protection from corruption. 8). **Aziz**: Self-worth. 9). **Jabbar**: Power and strength to heal. 10). **Mutakabbir**: Transcendence, growth. 11). **Khaliq**: Creativity, imagining possibilities. 12). **Bari:** Individuation as strive for freedom from faults. 13). **Musawwir**: Towards manifestation. 14). **Ghaffar**: Need for forgiveness. 15). **Qahhar**: Longing for Allah. 16). **Wahhab**: Continued blessings and abundance.

17). **Razzaq**: Gives gifts. 18). **Fattah**: Opening of the heart. 19). **Alim**: Knowing. 20). **Qabid**: Contraction. 21). **Basit**: Expansion. 22). **Khafid**: Slows down. 23). **Rafi**: Raises up. 24). **Mu'izz**: Self-esteem. 25). **Mudhill**: Humility. 26). **Sami**: Listening, hearing. 27). **Basir**: Seeing. 28). **Hakam**: True Wisdom. 29). **'Adl**: Balance and harmony. 30). **Latif**: Deep love and kindness. 31). **Khabir**: Inner knowledge and insight. 32). **Halim**: Tender, nurturing love. 33). **Azim**: Divine presence.

34). **Ghafur**: Total forgiveness as core wound hurt is healed. 35). **Shakur**: Thankfulness. 36). **'Alyy**: Transcendence. 37). **Kabir**: Infinite. 38). **Hafiz**: Protection from fear and despair. 39). **Muqit**: Provider of sustenance. 40). **Hasib**: Accountable and responsible. 41). **Jalil**: Divine power and strength. 42). **Karim**: Generosity. 43). **Raqib**: Devoted loving, deep concentration. 44). **Mujib**: Ask and listen for Allah's answer. 45). **Wasi**: Infinite omnipresence of Allah. 46). **Hakim**: Healing wisdom. 47). **Wadud**: Learning how to love. 48). **Majid**: Unexpected, amazing gifts of abundance. 49). **Ba'ith**: Spiritual awakening. 50). **Shahid**: Witnessing all dimensions. 51). **Haqq**: To be. 52). **Wakil**: Complete trust in Allah. 53). **Qawiyy**: Letting go of the need to always be in control because of fear. 54). **Matin**: Strength of perseverance and integrity. 55). **Waliyy**: Ability to receive unconditional love and to unify. 56). **Hamid**: Gratitude to Allah. 57). **Muhsi**: Knowledge that everything is important. 58). **Mubdi**: To initiate, to begin. **Mu'id:** Returning to the source. 60). **Muhyi**: Giver of life and vitality. 61) **Mumit**: Giver of death. Meaning transformation from the small deaths of one's ego self. 62) **Hayy**: everlasting energy for living. 63) **Qayyum**: continues to exist, to stand. 64). **Wajid**: Manifesting inner ecstasy. 65). **Wahid**: Infinite Oneness. 66). **Ahad**: Unique.

67). **Samad**: Continuous. 68). **Qadir**: Meaning, purpose, potential. 69). **Muqtadir**: Staying on your destiny life path. 70). **Muqaddim**: Patience. All happens at the right time. 71). **Mu'akhkhir**: Completing goals, finishing what you start. 72). **Awwal**: Pure potential. 73). **Akhir**: Already there. 74). **Zahir**: Fully present, fully visible. 75). **Batin**: Unseen calmness, the stillness of existence. 76). **Wali:** Safe and protected in relationships. 77). **Muta'ali**: Pure transcendence progress. 78). **Barr**: Realize that you are perfect, complete and truly loved. 79). **Tawwab**: forgiveness, compassion, including self. 80). **Muntaqim**: balanced reciprocity for deeds, no revenge. 81). **'Afuw**: Complete total forgiveness. 82). **Ra'uf**: Deep, inner, gentle love. 83). **Malikul-Mulk**: Reminded that you are always held in divine love. 85). **Muqsit**: Equal, just appropriations. 86). **Jami**: Integrated connection into whole self. 87). **Ghaniyy**: Fullness with a sense of being and having enough. 88). **Mughni**: Inner contentment, knowing Allah provides. 89). **Mani**: Divine protection, knowing you are safe. 90). **Mu'ti**: balanced receiving and giving. 91). **Darr**: Open your eyes and heart to see your mistakes. 92). **Nafi**: Purification to be able to benefit from the higher good. 93). **Nur**: Light of truth, pure love, wisdom from within. 94). **Hadi**: Awakening to Divine guidance. 95). **Badi**: Remembering to return to your true essence. 96). **Baqi**: Life goes on. 97). **Warith**: Return to oneness. 98). **Rashid**: Using inner intuitive and wise teacher guidance. 99). **Sabur**: Perseverance through to end of spiritual path.

Forgiveness

I decided to pull a Wazifa card. It was card 81 Al-Afuw Total Forgiveness. I was confused what forgiveness has to do with me personally at this time. I asked myself, 'Who do I need to forgive? I haven't felt hurt about what anyone did to me, in a while. There was recent animosity from someone who tended to hold a grudge with everybody. I restrained myself from yelling at her when she yelled at me. Alternatively, I thought of giving her the silent treatment that she sometimes gives to me. Over time, I gained compassion for her and prayed for her healing.

Perhaps, I needed to forgive myself? I did have occasional waves of regrets during the past two months, as I had memories from when I was in my 30s and 40s, I realized that I did the same annoying behavior, that I now have to tolerate from people twenty years younger than I. Like them, I wasn't aware of how my words or actions may have hurt other people and their feelings. Yet, older people patiently put up with my behavior. What could they say or do? They probably did the same to other people, like I did. I found myself saying aloud to the universe, "Wherever you are, this side or that side, I am so sorry. I'm so sorry. I didn't know. Please forgive me."

This was a few weeks before I read from the book, *Physicians of the Heart*'s, Chapter 8: The Family of Divine Forgiveness: A Way to Address Layers of Self-Isolation and Disconnection. Again, my heart filled with emotion and awe as I read and understood the meaning of each of the four Arabic names for forgiveness: al-Ghaffar, al-Ghafur, at-Tawwab, and al-'Afuw. The authors explain these names in relation to our developmental stages of spiritual growth.

In the beginning stage al-Ghaffar we are not able to consider forgiving because of shock and grief. Replaying the hurt over and over again in our minds. And may make the same mistakes over and over again. Yet, God's loving grace forgives us again and again.

Next step in the beginning stage is al-Ghafur, when we believe we have committed what we deeply feel is the worst crime or that the worst happened to us by another person, and consequently seems unforgivable. To forgive means to give up the grudge or revenge. Reciting al-Ghaffar and al-Ghafur opens the way to healing the wounds of painful memories and imaginings of revenge or the self-loathing, self-judgement, shame and guilt taking up all of one's thoughts. So that you can give up the grudge or revenge to gain compassion for self and others.

My hardest forgiveness task was to forgive my stepfather and foster father. Especially my foster father because I felt my adolescence and sexuality was stolen from me. They did not allow me to innocently play and explore. For decades, the hurt of feeling that I was way behind my peers in life skills, and would I never catch up, haunted me. As an adult, every time depression, loneliness, flashbacks and painful anxiety surfaced I hurt too much to be able to completely forget and forgive.

My first experience with some success with forgiveness was after I ran away from my second husband. I felt at that time that if he ever came after me, he wasn't going to wake up in the morning. He was the only person I honestly hated. I felt guilty for feeling this way, because I remember my grandmother telling us when I was a little girl, "Do not hate anyone. And God don't make ugly." Me deciding that I may have to kill him, gave me an odd sense of relief. I was already angry at Allah for giving me a second husband worse than my first husband!

After a while though, I did get tired of suffering, with my mind full of all the horrible cruel things that my second husband did, bringing to the surface constant memories and bodily flashbacks of what my stepfather and foster father previously did to me. I wanted to be able to concentrate and be professionally successful as I was before marrying him. So I decided I would forgive him but mostly for my sake, not his. This was only a few months after the divorce. I was still afraid of him but I wanted me, myself and I, back.

Years later, when a friend told me about the expression, "not letting people live rent free in your head" I understood immediately because I'd experienced this. After escaping from my second husband, there was no room left in my head to think, plan or create new dreams. I prayed for relief from worrying what he would do next, and from the painful memories of all he had done. My guilt and embarrassment over marrying him so quickly without getting to know him, nor having proper religious counsel, plus being divorced twice made me feel like a failure, and sent me into major depression.

At-Tawwab is a higher stage of forgiveness, when we are able to turn away from focusing on faults of self and others, arguing who's right or wrong, to instead turn towards Allah because Allah is always continuously forgiving you with mercy and blessings. You let go and let God, then you are able to open to joy and ease. This was true for me, although I believed I had turned my back on Allah with anger, I was blessed many times over with whatever I needed. These blessings restored my faith in Allah.

Gradually I came to the understanding on my own, that as I forgave myself, I was able to have compassion for others. Letting go of the grudges I carried for years because somebody said something that I didn't like to me or didn't answer my phone calls. Plenty times I said what I hadn't meant to say or was silent when I should have spoken. One day I observed these mistakes happen frequently when we are tired, then we say and do things that we really don't think or plan to do that hurts other people. We forget, just like children are obstinate, mean, and destructive at nighttime when sleepy, that adults temper tantrums are much worse and have long-term consequences. Like why don't we take ourselves to bed at a reasonable hour?

Perhaps my healing went deeper because my mother in spirit, along with other ancestors and spirit guides took me step-by-step through the stages of grief and forgiveness over the course of several years. They put me in specific situations that I wouldn't have known about or chosen for myself. Allah is truly the best of planners. We do still have free will. Although these were really tough challenging situations that most people would not have entered into, and certainly would not have stayed. I also used the oracle cards and I Ching for guidance in making major decisions, for emotional and spiritual growth that led to perseverance and success. Thanks to the help of psychic mediums at Church of the Spirit for bringing through spirit messages of parents and spouses asking for forgiveness and giving brief advice on doing different now. They also gave encouragement and validated I was on the right path and understanding.

A new psychotherapist also helped me release the last of the effects of past trauma. The details of how this was done is the subject of a forthcoming coming book.

Why I pulled the card, Al-Afuw, makes sense to me now. Al-'Afuw means to completely forgive, to have released and healed the memories of the hurt from one's own heart and mind. A peaceful oneness with all that is. It's been a long journey over my adult lifetime to obtain the freedom of full forgiveness.

Soon after publishing my first book, I felt much lighter as I noticed most of the old feeling memories, thoughts and hurts were gone. Other memoir writers related they experienced similar healing. Forgiveness may be the main theme or message from my books. Hidden from my awareness until nearly finished writing these last chapters.

The authors' *Physicians of the Heart's* explanation of these four names for the stages of forgiveness goes much deeper than my simple examples from my younger years. Having to go through a "dark night of the soul" during my middle years on my way to forgiveness, was not easy. Eventually, I surrendered to being able to love and trust the universe to provide, and to heal other people's animosity. In the process, with age I let go of unnecessary fears and worries of what others may think. I still can have momentary traces of a hurt, bruised ego. Most of this forgiveness process I learned on my own. I wish that we had the community support that indigenous cultures and traditional Sufism had for emotional and spiritual growth. And wish I had the book, *Physicians of the Heart,* sooner because I learn more each time I read or reread it, as it still touches my heart.

Sufism

Intrigued by this different perspective of Allah and the Quran, as pure love and healing sounds, I'd like to learn more about Sufis. Particularly to learn about the "guru" process to help students prepare for and while they're in a natural ecstatic state, but most importantly afterwards, to aid them through the immense changes in consciousness and thinking that results in major life transitions.

Many people think meditation is for staying calm, but when you meditate regularly you see the truth of situations. Regardless of how others are swept up in popular illusions and lies, you can no longer. This causes temporary inner discomfort and confusion along with conflicts in relationships because family, friends, coworkers don't want their bubble burst.

I wanted a personal guru but never had one. There is a saying, "When the student is ready the teacher will appear." So I became my own guru and decided one day I would be a guru for others. Several people asked me to be their spiritual counselor, however they weren't invested in doing their personal development work. They either just want to talk, get advice they mostly didn't follow, or they would ask me to do spiritual readings for yes or no answers. I'd rather help students who are dedicated to improving their own life and others, and who will eventually be able to do their own spiritual work.

A friend from Senegal in 2019, introduced me to some of the cultural aspects of Sufism, when she told me about Sheik Ahmadou Bamba. Later, I learned about women contributions to Islam, honestly astonished because we rarely heard about woman scholars or mystics. *Wrapping Authority: Women Islamic Leaders in a Sufi Movement in Dakar, Senegal* is about

Sufi women's religious participation and spiritual leadership. Senegal is located in West Africa and has a 96% Sufi Muslim population. Another book is, *Women of Sufism: A Hidden Treasure: Writings and Stories of Mystics Poets, Scholars and Saints*, is about Muslim women's contributions from other countries.

There is much more I want to learn about true Islam and the deeper spiritual meaning of all religions. I'm starting to see what my mother loved so much about Islam. How her introducing me to Islam when I was a child, influenced who I am now in fulfillment of my destiny.

Chapter 8: Facing Death and Loss

Many people are afraid of death in the United States and won't talk about it, although there's been a pandemic for almost three years. The only way I hear people talking about death is when they tell friends and family that if they don't get vaccinated they're going to die. Tired, wary of burying their loved ones, they wonder why it's not in the media that death wasn't from COVID, it was cancer, heart attacks, strokes, murders and suicides.

One aspect of Sekert, that I have been a bit afraid of, started with my aunt when I lived with her, there was a pattern of getting to know people for only a couple of years during which they feel an intense need to talk about their lives, guilts, and regrets to me, and then somehow I'm surprised when they pass away shortly after that. This happened with my foster mother who I had not seen in almost thirty years, we got close although it was just with phone calls, and then she passed away. Same with a couple of neighbors, one that I mentioned in the first book that I wrote, *Mother's Love from Beyond*, we had great love for each other. To the end, James thought he was going to get better, just have physical therapy and come back home. When he was in intensive care, he cried and said he didn't want to leave me. He died two days later. This made me not want to make any more friends with my neighbors in my apartment building since most of them are older than I am.

Perhaps it is my calling, my life purpose, especially since I had a near death experience to help people during their end of life transitions, and to assist families with grieving. Instead, I've avoided this assignment. During the COVID pandemic, I've had to step up to comfort more and more friends and family members. Most people were dying of other causes such as heart attacks, strokes, and cancer. The media's extreme focus on COVID leaves many people isolated, not knowing what to do, and grieving on their own without a nation wide effort to provide support.

Being born during a Saturn period meant lots of other types of losses throughout my life. Writing my memoirs was emotionally challenging, as I realized the World Issues Program at the School for International Training closed the year after I graduated, the ORAP college closed temporarily, and decades later Argosy University closed just before I was about to graduate. All due to impending global financial crises. It was a shock to see that Lowry Air Force near Denver Colorado where I received technical training was long gone. It's not like I can show future generations these locations and say 'Look, that's where whatever used to be.'

Sekert is also our ability to manifest. Usually we think of manifesting as picturing what we want. But whatever we dwell on, daydream about, even negative thoughts can also come true. Knowing this, helped me understand the next part of my summer solstice 2021 spiritual guidance reading: I Ching Hexagram 11 (lines 3, 4, and 5), into hexagram 58. Sacred Path card: 13 Coral Nurturing.

I Ching hexagram 11 Peace and Harmony means a time of social harmony, peace and sharing of prosperity, knowledge and influences. Fighting ends.

Line 3: Changes in the natural cycles of life are to be expected. Therefore prosperity will decrease with time, some evil and disagreements return but you shouldn't become sad. Maintain inner peace and enjoy what you have.

Line 4: Be neighborly without boasting of what you have.

Line 5: Uniting with others and being on same level keeps the peace.

Hexagram 58 is similar to Het Heru concept of Joy. Joy that comes from within in. Joy is a choice. Reach out for joy. In life there is both good and bad. It is possible to have both good and bad experiences happening at the same time. When I look back on my younger adult years I really did not know what joy or happiness was.

My Het Heru destiny to fulfill is to know joy and experience joy. Although I usually identify my inner feelings as calmness, this past year many people described me as joyful.

How do I maintain joy when the COVID pandemic and the climate change crises gives me, probably most of us, lots to worry about as we read articles, listen to and watch news media, plus our own experiences and observations. I saw a PBS special documentary about Jesus and what life was like during his time, with the old struggle of good versus evil cruelty.
To my embarrassed surprise, there was then the new idea of apocalyptic events to come and save us all. I have to admit that the idea of an apocalypse gives me comfort. Such as, in the back of the book, *Phoenix Rising*, is a list of predictions that were given back in the 1980s by an elder Native American medicine woman. Most of these predictions have come true during the past three decades. Natural disasters, freak accidents due to

carelessness, a description of Trump-like leaders, with near misses of Third World War (WWIII) and threats of nuclear exchanges. Also the COVID-19 pandemic is mentioned in the book, *Phoenix Rising*, including the possibility that there could be a man-made accident from a lab. Could COVID-19 be that? Especially since we keep getting contradictory information from the CDC about COVID-19 and the vaccinations effectiveness. We have all been exposed, double exposed, and overexposed to the "virus." So shouldn't we all have herd immunity naturally by now? The elder medicine woman also predicted that people will refuse to go to work because there are no longer any benefits, not even a living wage. Hence, "the Great Resignation, Lying Flat, and Quiet Quitting." Could the chaos of the Trump administration have been staged on purpose to entertain, distract, shield the public from reacting to how serious our domestic and global economic and food shortage problems are? The consequences of overconsumption, treating the environment and essential human labor as disposable.

Sekert also represents the foundational structure of buildings, projects, organizations and society. If the foundation is not correctly built or maintained it will collapse. We've hurriedly thrown together buildings and programs, that now can't be sustained. Sekert is Time. Time to learn from our mistakes, and start from scratch erecting new sustainable, healthy communities.

Although this feels stressful going through major changes, it is amazing to watch all of these Native American predictions unfold, each event bringing us closer to the end days of true peace, equality, and harmony with the environment. While we may arrive kicking and screaming, I can see this new era happening in my lifetime.

I've made a commitment to reviewing my solstice spiritual readings once a week on Saturdays (Sekert's day). Otherwise, with a busier schedule I have less time to remember and focus on my spiritual goals. What I've needed or desired, including finances simply shows up without me doing rituals or even praying for it. Perhaps these are rewards for living life correctly, with guidance from my solstice readings, intuition, and attempts to live out the principles and personalities of the ancient Khametic Paut Neteru deities, saints, attributes of Allah, and wise descriptions of totem animals' behaviors to the best of my understandings.

The other commitment I made, is developing my mediumship skills. Sekert aids in the connection between the Earth and the unseen heavenly world of the Source of pure love, knowledge, and ancestral spirits who have passed on, and those waiting to be born. Sekert is our ability to communicate with our spirit loved ones, enlightened ancestors (Shepsu) and spirit guides. Psychic mediums and indigenous traditional healers are able to relay these messages.

Chapter 9: A Friend Responds Through a Medium Message

My first book, *Mother's Love from Beyond: A Healing Journey of Grief and Loss*, tells the story of how I was introduced to the concept of mediumship. After it was published, I received the following message in September 2020, during a private reading on the phone with the medium Cher:

"So do we have a question to start with?"

"We do! There is a friend that I have not seen or heard from in a long time, and she lives in another country. I've wondered how she is. She came to me in a dream the other night."

"Okay, what's her first name?"

"Inviolatta."

"That's pretty. Do you think she's made her transition?"

"I've been thinking not yet, but now that you asked, I'm not sure I get that feeling."

"Okay, because when you said her name, right away a woman's face came in with a big smile. Would it be appropriate that she would wear some sort of headdress? Not a hat but some sort of head dress that would cover her forehead?"

I hesitated before answering. "Does it look similar to a cloth beret?"

"I get more of a wrap around her forehead. Not so much like a French beret but more like if I were to wrap my head in a scarf. I would cover my forehead and then I would wrap the rest of my hair."

"Maybe."

"Because I'm getting this woman coming through with a big smile. A headdress, that's what she's calling it. I'm also seeing hoop earrings on her. I get the feeling that maybe the headdress is more about her returning to nature. Returning to her natural state. I don't know if she would have dressed like this per se, but kind of symbolic of returning to a starting point. Does that make any sense?"

"Yes"

"Do you remember the woman at church who was a naturopath? She moved back home to Africa. This puts me in mind of your friend. This does very much feel like your friend."

"I'm glad."

"I'm asking her to give me a little bit more to identify her. She's got lots of books around her. And I feel like this person was very curious. She had so many interests. Now she's showing me herbal plants. This is where her interest have taken her. She's working with herbal plants. Does this fit at all?"

"Yes. You can keep going."

"All right, but it's hard if I don't hear from you to know if I'm on track."

"Well, you know me. I am able to put the pieces together."

"Right. I do get her being very, very happy. So when you asked how she was doing, she's coming through very happy. She's showing me bare feet."

"Yes!" I said excited.

"I'm hearing 'bare feet and grounding.' Did she work with you on your feet? I feel like she wants to continue. She's saying she wants to continue. She's sending you energy as if she is actually working on your feet. She comes in and I get her putting her hands on your ankles. So in spirit she's a very powerful healer. This may have been more of an interest on this side. But she's really blossoming on the spirit side. And she's a wonderful healer. She comes in and she has her hands on your ankles. I see your feet. She sending you wonderful wonderful healing energy. So it's not so much about her but what she brings for you at this time.

I'm also getting a lot of music coming in. There's a lot of drums. It's not really a Congo drum. They are using the word tribal drum. And the music is really wonderful. It's very uplifting. So she just comes in with a lot of, the word is native, a lot of native energy for you. And I see that energy traveling and moving up into your shoulders and down your arms to your hands. This is a real transfer of energy from her to you. And I feel like, as we know with your work that — oh that's interesting — lot of your healing energy is with words and thoughts. She centers this energy from the heart chakra into your hands. So I feel like this has to do with your writing now. And I hear the word collaborate. She's going to be someone who will be collaborating with you.

"Oh wow!"

"Very, very powerful what comes through. So I see you writing, but then it feels like you get stuck and it could be, I'm not sure how to express this. You're not happy with something that you've written and that's when she comes in. She's showing me she's pulling apart some threads. You know, like how knitters roll their yarn into a ball to keep it from getting tangled up?"

"Yes."

"She is coming to help you detangle your thoughts so that you can express it the exact way that you want it to be. This is going to be fun! (Laughs). That's what she says, 'This is going to be fun.'

There is a real sense of sisterhood that comes through with her."

"Yes, very much."

"There is a strong sense of sisterhood. I feel like the work you were going to be doing with her, as the vibration expands, it is going to bring to you more sisters. That feels really good. And that happens on both sides. She has a couple of sisters that she works with, and she will bring them through when she needs to. But for you, on this side, that vibration is going to bring in more sisters and that feels really good.

"Yes."

"Do you share your writing while you're creating? Do you talk to people about what you're doing?"

"I have, if I know what you mean. I don't share exactly what I'm writing. But this has been different for me because I usually do things alone. I have told people that I'm writing my book and somewhat about the process. Yes, I have found that discussing it actually helps me get more clarity."

"She's showing me something like a writers' workshop, where people are sitting in a circle. It's another type of collaboration as writers talk about their process. So she brings that in for you. Certainly doing something on Zoom could be easier than meeting in the flesh. Discussing the process feels like the most important. Just being with other people. I think a writer's life can be lonely. Can be very singular. And so she brings in this workshop idea so that you again are in community with other people. There is a wonderful exchange of ideas. Not so much of ideas of what you are writing about, but talking about the craft. That's her word, talking about the craft. And that just feeds you. Finding other people like you, other writers gives you energy for what you want to do."

"Now she's bringing in small oranges. I don't know if these are mandarin oranges but they are that size, maybe a little bit smaller. When you take a bite, it energizes you. So she brings that in for you."

"Okay."

"Are there bright colors in your apartment?"

"Yes."

Good. It is important to have bright, bright colors. I'm getting a beautiful yellow coming in. I'm getting a red with some blue in it so it's not a harsh red, but a kind of softer red. And then an orange color. I don't know if that would be the combination. I'm not sure if it's a painting or a fabric but she's bringing in those colors for you. It feels like, especially with winter coming that you, the word is 'need.' You are going to need to have bright, bright colors around you."

Cher was quiet for a few minutes trying to see what else, then she continued, "I feel like we get stuck. It is winter and I feel like I'm stuck. She really wants you to look at how do you take care of yourself. But I don't know if this stuck is more emotional with your writing or physically stuck with the weather. It seems that with winter coming it's going to be more difficult this year. I want to take a long sigh." (Cher makes a big sigh, deep breath sound, and then laughs).

I too sigh loudly.

"After this summer."

"Right."

"We're going to be stuck some more and it is going to be like yeah. So having some bright colors around you is going to be helpful. And I want to have around you some things that you enjoy looking at. And it feels like you have these items but they may be put away like in a cupboard or something."

Yes."

"Leave a couple of things out that bring you joy when you look at them. She's really working to set you up for wintertime because it feels like it's going to be a long one. Long but productive. So that's something to look forward to. I get your friend leaving now and someone else is coming in."

Reflections on the Medium Message

It wasn't until later in the year that I found an old Facebook messenger message from a mutual classmate reported that Inviolatta had passed away two years prior, because I only occasionally go to my Facebook page and didn't know I had to sign up separately for Facebook messenger. Although I had not received emails or letters from Inviolatta for more than two years, in my mind was the possibility that she was still alive. Power outages were frequent when it rained, so it was not unusual for there to be no phone or internet access. Snail mail took months and wasn't secure. Zimbabwe had economic problems, with civil unrest and hearing reports of people being tortured or killed for any disagreements with Mugabe, would've been dangerous for Inviolatta and I to exchange emails.

Inviolatta previously worked for years as a schoolteacher, then later a school principal. Hence, the psychic medium Cher seeing her with books. Later Inviolatta changed to doing community work through ORAP that included administrative duties of balancing the books. Then she came to the United States to go to the School for International Training (SIT) to get a bachelor's degree from the World Issues Program. That's where I met Inviolatta.

Inviolatta gave me a going away party and her nephew video taped us dancing. She danced in her bare feet. On the SIT campus in the United States, Inviolatta sometimes wore a braided wig, after she had tried to get a perm that made some of her hair fall out. So the next year, at home in Zimbabwe she had very short natural hair. I've not seen her wear a headdress, nor traditional clothes.

What is amazing about this mediumship reading is the message applies more to winter 2022, than the original predictions for 2020-2021. I reviewed the audio recording of the message as I was writing in this second book about Zimbabwe and now understood why I frequently felt Inviolatta's presence, helping me to remember. With my first book in 2020, my writing flowed, and I finished a major draft in six months. Writing in 2022, about my Zimbabwe experiences I felt stuck, as it was challenging to put into words and also emotionally difficult because I miss everybody there. Zimbabwe is my second home.

The writer's workshop idea? Well, I wanted an African American editor this time, who would understand or at least be willing to learn about African American, Native American and other indigenous cultural beliefs and spirituality. Two Black writers' editorial companies turned me down, one editor saying that she wasn't comfortable with the "occult." Occult? Astrology and divination are the occult? The good thing is one of websites offered a Black writer's group. A commitment is required to attend regularly. There is a small annual fee but for me it was worth it.

The COVID-19 pandemic partial shutdown, mask mandate, and social distancing continued into 2022. I really couldn't complain much about the six months full lockdown in 2020. But it's now two years and counting! Cher knew that I usually get mild depression, mostly less smiles in the wintertime because using a wheelchair limited my independent travel outside when it snowed. Literally stuck in the house.

My new couch in my living room is a burgundy red, with two large off-white pillows with a few thin red and orange stripes. Cher hasn't come to my apartment and I hadn't told her about my furnishings. The cloth slipcover, at that time, was a bright red. Later after this message from Inviolatta, I sewed a yellow cover to replace it with a waterproof fabric I already had, but planned to hide it underneath the bright red cover. The yellow cover still brightens my home year round.

Stored away in boxes in my bedroom are my large watercolor paintings. Frames that size can be expensive. A neighbor offered to hang them for me when I first moved here sixteen years ago. But then I went to graduate school, within ten years tall bookshelves covered my walls instead of pictures. This past summer, a colleague Denise came to deliver a big box with the little dolls and miniatures I made for a play therapy demonstration. She visited a little while. Seeing my large sunflower acrylic paintings propped up on some boxes in a corner in the living room she got excited and inquired if I had more. I pulled out some of my paintings and showed her. Denise loved the bright colors and said, "I have frames at my house and am happy to help you hang your paintings. She also fussed at me. "Our creativity needs to be where we can see it. Even if you tape it up on the wall."

Probably a message through my colleague from Inviolatta then, as I'm now reminded that I painted a picture of one of Inviolatta's favorite flowers and gave it to her while I was in

Zimbabwe. In one of my boxes is also a large painting of the Zimbabwe flag and other symbols.

In the backyard of her beautiful ranch style home, Inviolatta had a small garden. However, as far as I know she only grew collard greens, not herbs. If she knew about herbs, she didn't talk about them. Her parents and family lived out on the farm in the rural villages, so it is possible that perhaps by watching her mother and other elders she learned about herbs.

The woman wearing white who knows herbs, may be the traditional healer Leticia, that I studied with in the city. I wore white when I went to the clinic at her house, in a room filled with shelves of jars of herbs and other medicines. But she too had short natural hair and didn't cover her hair. She showed me how to play special tribal rhythms on her drums. Maybe Leticia passed over into spirit too.

It is possible that the headdress, that Cher saw, was only symbolic to help her identify that my friends were African. And Cher remembering our mutual friend from church the naturopath, helped identify what country in Africa, although Cher did not mention Zimbabwe.

My lower legs hurt with the cold and dampness of winter. The pain seems worse this year, especially from my ankles to my knees, as I've made the commitment to exercise and try walking forward with a normal heel to toe gait. I did pray for relief and to have my dream come true of me being able to go hiking again out in nature. In a recent mediumship practice, someone else saw a woman they identified as my mother, was massaging my feet and legs! My legs do feel better.

I'm grateful to have help and encouragement from spirit writing this book. A different main spirit guide, who is precise with words and grammar is leading. I don't argue I just follow.

All I know is, this was not my usual way of writing, but I like this no nonsense style. It's easier.

Chapter 10: Ochosi Revisited

In the process of writing this book I reread, *Ochosi: Ifa and the Spirit of the Tracker.* I was curious how the Ifa reading that the Candomble priestess Valdeci gave me in 1996, about Ochosi energy ruling my head, has influenced my life.

Ochosi protects the needs of the environment. In Zimbabwe, I witnessed elders' knowledge of elemental spirits in everything including the weather. Climate change is a result of all of us improperly using natural resources. Traditional healers knew how to restore balance in the environment. Their drumming brings rain during drought. Spiritual evolution is defined as being in perfect harmony with nature. Ochosi teaches us that everything in nature has a conscience.

My affinity for Native American culture may also be influenced by Ochosi's connection to Native American spirits and the people who are guardians of the land. Animals, especially birds have been my allies, giving me support, encouragement and lightening my mood. Red-winged blackbirds whom I hadn't seen in a few years now make their presence known again as they sing, then fly in front of me, similarly with bright red cardinals and their families, robins, ravens and hawks.

I really miss being out in nature and want to get serious about cabin retreats or even living again out in the countryside, in spite of having used a wheelchair and the COVID pandemic crisis. It may be possible that I won't need the wheelchair outside. I don't know, I haven't tried walking long distances beyond my apartment, nor up and down stairs or uneven terrain yet.

Ochosi gives us knowledge of the mysteries of plants. On my bedroom wall, I have a picture of George Washington Carver for inspiration. Plants talked to him and he listened. Sometimes before sleep at night, I would ask for a dream showing me what foods or natural herb I needed to heal symptoms I was having. Upon wakening, I would write down or draw a picture of what plant I saw in the the dream, and then go research it. Othertimes, books would open to pages of homeopathic medicines needed for someone else.

I did not know back in 1996, why the Cuban priestess gave me the cleansing herbs specifically customized for me. I simply followed her instructions for how to mix them with water and pour this over my head while standing in the bathtub. Nor what it meant for Ochosi's spiritual herbs to open human access to communication with the spirit realm. Nor did I know about mediumship then. I did learn a little about herbal remedies, gemstones, and baths for physical healing, but not about the cleansing herbal baths for spiritual healing that relieves psychological distress. Homeopathy is the closest I've gotten to using herbs to relieve psychological distress.

Thinking about it now, perhaps referrals to priest for the Ochosi spiritual cleansing herbs could open the way for my clients who do not have the capability to be introspective, to have personal insights relevant to changing their behavior, or to see the larger perspectives of how their consequences also affect others. Not everyone is able to think abstractly and apply what they learn verbally with talk therapy.

In my first book, *Mother's Love from Beyond*, I mentioned I started in mediumship classes at the Church of the Spirit.

However I stopped due to transportation problems, and after seeing curriculums for mediumship classes are mostly about spiritualism history. My African and Native American heritage already believes in spirits of our ancestors, so why have to read so many books to prove that life continues after so called death. It's like having to memorize Columbus and other European explorers' history for discovering countries that existed long before they were born! Plus my head is full from textbooks giving me a trillion words vocabulary and theories from years of graduate school. I want real mediumship practice! For now my spiritual guidance messages are admonishing me to get serious about committing to deeper levels of development for being a Seer and Healer. To learn the herbs as well as put more meditation and dreamtime into my daily life.

Ifa and Ochosi's Role

Ifa is a complex system of divination based on the concept of destiny and good character. You chose your destiny before you were born. Balance between self and the world is the basis for developing good character through spiritual transformation. Using divination helps you to be able to make the correct decisions at the crossroads. Consulting the Ifa oracles or a priest for which path to take and following that guidance will bring blessings from the Orisha because of your ongoing good character. Then obstacles will be removed from your path. These obstacles can be internal fears, doubts, confusion, ignorance, inexperience or the wrong motivation. External obstacles are injustice, oppression, poverty, natural disasters, personal illness, and misfortunes. It is important to know the difference between problems caused by your own internal obstacles such as your own thoughts, actions and behavior instead of only blaming external factors.

Ochosi is one of the Ifa orisha energies that can provide you personal guidance and clarity on how to heal and release fears and limitations that hold you back, as well as bring liberation and protection from societal injustices and laws. Similar to Ogun, he has the power to clear away obstacles that are in the way of your spiritual growth. Ochosi's role is to show us the the shortest path to our spiritual goals. Spirit certainly has presented me with inspiration by frequent, awesome miracles that show me the way and to keep me going forward with the hard life tasks.

Remembering the story the priestess Valdeci told me about how Ochosi was initially the warrior Ogun, who had to adapt his hunting method from using a machete, to using a bow and arrows in the Americans, I was really surprised to find a large bow with arrows at a store in downtown Bulawayo, Zimbabwe. Seeing it as a symbol of both African and Native American cultures, I bought it. The bow seemed delicate. However, when I shipped it to my sister's home, and complained because I wasn't allowed to carry it on the plane, she laughed at me, "A bow and arrow is a weapon after all!" This was before September 11, 2001, so it never occurred to me that airport security would consider me, or the bow and arrows dangerous.

"It Doesn't Matter Where You are Going. Any Road Will Do." Ifa Proverb.

This proverb reminds me of people I know, who come to me for help because they feel stuck, not able to move forward in their lives. Anxiety and fear of failure keeps them from their goals. American society makes these fears worse by pretending to offer numerous opportunities to choose from, yet fierce competition and discrimination only allows a few to succeed, even if your capabilities are the best of the best. More and more information is piled on for what each individual is expected to know. Weighed down, it is difficult to have confidence in making decisions.

As a healer and counselor, I do a lot of prayers on clients' behalf. I ask for heavenly guidance to show me a different way to help heal them. Honestly, sometimes I get frustrated. It can be difficult for me to understand and have empathy when some clients are the complete opposite from me. No inner faith or optimism to pull them forward on their own during tough situations. Not feeling connected to anyone or a higher power, when they pray they feel nothing happens. Nonetheless, I've been driven to help them to see their hidden potential and beauty. Most importantly, to show them that they are not helpless and therefore can begin taking responsibility for their participation in their own life. To truly accomplish this, supportive spiritually healthy families, communities, and countries are needed. Indigenous cultures understood that we are not meant to do everything alone. Together we have opportunities to improve our character by observing each and everyone around us, naturally showing us a mirror reflection of opposite qualities that we can develop in ourselves and appreciate everyone for being who they are.

The Ochosi book gives warnings to people who refuse to put serious effort into finding their own personal destiny and improving their character. Some people come to me for help but are very reluctant to following through on recommendations so that they can know what faith, peace, joy, and having a life purpose feels like for themselves. They suffer with depression, focused on not having achieved societal expectations of material and career success. Their time is consumed with cellphones, computer games, and television. Rarely having quiet solitude for creativity, sleep and dreaming to connect to self and the universe. Mostly they are afraid of possible loneliness, intense emotions and memories that need to be felt and acknowledged to be healed. Not knowing that underneath these uncomfortable emotions are peace, joy and connection. In contrast, I probably overdo solitude. It is because of my faith and optimism, even the tiniest amount, that I am able to persevere.

Ochosi helps put you on the shortest route to be in perfect alignment with your destiny. A destiny with lessons you agreed to learn in this lifetime before your birth. Well, to say, Ochosi "helps" is putting it mildly, because you will often find yourself in places and situations you hadn't consciously intended to go. I have mixed feelings and opinions about Ifa being based on the belief that when you are focused on developing a good character then you will receive the blessings of a long life with abundance and wealth — while those who have bad characters will be cursed by illness, poverty and infertility. It begs the question, why do bad things happen to good people?

This Ifa and other similar major religions' beliefs in divine punishments, is probably the feelings most people have when Ochosi's energy removes people, activities, and possessions that are not in line with your spiritual destiny path. However afterwards, Ochosi also gives inspiration, guidance, and opens the way for forging a new path that is much smoother and abundance filled. During the ignorance of my younger years, I had more crises that may not have necessarily been due to me having a bad character back then. Mostly, I just didn't know any better, although I adhered to religious rules. My life got progressively better as I committed to following divine guidance from consulting the oracles, and allowed spiritual transformations to happen to the best of my ability. Then as promised, the magic and blessings of Ochosi continues to awe me with abundance and miracles.

Carryover Soul

When I first read of the concept of a "carryover soul" in the books, *Spirit Song* and *Phoenix Rising*, I sobbed aloud. A carryover soul is usually thought of as the reincarnation of a grandparent in a later grandchild. West Africans believe similar. It could also represent some of the memories of ancient past lives that intrude on our present lives. I cried because this explained the loneliness I've felt as if I did not belong anywhere, felt so different than my family or anyone else, especially with my strong interest in indigenous spirituality and healing, love of and connection to nature, and how cramped I feel living in cities.

Lonely too, because those who have Ochosi energy will be sabotaged by those closest to us. Ochosi brings us the truth of who hinders our growth and who supports it. Acknowledging this truth was very painful. Since the Cuban priestess explained to me about Ochosi's task to always keep me on a cleared spiritual path means losing those dear to me, I've had less incidences of being sabotaged by those closest to me. Perhaps it is also because I've lived alone for the past sixteen years. And I'm more aware and observant of people who come into my life who only seem to focus on their own needs. Actions speak louder than words, became my motto. Therefore, I must first become aware of my own thoughts and behaviors that may be leading the other person on. What are my own motives? Am I over giving? Is it a habit of automatically giving or being sucked in to solving other's problems without realizing it?

I am the one who has to know my own intentions, make my actions match my intentions, and then allow others their natural consequences. I had to learn to stop rescuing people from their own choices and behaviors. Sometimes though, following and submitting to my I Ching guidance, means putting up with individuals that I know does not have my best interest in mind. Helps at least, knowing ahead of time that they may cause me to lose or sacrifice something. Usually it is a minor loss.

Where I probably experienced almost nonstop sabotaging, was trying to get through the clinical psychology doctoral program. I learned the hard way that although I spoke up for other's rights, justice doesn't always bring desired results. Even after I transferred to another university the dean and staff "kept losing my documents." A friend commented near the end, "Maybe all these challenges are telling you that maybe you could be barking up the wrong tree."

No, I knew I was to graduate, so I hung in there anyway because I checked in regularly with the I Ching, and Sacred Path, and Metu Neter cards readings along the way. Ochosi, Ogun, and Sekert energies combined gave me the ability to see and understand the bigger picture of the effects of economic decline, discrimination and racism factors to have the strength and courage to persevere. Of course, I asked the I Ching before I submitted my application to the university. The I Ching message was, that going through the doctoral program would mean by my being able to sacrifice for the benefit of helping others, I would reap rewards. I thought that meant that I would see abundance after I graduated with a huge income but to my surprise, I was given all that I needed materially and spiritually, along with family emotional support throughout the program. And much more after I graduated.

Ochosi is our ability to defend ourselves. I've taken a few self-defense workshops for women, a Tai Chi class and now do Qigong for exercise. But I've not had martial arts classes. Sometimes I tried to imagine how I would have defended myself while sitting in my wheelchair. Could I use the same tactics and strategies to throw a potential attacker off their feet? Perhaps I haven't thought much about physically having to defend myself, because when I call on Ogun (Heru Khuti) energy to surround me with protection then I'm usually safe in my travels.

We are also warned against having narrow minded expectations of quick solutions for how we want wealth to manifest. Ochosi energy is the wisdom, adaptability, flexibility and problem-solving capabilities for survival. Ability to stay focused on a goal, similar to how a hunter has to sit or stay motionless waiting for the right opportunity and time to advance. Transformation always takes place, one step at a time in slow steady increments that requires patience and persistence. In the United States, where we are used to immediate gratification expecting an instant fix, we may miss the many miracles around us. Spiritual growth requires consistent concentration, determination and patience maintained over several years. However, there are times when Ochosi does bring instant transformation, with instant changes in perception that penetrate to the deeper levels of your awareness and consciousness. Those overnight insights, epiphanies and "Ah hah moments" during the day that suddenly connect your understanding of your past, present and future.

I mentioned earlier about Heru Khuti's ability to assess what is obsolete and no longer needed, Ochosi also pushes us to evaluate and discard habits and items that are no longer working in our lives. This includes getting rid of clutter.

Chapter 11: Getting Rid of Clutter

After living in this apartment building for almost 17 years, in April 2022 I had an extra push, probably from Ochosi energy, to discard old items that I didn't use. The new building owners informed us that they were going to rehab the whole building. New bathroom and kitchen cabinets, countertops, stove, refrigerator, laminate floors instead of carpets, paint, blinds, toilet, and lighting. This would be done five apartments at a time starting with the 11th floor.

They would put us up in a nearby hotel for a week, in my case two weeks because I live in an ADA accessible apartment, and give us a gift card of $180 for meals each week. The hotel would provide the usual continental breakfast, but because of the pandemic their restaurant was closed so we would have to order in, or go out to nearby restaurants. Using Door Dash would use up my money in a few days. The ADA accessible apartments were to be done last, in April, which I was grateful for because my wheelchair wouldn't go through the snow. With the continental breakfast of waffles, toast, cereal, and mostly fast food joints in the college campus area, I had to go hunting for healthy gluten-free, and vegetarian food.

Friends asked me if I was excited about the move. I had mixed feelings because of course, who wouldn't want a clean new apartment? The catch was although the owners originally told us that movers would come and pack us up, they later told us that the movers would only come on our move out day. They supplied the cardboard boxes, tape, bubble wrap, and packing paper. This is a low-income senior building with old folks and a few middle-age people with disabilities, how were we to pack ourselves? Our newest manager, after a secession of managers, informed us at a meeting that we would get fined if our apartments weren't left clean on moving day! She told us that we had families and home care agencies that would help us. Not understanding most tenants were in their 70's and above, some in their 100's may not have adult children. Perhaps they did not birth them or outlived their children, or have conflicts with them, either one stayed intoxicated, or they live across the country. Further, certainly nothing was business as usual during a pandemic.

Even before the pandemic it was difficult to acquire reliable, affordable home care services. As tenants, we soon found out how exhausting and almost impossible it was for us to do constant sorting, lifting and walking back and forth to pack boxes. Each day, I packed up the personal items that I didn't want misplaced or broken into smaller boxes, that I had to buy myself because I couldn't lift their so-called "small" boxes. Later I discovered that the company the building buys the moving boxes from, does sell a smaller size, so again why weren't they taking us into consideration, although I asked for them?

I was awake most nights mentally strategizing how to make it easier. One woman who used a walker finally told the manager that she couldn't do it. She hurt her back and her shoulder with the lifting, and it was so tiring. I had already told the moving coordinator that I couldn't have all those boxes in the way of me maneuvering my wheelchair. On rainy and snowy days, I'm unsteady on my feet and have more pain in my knees. So I'm glad someone else spoke up. When I went downstairs later to get more packing supplies from the office, the moving coordinator told me someone would come during the last few days and help me pack. I was glad because I spent four days resting in bed after also hurting my back and being so tired. Plus, I had bruises on my lower legs from bumping into boxes, that forced me to stop doing as much as I was doing.

Somehow we managed, as we wondered if the construction crew and the management of the building considered us as people. The construction crew used the two passenger elevators to move heavy new supplies, huge carts with debris, and for moving tenants' furniture in and out. They of course broke one elevator, and then the other elevator which meant that we had to wait and wait to ride the elevators. What about when we needed to get to appointments on time? They would turn off the water without notice. Some weeks they gave us letters that said that the water would be turned off a couple of days that week, supposedly so we could prepare, however the water was off all day each day that week. We'd get up early in the morning and there's no water. What about older people with incontinence challenges? It also meant we couldn't do laundry. At the meeting last year, they told us that we were going to get a new laundry room. There were only two washers working, with construction workers going through the laundry room, miserable anyway with the outside door open, blowing in cold air on us. In the fall, they took out the remaining washers and dryers, having us to go two block away to the laundry mat in the winter months before the new machines came. COVID supply chain shortages was to blame.

And then they want to fine us if our apartments aren't clean on move out day? Who would have the energy by then after packing, and the stress of our routines and sanity being interrupted, with the constant sound of drilling and hammering?

Meanwhile, I made it my goal to give away or throw away as much as possible, by for every two boxes I packed I would discard almost one box full. I've collected a lot over time of course, but also because I use a wheelchair when I go outside, I got in the habit of preparing for rainy or snowy weather. Starting in October, each time I went to the grocery store I would buy double my usual amount. At back-to-school sales I bought enough paper, composition books, pencils, pens, erasers for the year. Not being able to be at the campus library in the wintertime, because paratransit vans would drive me from one end of Chicago to the other taking sometimes three hours instead of a half hour to get me to and from the University. As a result, I bought textbooks to read at home. This included other books for research papers. I really should've taken out stock in Amazon over ten years ago!

There were positives, as packing built my stamina and muscle strength with lifting, walking back and forth across the room, and from room to room to box similar items together. It felt like I was on my feet constantly. Better than an hour's workout at the gym! My apartment is now cleaner than it's been in a decade, as I dust shelves and sweep out corners. Seems silly since the construction crew will tear out the carpets, cabinets, and closets but dust was making me sneeze even with an air filter.

All of the sorting, discarding and finishing old projects is symbolic of my finishing and being done with the past. With a mixture of initial overwhelm, waves of panic, loss and grief then relief, I somehow felt safe enough, after all these decades to be able to empty out. Letting go, releasing what is no longer me. Moving on with my new, yet unknown me. Ochosi certainly didn't make it an easy transition! Perhaps it would have felt better, if I had gotten rid of the clutter, but not had to empty out my insides. Or known previously what I was physically and mentally capable of.

Chapter 12: Spiritual Transformation

Ochosi has certainly kept me returning again and again to making spiritual transformation a priority, in spite of my other plans. Although I spent many years in college, in my home life there were always crises that required faith and inner changes to get through: my near death experience occurred during my first year of nursing school, I divorced soon after graduation. African spirituality came into my life a couple of years before moving to Chicago to go to an art school that became a bridge for me studying abroad in Zimbabwe. Returning to the United States very ill, I became physically disabled spending ten years recovering while going through menopause and an emotional long dark night of the soul. Very grateful when I discovered the Church of the Spirit and mediumship during my first year of the doctoral clinical psychology program.

Family and friends say that they are proud of me for all my academic accomplishments and degrees. However, there were plenty of times that I've cried and asked God, "Why did you give me a registered nurse degree and only let me work as a nurse for a few years? Then have to return from Zimbabwe with a debilitating illness that didn't let me use my bachelor's degree. The Great Recession of 2008 began two years before I graduated with my master's degree in counseling. It wasn't just me who wasn't getting hired. When I talk to my schoolmates no matter what kind of counseling specialty — community, school, family or rehabilitation counseling they had to take on other unrelated jobs. The COVID-19 shutdown sidelined me for a year. At my age, I could almost give up. Why not just retire early and live on Social Security benefits? The corporate system makes sure that you're never done with "education." In Illinois, at least a year of a postdoctoral clinical psychology fellowship with supervised employment is required before you can apply to take the licensure exam, the EPPP (Exam for Professional Practice in Psychology).

But why? Why? Why? Why? I studied and worked hard, paid my own tuition throughout community college, then irrationally accrued student loans on top of student loans for a bachelors and two graduate degrees. What was the purpose?

Ochosi gave and took, gave and took. It took me years to get through my thick head, what letting go of attachments meant. The COVID pandemic crisis released the rest of my fears and attachments to people, places and things. I did not know this was a requirement for reaching my goal of getting to know what it's like to "just be." This journey "to just be" that started out 30 years ago.

Now, I no longer cry over not using my academic degrees. I've since realized that my college education helped me and others who have crossed my path or have come along for portions of my journey. The anatomy, physiology, microbiology, medical terminology, and pharmacology knowledge helped me survive life-threatening illnesses when doctors didn't have a clue what to do with me. I learned more after nursing school than during nursing school. Fascinated by psychiatric nursing courses, wanting to learn more about human behavior, I saw back in the 80's that most people wouldn't be in the hospital so frequently if their social needs in their homes and communities were addressed. Traveling abroad opened my heart to valuing people, and my eyes to see there are many perspectives and ways to live. Otherwise, I was previously stuck in thinking there is only one way, and being the best at that.

Ochosi teaches us to have balance between self and the world. This certainly taught me the hard way not to go to extremes in life. Being a strict vegan, with no salt or processed sugar in my cupboards for ten years, followed by ten years recovering from the resulting disabilities was my most challenging lesson to learn. Yet those ten years both took me down into the dark night of the soul, and raised me up at the same time.

Each of the Zimbabwean traditional healers told me their stories of how they became gravely ill, almost dying, bedridden some with paralysis requiring others to nurse them back to health. One of the traditional healers told me she temporarily had psychosis. However, at that time I was focused on gathering information for my research thesis assignment about the Zimbabwe healthcare system. They told me their stories more than once, but I wasn't thinking it could happen to me. After all, I had already almost died in 1982 returning to Earth with psychic abilities.

I completely forgot about a magazine at the Healing Earth Resources bookstore before I went to Zimbabwe. It was closing time, so the clerk was turning off the lights while talking to my friend Paula. I was standing by the magazine rack reading an article about Native American and other indigenous cultural beliefs that if you don't use your psychic and healing gifts and talents then you could become very ill or even die. The clerk hurried us out the store and gave the magazine to me for free.

When I returned to the United States, from Zimbabwe, I was only focused on survival and coping emotionally. I did vaguely remember a traditional healer who said he had discovered an herbal cure for AIDS. Would I please help him promote his herbal remedy in the United States? Was the decline in my health a punishment for totally forgetting his request? Unemployed and homeless in the city that was still new to me, I didn't have connection to people to network with, to tell them of his discovery. The friends I had prior to going abroad didn't understand my need for physical, mental, and psychic readjustment.

The true wounded healer heals one's self and then others. First, I had to heal myself physically, as doctors told me there is no treatment in Western modern medicine for degenerative neurological diseases. Second, I had to find ways to heal emotionally and socially. It seems that I also had to go through all these Ochosi trials and tribulations in order to prepare me to understand what my future clients have gone through.

Chapter 13: Career Path

Remember my second Metu Neter card career reading back in 1994? Tehuti tu tchaas /Tehuti tem maat. Tehuti represents a teacher, expert, spiritual counselor. At that time, I was new to African spirituality and didn't know what Tehuti meant except that I was to use the oracles and intuition for guidance.

I try to regularly consult the oracles. Have to be honest here, my bad, because sometimes I do get busy and am already in a situation or relationship, and only remember to consult when I start to have trouble. Plus, since I'm usually blessed with abundance, then I get lazy and overconfident.

For my careers, including choice of clinical training sites, I do regularly consult the oracles. Soon after graduation in 2020, I did oracle readings concerning where I should do my postdoctoral fellowship. No matter what location I inquired, the guidance was for me to nurture myself first. Guidance from the, *Soul Lesson and Soul Purpose Oracle Cards*, and the I Ching readings were for me to rest, to work on my own faults, with the possibility of being misunderstood because of cultural differences, and it was not the time to start anything new. Ever busy between resting, during these two years of being unemployed, I enjoyed being able to participate in community events, express my creativity through writing this book, making African American dolls and culturally appropriate miniatures for sandtray therapy. It was great to be able to finish projects I started years ago, easing my guilt for having accumulated all those supplies. And to not have to rush.

Of course, I wondered were there problems with my health that I wasn't aware of, and how to improve my health. So I consulted, *The Medical I Ching: Oracle of the Healer Within*, and received hexagram 52 Keeping Still, lines 1 and 2 into hexagram 26 the Taming Power of the Great:

There could be diseases from chronic stress and serious accumulations of toxins. Fair prognosis when get prompt treatment. Keeping still refers more to inner stillness and calm than being physically still.

I was recovering from repeated trauma and challenges that everyone else was also having since 2019, so I did have some mild depression and anxiety that caused me to doubt myself. Physically, painful leg and foot spasms with ankle swelling kept me awake at night. I certainly didn't want the lower legs paralysis to return. With the COVID pandemic extending past a year, I knew rest and self-care was the best way to prevent illness, so I obeyed. In the meantime, I quietly prepared for when the time was right for me to return to being out in the world.

Later, I did get a few days of COVID symptoms of severe headache, sinus infection, mild pneumonia, cough and mild fever mentioned in the Medical I Ching interpretation of hexagrams 52 and 26. Gradually I had to acknowledge other reasons why heaven instructed me to take not one year, but almost two years to rest. My physical health stayed strong as I had the luxury of drinking enough water, regular sleep, healthy meals and bowel movements.

However, I'd have waves and waves of uncomfortable memories of losses and regrets that I hadn't realized didn't have much to do with my childhood, or young adult years that I wrote about in my first book. It was mostly from the trauma I suffered in graduate school. Some of this trauma and grief is not unique to me. If you think about practicums and internships where we go to different cities, have supervisors, colleagues and clients that we establish relationships within a year and then we move on to the next location for a year. During my internship I was going to five different locations, each on a different day of the week with four different focuses at a private school, medical clinic, community mental health center and a mosque. Starting relationships and projects with others and never getting to finish it, for reasons beyond my control. The COVID pandemic shutdowns abruptly closed all of these locations in March 2020 without us ever having an opportunity to say goodbye. Same with the university I attended for six years that abruptly closed exactly a year prior in March 2019. Add this onto my previous losses and it really added up, taking a toll on mind and body. I needed this time to grieve and to get my sense of self back.

Out into the World Again

After a while with the COVID closures, I began missing interacting with people and being useful. So, I was pleasantly surprised in January 2022 to receive favorable guidance and insight into the effects and benefits of doing my postdoctoral training at EMAGES with Dr. Hattie Wash:

Metu Neter cards: Tehuti tu tchaas/ Maat tu tchaas, Sacred Path Card: Sacred Space/Respect, and I Ching: Hexagram 15 Modesty

Metu Neter cards: Tehuti tu tchaas/ Maat tu tchaas means this could be a place where I could experience a contented, joyful sense of well-being and successful time, as long as I consult and follow a sage and the oracle's advice along with my intuitive wisdom.

I later discovered, when I started my postdoctoral training at EMAGES in April 2022, I would indeed be following a sage. Dr. Hattie Wash is full of wisdom and I'm continuously amazed at her truly intuitive guidance. Tehuti is an expert, a teacher and after forty years of experience Dr. Wash is certainly an expert! She is also an example of a long-term pioneer, compassionate leader, and she encourages us to also persevere in moving forward with new ways to help our people. It was definitely a Maat situation as I would not initially receive a full stipend, because most African American community mental health clinics lack funds and clients don't have insurance. I told her that was okay with me because I was there to be of service to her and the community. Her wisdom and training is more precious.

Sacred Path Card: Sacred Space/Respect. This card is a reminder about acknowledging mine and other's personal space. I do this by standing in the doorway to rooms or offices to ask permission before interrupting their thoughts or tasks before entering. It is also about respecting my own self and not neglecting my own personal needs, such as rest, nourishment and sleep while providing for other people. Along with hexagram 15, it again reminds me to respect other people's cultures, beliefs and life choices. I listen and learn from clients' daily struggles, yet creative ways to survive emotionally and socially.

I Ching: Hexagram 15 Modesty. The need to be humble and modest by being on the same social level as the average person. In this situation I too have low income like my clients, but my education allows me advantages that other people might not have, especially those from inner city areas. Again hexagram

15 reminds us to be balanced by not going to extremes. What's interesting about the guidance from the book, *I Ching Praxis,* is reference to credentials: Line 1: could succeed without showing off one's credentials; line 2: use your reputation and credentials to serve others; line 3: it's possible to earn credentials by completing your program or project; line 4: humble yourself while doing your very best; line 5: may be criticized by others regarding your credentials but what you do shows your abilities and strengths; and Line 6: may only be influential within your small community although you have well known credentials and wealth.

Since I received hexagram 15 straight up, with no lines stressed, is it possible that it really doesn't matter whether I get licensed or not? The EPPP psychologist licensure exam theories questions are outdated, with confusing wording that makes it more of an extensive vocabulary test, instead of helping clients. And as far as the importance of learning and memorizing research studies results, most grandmothers will tell you, "I could've told you that!" African Americans and other multicultural people tend to fail the state exams because the questions are abstract and as we are relational people, we usually try to imagine stories as to how the information may apply to our clients before choosing our answers. Reflecting on the advice from hexagram 15 as it unfolds, I'm seeing how every line regarding credentials applies depending on what perspective and position you are in, or looking at.

On a practical level, emotionally it was frustrating trying to balance graduating with a doctoral degree in clinical psychology, as Dr. Mateen, but now learning a lot of new information and techniques specific to African American clients that wasn't taught in the curriculum at universities. How do I be humble and open to being taught, yet still be able to contribute? With so much to learn, I did at times doubt myself. The stress of the pressure to prove myself, that I didn't really want to ever have to do again, even among other African Americans. I had had enough of that in predominantly white institutions, plus often being considered dumb because I used a wheelchair.

The all African American staff at EMAGES is generous, caring but uses an honest and direct approach probably from years of counseling men. Being authentic is what I've prayed to manifest within myself and with others. Determined to not be at any agency so focused on theories, rules and policies that we couldn't be ourselves. Although I'm grateful to be in this loving, accepting environment I still had to get used to allowing myself be vulnerable again. To be able to keep my vows to be my authentic self no matter what. Hoping that the staff would want me just as I am, I gradually let go of my worries as I decided to take each day as an unexpected new day, eager to learn.

This meant not worrying about being there, in a postdoctoral fellowship position or credentials, as much as being able to learn enough to stay on afterwards and continue to help men and their families. However, as I've previously done okay with passing exams, my credentials are needed for the success of the community mental health center, because state accreditation requires that it have licensed staff. Yet it creates barriers for African Americans to become licensed. It is a vicious cycle as we are required to have licensed staff in order to train and supervise other African American psychologists to become licensed psychologists.

I'm grateful to be trained during my postdoctoral fellowship by Dr. Hattie Wash using the philosophy and recommendations in her book, *Culturally Specific Treatment: A Model for*

The Treatment of African-American Clients. Her counseling and therapy interventions are designed to acknowledge all areas of an individual's life. She explained this as four main relationship areas: biological effects on the physical body, social interpersonal, spiritual, and political/economic including the effects of racism. African-centered worldview is relational, "I am because we are." Individual talk therapy that we were taught in universities, doesn't make sense when there are multiple societal influences beyond an individual's control. Neither does family therapy make sense, based on old white middle class values of a "nuclear family" in the suburbs where the husband works, and the wife stays home. African families were extended families with several generations living and cooperating together in the neighborhood community. Dr. Wash incorporates group therapy to help clients learn to receive and give support, to communicate, appropriately express feelings, gain a positive sense of self, respect others, and follow through on goals. Thus preparing us to restore healthy families and communities. One of my passions, as you may have noticed from reading this book and my previous book, is helping to develop ways to reestablish healthy communities.

Chapter 14: Another Tough Assignment

My postdoctoral fellowship trained me how to counsel mostly men for life stressors, substance abuse, sex offender treatment, and reentry back into society after prison or during probation and parole. This requires compassionate listening and understanding as I hear life experiences from men's perspectives. Initially it was hard to listen and not be triggered by a lot of emotions. Amazingly I didn't have flashbacks. Perhaps this is because I've already done my own hard healing work over the past few years.

But still! Counseling mostly with men was not initially one of my career plans, although I know families and the world can't be healthy and whole without men participating in intergenerational healing. Being immersed in Muslim culture for my internship wasn't on my radar either. That tough assignment came from my mother in spirit. This tough assignment of counseling men is probably from my father also in spirit, because I've asked my father to help his sons and their sons as they have repeated his same mistakes. It's not only my father's fault, it's how most men in the United States were taught to believe and behave, regardless of the dire consequences of their actions. Families without fathers is repeated generation after generation. Fathers required to work excessive long hours away from home. Or stay away from home because of the shame of not being allowed to work. Disrespected at school, on the job, in the streets and at the mall, angry, frustrated, with a sense of hopelessness looking for a way out. America supplies the booze, drugs, pornography, video games and movies promoting excessive sex and violence as normal. A selected few get sent away to prison. Those with money go free back into society, and business as usual continues. People poor and rich are sucked into the fantasy of the highlife. Men's energy and money is more focused on winning in the sports arena then making the world a better place. Even when fathers are home, sports games may take priority over the home. Teaching boys to communicate in coded sports' abbreviations but not communication skills for loving friend, family, and community relationships.

Why was I given all these difficult assignments? Well, being in the Heru Khuti clan, why not? Heru Khuti energy is true justice, which means providing rehabilitation more than simply severe punishments. Sure, I have what it takes to yell and insult like a drill sergeant. However, Heru Khuti upholds the natural laws of Maat. On the Maat card, you'll see she holds the balance scale, but she is not blindfolded. The ability to do the right thing comes from inside each person. However, we must show people that they can have a peaceful, calm loving heart by providing safe, healthy families and communities. Instead of constantly showing us the opposite by surrounding us in the workplace, schools and media with lawlessness, greed, indifference, and violence. Our whole country, and the world needs rehabilitation and therapy!

A tough task, but we have to start somewhere. I'm grateful for the opportunity to join with others in their efforts for moving forward our human evolution. Being in the Heru Khuti and Snake clans means that I can take being bitten, attacked repeatedly, yet get up and keep going promoting truth. Sekert energy gives me the foresight, perseverance and ability to manifest towards long-term goals even if it takes decades or centuries.

This assignment from heaven also helps heal me. It takes me closer to the last aspect of my Het Heru destiny, sexuality. Even though I was sixty-six years old, the group therapy sessions with the men initially had me frequently horny and thinking about sex, like I've never felt before. What am I to do with this? Is this the way men feel, miserably physically aroused so much that they have to do something with it in order to get relief? I am an empath, meaning I feel people's emotional and physical pain, but I wasn't expecting to have to cope with this intense hot sexual energy down there, in order to understand my clients' dilemmas!

For years, men tell me, "I love your smile." "I love your voice." "Can I get a hug?" "Your Spanish is sexy." Some profess their love for me.

When men give me a compliment, I compliment them too. It's not flirting, it's my way of decreasing the gender bias. Men can be allowed to look good, have feelings, and to be authentic too.

What they feel is my peace, calm and genuineness. My Het Heru Oshun is still there with smooth facial skin, natural red lips, a slim body, subtle curves, that make me look younger than my age. Perhaps I am a little too thin, as I slide into elder age busier than before, walking more, my weight in the same range between 128 and 132 pounds, same as it's been for decades. Tell, tell aging signs as skin on my neck and arms and pants sag, and my body hair grays. Oshun is what people experience as I bring harmony and creativity to the therapy groups, helping to synchronize the co-facilitator counselor's and clients' ideas and needs. Showing everyone real love and concern.

I could laugh, giggle, play, and sing more but I'd hold back. Automatically conditioned to fear my realness will be misinterpreted. Perhaps I could try wearing the Muslim woman's burqa and niqab to cover my face, hide my smile. And not open my mouth. No conversations, not even about the weather? I don't want the men fighting over me. There shouldn't anything to fight over because I treat everyone the same. Most people who have had near death experiences share of the unconditional love they received. Their friends and family may get a little jealous because we've been socially conditioned to be possessive and loyal to a few.

Reading the book, *Boys and Sex: Young Man on Hook Ups, Love, Porn, Consent, and Navigating the New Masculinity*, helped me understand that men's perspective and limited sexuality hasn't changed much since I was a young woman. Fear of true intimacy continues, as lies and stereotypes are circulated in locker rooms, on smartphones, and the internet instead of real sex education. This promotion of idealized sex generates billions of dollars, therefore companies don't care how it destroys families and people's lives.

Hopefully we can now restore the beauty of true sensuality, sexuality and love. When we feel satisfied and whole inside and nurtured we also feel the sensual energy in the genital area. A creative project or achievement, a home cooked meal. The nurturing closeness of a mother who cares. Curious why men have fantasies of bigger, and bigger breasts, yet, cite indecent exposure when mothers breastfeed babies in public. This closeness and connection of being supported, understood, heard, valued and appreciated can be provided by anyone — not just mothers.

Recently, a coworker gave me tickets to the Black Ensemble Theater play, "A Taste of Soul." The sensually enticing music, voices, dancing, bare legs and cleavage temporarily taking us back in time to memories in trance, to the 70's and 80's. All this is Osun energetic creativity, with the sparkly costumes and colorful stage props, along with mouth watering soul food recipe stories. Gradually I allowed in the pleasurable, fun, fun, fun! Sensually, I could have taken in more. Natural and free. Free to be innocently me and you.

Chapter 15: Applying Accumulated Wisdom to How I Provide Psychotherapy

IChing hexagram 33 Retreat. There is return after retreating, when the time is right. Here again I was returning to my career after having had to retreat and change directions several times. This time I am returning as an expert myself, with decades of acquired wisdom and formal training. Fulfilling my second Metu Neter card career reading Tehuti tu tchaas/Tehuti tem maat in 1994, now changed to Tehuti tu tchaas/ Maat tu tchaas in 2022.

I provide spiritually integrated psychotherapy for those who are interested. Meaning, for example, if a client mentions that faith helps them cope through prayer and gospel music, then we may sing gospel songs together and explore how the lyrics pertain to their life. Others may be already working on personal growth and health but are now challenged with crises that either test their faith, or renew faith with spiritual mystical experiences or miracles. Some people are astonished to learn there is an explanation for their and loved one's behavior, and glad to have their natural talents and intuition validated.

For clients with very complicated situations when I'm not sure how to proceed, I consult with my supervisor, as well as the I Ching and Sacred Path Cards at home. When I recently did this, I was amazed that the oracles accurately described the client, her situation and actually gave me similar advice as my supervisor! The use of divination is essential in African and indigenous healing practices. I don't tell clients I occasionally use divination, I just follow the guidance. However, for best results it helps to have the client, family and community's belief and participation.

Intergenerational Healing

Ancestral healing is not only for you but also your parents and their parents and grandparents. I've noticed that as I've done my personal healing my siblings have also changed and healed without going to therapy. Ancient indigenous cultures used multiple methods, some similar to how Dr. Brian Weiss recently accidentally discovered past life regression. We are collectively, globally healing as the internet and books allow us to communicate and share experiences. The truth shall set us free. Ancestral healing, well known in indigenous cultures, can now be taken to a higher level.

Much more than setting a plate at the table, talking to and remembering our ancestors. What if your core issue is that you are your grandmother who came back as you, and you are carrying her pain and fears? The psychiatrist prescribes sedatives, antidepressants, and antipsychotics medications, then perhaps in desperation gives electric shock treatments. Yet, your symptoms are still not improving. There are many people in this situation who seek relief for emotional pain and are given pills instead of getting to the real source of their pain. People need community and spiritual support, not more "newer" and newer psychiatric medications advertised on television to try since the other antidepressants didn't work. Nor tired family and friends happy for you to "Go take a chill pill."

A majority of physicians and mental health professionals weren't trained to know the difference between clinical depression versus spiritual depression. Spiritual depression as described in the book, *Sacred Contracts,* is when you feel empty inside, disconnected from everything, feel abandoned, without feeling divine love, caring and a purpose for living. Another description of spiritual depression is a "desert period," from the book, *Soul Perfection*, an overwhelming feeling of being absolutely alone, afraid and although there are other people around it's hard to believe that anyone loves you. Or to have faith while you are tested by frequent obstacles.

Everyone will go through one or more of these long desolate periods in life. We've heard somewhat, about midlife crisis and menopause. Other cultures teach that everyone experiences major shifts that occur near puberty, at age thirty, and again near age sixty. To prepare for these common life transitions, indigenous cultures have rites of passages, initiations, and mentorships. In the United States, we expect people to stay the same throughout their lives and only celebrate transitional events with symbolic one-day parties and feasts. After that you're left on your own, to sink or swim.

There used to be convents and monasteries for young people seriously interested in a spiritual life and undergoing mystical experiences, where they were guided and protected. Now each person is scared to go through emotional and spiritual transformations on their own. People need community and spiritual support during these times.

More and more people are surviving near death experiences and other spiritual experiences with few places to go for aftercare guidance. Not knowing of natural ways, desperately wanting to replicate mystical states and connection they try out the latest street drug to temporarily obtain visions and ecstatic highs. Or turn to addictions to numb or to temporarily feel better, which could lead to unintentional criminal behavior.

The world's future is uncertain and frightening for younger generations who grew up with more media exposure to chaos, disasters and climate change. Young and old, we are all consciously or unconsciously seeking understanding and better lives, often wondering what is the purpose of bothering to keep living? True healing is integrating the ways and wisdom of our ancestors to restore whole, balanced, healthy, supportive communities by getting to know and valuing each individual's destiny and personality, as well as the community's purpose and contribution to the world.

Chapter 16: Work on What Has Been Spoiled

September 30, 2021. It was kind of late to be doing a birth chart at 65 years old. However, I noticed that my previous I Ching birth chart time, done in 2008, was off by 30 minutes. The interpretation didn't make sense to me, as my other adult destiny readings did, as related to my life history.

"Hexagram 18 Work on What Has Been Spoiled/Decay. Working on what has been spoiled has supreme success and order comes into the world. It furthers one to cross the great water (meaning take on the challenges and risks to go beyond usual routine). The image of decay. Thus the superior one stirs up the people and strengthens their spirit." (Wilhelm & Baynes, 1950).

For further understanding, I consulted the book, *The Astrology of I Ching*. My life task would be, and has been, correcting the mistakes and habits of my parents that I've inherited. All of us healing and letting go of the old, so that we can bring in the new. Not understanding this earlier, has meant being depressed over not having children and a full career like my siblings. I am the only one of my mother's children that doesn't have children. Nor have I owned a home nor retired from one job with benefits. Instead, I was free to have the time, money, and education to pursue therapy to focus on healing myself. In so doing, I saw my close siblings also heal and change without going to therapy. Hopefully, we are making a dent in breaking the family cycle of abuse, to neither be the victim nor the perpetrator.

Hexagram 18 Work on What Has Been Spoiled extends beyond family to include communities and governments. As you have read in my memoirs, I have worked on what has been spoiled for most of my adult life, without consciously knowing these tasks were part of my destiny.

A friend requested I pull a Jewish Kabalah, *72 Names of God* card, after I told him about the ninety-nine names of Allah book and cards. Repeating the specified prayer on one of the cards, and carrying the card with you opens the way to safety, contentment and more. Did I have room to add another similar culture's beliefs? Curiousity and dedication won out. I asked the question, 'What do I need to help me through this stage of transition, and best be able to help?' It should be no surprise that it is 61 Water: Vav Mem Bet, with the meditation prayer: "With this I purify the waters of the earth and awaken the forces of healing and immortality." This card reading certainly does relate to my interest in helping others heal and to understand the continuity of life.

It seems odd to end this book here. And I was going to, but then during editing I realized I left out the third orisha that the Candomble priestess told me ruled my head, Osaala. It took me awhile to find out that Osaala is a Spanish language intonation for Obatala. Afterwards, I did not give conscious thought to Obatala. I didn't wear white nor do any prayers or rituals for Obatala. Ashamed that I honestly forgot Obatala all these twenty years.

Tears come to my eyes as I read the attributes of Obatala, from the book, *Obatala: The Greatest and Oldest Divinity*. His attributes describe me in my older years, as I return to what I consider is a career. Gentle, quiet, calm and patient, yet is a leader with good character who serves humanity to help reform the world from chaos and distress by finding solutions to problems whenever needed. And to redeem generational curses. More tears. Sounds similar to "work on what has been spoiled." Helps others to fulfill their destinies. Orisha means destiny. May have a disability or assist those with disabilities. No alcohol and avoids red meat. Able to find peace and harmony to overcome fear and sorrow. This attracts blessings for self and others. I've been wondering how abundance comes easily to me. All of this is true.

I've shied away from being a leader but that's what I'm called upon to do. People criticize my calm and patient style, especially since I counsel clients who had rough backgrounds. I was recently doubting my approach, thinking, well maybe I should be tougher. No, this is how I am meant to be. I'm always automatically problem-solving, even in my sleep. What does this person or another need? Each person has unique needs. You would think this would drive my head crazy. Reading this about Obatala helps me understand, instead of resist, my destiny role. A role I've been doing all along without knowing. Obatala exists in modern society. We could all strive to live the virtues of Obatala.

Conclusion

Writing this book took some unanticipated twists and turns. It started as one book and became two separate books. There were long pauses as I awaited intuitive guidance for what direction to go next. The ending was completely unexpected, as I was astonished to learn more about my hidden destiny path after all these years. Faith, trust and regularly following the oracles led me to these revelations.

Hopefully, you have a trustworthy spiritual counselor or mentor to help with interpretation of your divination, in regards to your personal growth and situation. In life we learn by doing, by experiencing, not by continuously reading or listening to lectures, or memorizing scriptures. A genuine spiritual counselor can guide you through because they've also been through what you're going through. Especially through the longer periods of intense individual and collective societal growth. The resultant peace, courage, confidence, joy, miracles, and abundance is worth the effort.

With meditation and reflection, you will connect to your own knowledge and experiences. Trust what you intuitively know and your honest observations of the world. Everyone, each person has an important piece of wisdom to share that was broken apart centuries ago, that is gradually coming together again for the whole betterment of all. My intention is to introduce you to indigenous ways that were taken away from us. So that you are no longer afraid of your own culture, nor of people who live their cultures. I showed you how I apply what I've learned to my everyday life. Now it is your turn.

With deep respect for indigenous cultures and the people who truly have the knowledge I thank them and yield to them. My prayers are for all indigenous communities globally to be recognized and respected, most importantly their culture and lands returned to them, and allowed to be restored to healthy ecological balance. Exploitation and stealing resources from people here in the United States and from other countries ceases. Amen.

In my upcoming third book, *Getting to Know Yourself and Others: Multicultural Personality Studies*, to better assist you, I go more in depth, giving personality descriptions beyond my own experiences.

As you can see, I could have delved even deeper into learning and living any specific one of these ways of divination knowledge. It would be helpful, for other dedicated people to follow my lead and write books about how the use of divination changed and enhanced their lives.

All the best.

Books and Articles

I purposely did not write this book in a scholarly way, with huge academic words, book quotes and citations. This is because we all have this knowledge and information within us. Books are just one way to share and communicate with each other. I believe there really is no such thing as an expert, it is simply one person sharing their opinion and experiences. The so-called expert may have done the research and statistics to find how many other people might agree. And they had the money and the time to get published. But life is always changing. Meaning what was true two weeks ago, may not be true today. And the authors may live in a completely different situation than yours, and therefore the advice may make no sense for your current life situation. Books are a way to have a long-distance conversation, often with a stranger. But inside us is enough commonalities that we don't feel alone. Here is a list of books whose authors think similar to my experiences, and some who don't.

African Names: The Ancient Egyptian Keys to Unlocking Your Power & Destiny. Hehi Metu Ra Enkamit. (1993). Ser Ap-uat Press.

Black Panther (2018). Movie. PG-13.

Boys and Sex: Young Man on Hook Ups, Love, Porn, Consent, and Navigating the New Masculinity. By Peggy Orenstein. Harper Collins Publishers.

Case Report: Florence Nightingale's Fever. (23 December). BMJ 1995; 311: 1697.

Culturally Specific Treatment: A Model for the Treatment of African-American Clients. By Hattie Wash, Psy. D. (2018). Lulu.

Florence Nightingale: The Case for Brucellosis. (2019) Health. Steemit.com

Florence Nightingale's Long COVID. Sarah L. Mauer. (24 November 2021). Nineteenth-Century Context. Taylor and Francis online. https://doi.org/10.1080/08905495.2021.1987776

Holistic Tarot: An Integrative Approach to Using Tarot for Personal Growth. By Ben Bell Wen (2015). Berkeley, CA: North Atlantic Books.

Guardians of the Soil: Meeting Zimbabwe's Elders. By Chenjerai Hove and Ilija Trojanow (1996). Baobab Books.

Heading Towards Omega: In Search of the Meaning of the Near-Death Experience. By Kenneth L. Ring. (1984). Harper-Perennial.

Holistic Tarot: An Integrative Approach to Using Tarot for Personal Growth. By Benebell Wen (2015). Berkeley, CA: North Atlantic Books.

I Ching: A New Interpretation for Modern Times. By Sam Reifler (1974).

I Ching: The Tao of Drumming. By Michael Drake. (1991). Talking Drum Publications. (paperback). Random House Publishing Group. (e-book).

I Ching Praxis: Forty Years of Practical Insights into the I Ching. By Ra Un Nefer Amen (2014). Khamit Media Trans Visions, Inc.

Isese Spiritual Workbook: The Ancient Wisdom of the Ifa Orisa Tradition. By Ayele Kumari, PhD. (2020). Ori Institute.

Left to Tell: Discovering God Amidst the Rwandan Holocaust By Immaculee Ilibagiza. (2006). Hay House.

Light Emerging: The Journey of Personal Healing. By Barbara Ann Brennan. (1993). Bantam Books.

Love, Medicine, and Miracles: Lessons Learned about Self-Healing from a Surgeon's Experiences with Exceptional Patients. By Bernie Sigel M.D. (1990). HarperPerennial.

Mary Magdalene Revealed: The First Apostle, Her Feminist Gospel, and the Christianity We Haven't Tried. By Meggan Waterson. (2019). Hay House.

Medicine Cards: Revised, Expanded Edition. By Jamie Sams and David Carson (1988, 1999). New York: St. Martin's Press.

Medicine Cards: The Discovery of Power through the Ways of Animals. By Jamie Sams and David Carson (1988, 1999). New York: St. Martin's Press.

Metu Neter Cards. By Ra Un Nefer Amen (1990). New York, Khamit Corporation.

Metu Neter Vol. 1: The Great Oracle of Tehuti and the Egyptian System of Spiritual Cultivation. By Ra Un Nefer Amen (1990). New York, Khamit Corporation.

Mind Over Matter: Scientific Proof That You Can Heal Yourself. By Lissa Rankin, M.D. (2013). Hay House.

Mother God: The Feminine Principle to Our Creator. By Sylvia Browne. (2004). Hay House.

Mother's Love from Beyond: A Healing Journey of Grief and Loss: A Memoir. By Haneefa Mateen. (2021).

Mystical Traveler: How to Advance to a Higher Level of Spirituality. By Sylvia Browne. (2008). Hay House.

Obatala: The Greatest and Oldest Divinity. By Olayinka Babatunde Ogunsina Adewuyi (2013). River Water Books.

Ochosi: Ifa and the Spirit of the Tracker. By Awo Fa'lokun Fatunmbi (1992). Original Publications.

Organization of Rural Associations for Progress ORAP Zenzele College Student Handbook, Grassroots Development and NGO Management 6. (August 18, 1997).

Our Lady of Kibeho: Mary Speaks to the World from the Heart of Africa. By Immaculee Ilibagiza. (2008). Hay House.

Past Life Oracle Cards. By Doreen Virtue and Brian Weiss, M.D. (2014). Hay House, Inc.

Phoenix Rising: No-Eyes' Vision of the Changes to Come. By Mary Summer Rain. (1987, 2011). Hampton Roads Publishing Company. BookNook.biz (e-book).

Physicians of the Heart: A Sufi View of the Ninety-Names of Allah. By Wali Ali Meyer, Bilal Hyde, Faisal Muqaddam, Shabda Khan. (2011).

Physicians' Untold Stories: Miraculous Experiences Doctors are Hesitant to Share With Their Patients, or Anyone! By Scott J. Kolbaba, M.D. with 26 other Physicians (2016).

Pain, Pain, Go Away. By Vicky Uhland. (Winter 2015-2016). Momentum. National Multiple Sclerosis Society.

Physicians' Untold Stories: Miraculous Experiences Doctors are Hesitant to Share With Their Patients, or Anyone! By Scott J. Kolbaba, M.D. with 26 other Physicians (2016).

Race, Gender and Imperialism in the Wonderful Adventures of Mrs. Seacole in Many Lands. C. Janneck, G. Cypher, A. Rivera, K. Schommer, and O. Hayes. Women in the world global connections and British women's travel writing 1780–1860. Https://britishwomentravelwriters.wordpress.com

Return of the Rishi. By Deepak Chopra. (1991). HarperOne.

Sacred Contracts: Awakening Your Divine Potential. By Caroline Myss. (2002, 2003). New York: Random House Company.

Sacred Path Cards: The Discovery of Self through Native Teachings. By Jamie Sams (1990). New York: HarperCollins Publishers.

Sacred Path Workbook: New Teachings and Tools to Illuminate Your Personal Journey. By Jamie Sams (1991). New York: HarperCollins Publishers.

Soul Lessons and Soul Purpose Oracle Cards: The Most Direct Path of Spiritual Peace and Personal Fulfillment. By Sonia Choquette. Hay House, Inc.

Soul's Perfection: Journey of the Soul series, Book 2. Sylvia Browne. (2000). Hay House.

Spirit Song: The Introduction of No-Eyes. By Mary Summer Rain. (1985, 1993). Hampton Roads Publishing Company.

The Astrology of I Ching. (1976, 1993). By W. K. Chu and W. A. Sherrill. Penguin Books.

The Forgotten Child of Zimbabwe. By Debra Chidaka Akue (2017). Christian Faith Publishing.

The Harlem River Arrangement: The I Ching Transcripts. By Ra Un Nefer Amen. (1984).

The I Ching or Book of Changes. By Richard Wilhelm and Cary Baynes. (1950). Princeton University Press.

The Illustrated I Ching Workbook. R. L. Wing. (1987). Aquarian Press.

The Medical I Ching: Oracle of the Healer Within. By Miki Shima. (1992, 2011). Blue Poppy Press.

The Medicine Woman: Inner Guidebook: A Woman's Guide to Her Unique Powers Using the Medicine Woman

Tarot Deck. (1991, 2012). By Carol Bridges. U.S. Games Systems, Inc. Stanford, CT 06902.

The 99 Beautiful Names of Allah. Physicians of the Heart: Wazifa Card Set. By Shabda Khan, Faisal Muqaddam, and Bilal Hyde. (2022). Mandala Publishing.

The 72 Names of God: Meditation Deck. By Yehuda Berg (2004). Kabbalah Publishing.

Women of Sufism: A Hidden Treasure: Writings and Stories of Mystics Poets, Scholars and Saints. Selected and introduced by Camille Adams Helminski. Shambhala Publications.

Wrapping Authority: Women Islamic Leaders in a Sufi Movement in Dakar, Senegal. By Joseph Hill. (2018). University of Toronto Press.

Zimbabwe Country Report on Human Rights Practices for 1998. U.S. Department of State. https://1997-2001.state.gov

Zimbabwe Human Rights NGO Forum: A Consolidated Report on the Food Riots 19-23 January 1998. Report Compiled by the AMANI Trust on Behalf of the Zimbabwe Human Rights NGO Forum.

Zulu Bone Oracle. By Ulufudu (1989). Wingbow Press.

Author's Bio

Haneefa Mateen has a wealth of life experiences and knowledge from exploring healing methods for mind, body and soul. A natural teacher, healer, and artist she shares more of her wisdom. Her books are accessible, easy on the eyes, available in large print format.

She has an associate's degree in registered nursing, bachelor's in International Studies, master's in Rehabilitation Counseling, and a doctorate in Clinical Psychology. She currently does spiritually integrated therapy and healing, and is active in African American community cultural events.

www.ingramcontent.com/pod-product-compliance
Lightning Source LLC
Chambersburg PA
CBHW052129070526
44585CB00017B/1761